THE STRONGEST WEAPON

The true experiences of a secret agent in the Second World War. Notburga Tilt recounts vividly how she bluffed and flirted her way to many a German heart, how she suffered torture and severe flogging at the hand of the SS, and how many times she was near to death.

She was born in Graz in 1923, the only daughter of Anton and Margaretha Triller. The family was a large and famous one and her early years were spent in the splendid environment of the wealthy and beautiful — then, while still a schoolgirl, the Nazis swarmed into Austria, Chancellor Dollfus was murdered and the country ceased to be a democracy. There was Jewish blood through intermarriages in the Trillers, thus an immediate purge against them set in, yet they remained united, courageous and outspoken in their condemnation of Nazis. Notburga herself discovered how a Nazi official was starving the owner of the property he had confiscated (in 1938) to death in an attic — because she was a Jew; a senior member of the Triller family was murdered and his dismembered remains sent to his widow for burial . . . then was born the burning obsession to bring down Hitler, whatever it should cost her. She was young but soon discovered that she held in her grasp the strongest weapon, guaranteed to bring any German to his knees. The information these men parted with played an important part in the final victory of the Allies. For her part, Notburga was involved in all the stark horror and tyranny she wished so desperately to end.

THE STRONGEST WEAPON

NOTBURGA
TILT

ARTHUR H. STOCKWELL LTD.,
Elms Court Ilfracombe
Devon

First published in Great Britain, 1972

SBN 7223 0344 - 0
PRINTED IN GREAT BRITAIN BY
ARTHUR H. STOCKWELL LTD.
Elms Court - Ilfracombe
Devon

CONTENTS

ILLUSTRATIONS

Photograph by Jessie Gibbs

The Author

PREFACE

In preparing this book, I chose to start with an introductory chapter about myself.

I would like to pay tribute to those people who walked with me all or part of my way. Some of them are dead, executed by the Nazis. Their constancy and courage I will always remember, hoping that their souls will now have the so much desired freedom.

To those compatriots, who managed to escape Hitler's Inferno, I say "Thank You", and salute you for the trust and faith you put in me. It was this very confidence which gave me the strength to fight on, when all odds were against me, until Victory was ours.

The multitude of Nazi victims all over the world . . . dead or alive, who are still cloaked in anonymity, will bear witness of my experiences and cruelties undergone.

Since I have pledged myself to champion freedom, with all its consequences, I have been sustained by the courage of people from many Nations. I owe it to them and to myself that this book should maintain the integrity of truth, hence the delay – I had to master the English language before I could present my story.

"Truth is not always probable: but truth is stranger than fiction."

Notburga Tilt

FOREWORD

Burgi Triller was seventeen years old when she joined the army of nameless Resistance-fighters against Nazi tyranny.

People like her were strictly *volunteers* who risked their lives in an unequal fight against oppression and inhumanity.

Indeed, the Austrian Resistance made her own vital contribution to restore her sovereignty and on behalf of the Allied Forces.

2,700 Austrians were sentenced to death as active Resistance-fighters, and executed.

16,493 were murdered in Concentration Camps.

9,687 died in Gestapo dungeons, and 6,420 in other prisons.

65,459 Austrian Jews perished in Gas-Chambers or were put to death under gruesome tortures.

On February 18, 1942, the British Prime Minister, Winston Churchill declared: "We are fighting to liberate Austria," asking the Austrians to fight alongside the British and their Allies.

1,500 managed to join the British army and many of them were killed or wounded.

Although this book is a personal account, it is part of the historic and heroic battles the Resistance-fighters fought all over Europe.

Today, some of the events as described in this book seem incredible, but it proves how personal initiative and originality plus courage, could succeed.

Not all of the Brave made it and many girls were caught and beheaded, sometimes for rather trivial offences, yet Burgi Triller got away.

How did she do it?

Read her unique and enthralling story and ask yourselves what you would have done in her place.

Prof. Herbert Steiner, Csc.

Wissenschaftlicher Leiter des Dokumentationsarchives des oesterreichischen Widerstandes, Altes Rathaus, Wipplinger-strasse 8, 1010 VIENNA.

CHAPTER 1

MY CHILDHOOD

I was born on January 21, 1923, in Graz, the second largest town of Austria. My brother Toni was nearly seventeen years older than I and attended, at the time of my birth, the Academy of Commerce. Due to devaluation after the first world war my parents, Anton and Margaret Triller, lived very modestly on my father's hundred per cent invalid pension, awarded to him for the injuries received at the Italian Front in 1917. A young lieutenant from his regiment, Alfons Gorbach, also wounded and lying next to him in the field hospital, over the years played a big part in my father's life, and rose, in 1960, to the position of Chancellor of Austria.

Our family was a large and famous one, most of the male members were serving officers who distinguished themselves for Austria. The women, feminine and beautiful, made splendid and wealthy marriages. As my father was always considered an excellent speaker and honest adviser his services were in great demand, thus widening our circle of friends enormously.

At the age of four I attended a private Kindergarten and became a real handful for my teachers. Despite this fact, they liked me and recognized my artistic abilities in singing, dancing and poetry. At the age of six I was transferred to another private school which was acknowledged as the best in Graz. There were Professors for every subject, my favourite was a Professor Holman who taught music and singing. When he produced Mozart's, *Die Prinzessin und der Zwerg* I had reached the ripe old age of nine. Holman gave me the second lead, Helga being placed first, although it was a far cry from my own choice of casting, thus I made an all out effort to learn the entire opera of twenty-six pages. Accompanied on the piano by my grandmother, Her Excellency Mina von Bolzano, it took me two months to do it. One week before the final rehearsal I had had enough of singing my role and exclaimed before the cast of some forty-eight people: "I don't look like a *Zwerg* (Dwarf) so why should I play this part?" Holman looked flabbergasted, the others were bursting to laugh, whilst I just stood there awaiting an answer. Angrily, the Professor challenged me to sing the entire opera myself and, when I maintained that I could, flung up his arms in despair. Realizing that I had made a firm statement, I asked him to accompany me, thus he took me up, playing the introduction. Suddenly my throat went dry and I cleared it noisily – Helga's giggling was evident. However, one look at my co-star and I knew what I had to do . . . sing . . . or be laughed at for boasting. All nervousness vanished and stepping forward I sang every key required, high and low, even improvising the chorus by gesturing about, demonstrating my ability and versatility. Wild applause followed, with some of the teachers shouting at the tops of their voices: "Bravo, Burgi, bravo!" Professor Holman, padding his forehead with his handkerchief, finally managed to restore order, asking me point-blank: "And who may I enquire have you in mind for your part?" To which came my prompt reply: "Helga, she's got the right features for a Dwarf." Helga was in tears and pandemonium broke out. In spite of my undiplomatic statement I was adament – I would not sing the *Zwerg* whatever the consequences . . . even dismissal from the opera. Holman dispersed the rehearsal but ordered me to stay and I expected the worst but all he said was: "Now that you have convinced me that you can sing, if need be all the parts, I only hope Helga will recognize your genius . . . and sing yours."

Further school plays followed, the most memorable being my part of Prince Eugene of Savoy, Austria's famous Field Marshal and hero, and performed for the visit of the

Minister for Education from Vienna. Weeks of rehearsals with hard work under the direction of Professor Holman culminated in a production of notability. Props and scenery were on loan from the grand opera and my costumes made to fit me perfectly until alas . . . one week before the actual performance I developed mumps. In the emergency two doctors raced to my home, followed by Holman and various Professors from my school. Luckily the inflammation was not too bad and, with medical aid fit for a prime minister attending the opening of Parliament, the swelling receded and I was declared free from contagion on the morning before the performance.

Wrapped up warmly like an Eskimo, I was taken to school and dressed for my role. Somehow the white powdered wig and the three-cornered hat seemed to transport me back into the eighteenth century. The costume suited me splendidly and, for a moment, I wished that I was a boy. Poignantly the stage was covered with red-white-red flowers – the Austrian colours – against a magnificent background (on canvas) of the Belvedere Palace, once given to the Prince by the Empress Maria Theresa for his victories against Louis XIV. Suspended in the air, above the centre of the stage, was a large Austrian eagle with outstretched wings, a gold crown on its head, a sword and sceptre in its claws.

The College Theatre was filled. The suddenness of my entry surprised me but I stepped forward, drawing my sword, and started my first of fourteen verses. Suddenly crash . . . bang . . . a board of the stage gave way and my elegant booted leg went down. There was a gasp from the audience, followed by suspense one could cut with a knife . . . until I smiled, pulled out my leg and started from the beginning. However, before I could say the opening line of: "Prince Eugene, the noble Knight . . ." the people stood and applauded, I presented my sword in a military manner, like an officer reporting that his men were ready for inspection. The excited audience continued to applaud until Professor Holman asked for silence.

I delivered my long poem faultlessly, with every word audible to the last row, and was rewarded by five curtain calls, a basket of fruit, and a box of bonbons made especially in

Vienna. Speeches followed. Then Holman came to my dressing-room and embraced me enthusiastically, saying: "You made tragedy into triumph my girl, I shall never forget it." Both of us were dabbing our eyes . . . for me perhaps a childlike awareness of growing up caused the emotion.

One year later Chancellor Dr Engelbert Dollfuss was dead – murdered by a Nazi disguised as a policeman. The first of the Nazi outrages. Although the coup was put down the flame of unrest never died and a feeling of worse to come cast gloom over the whole country. Unfortunately, only a few realized the dangers – over one thousand people were killed in this last dramatic act of democracy in Austria. Hitler and his followers in Germany and Austria made no secret of using all their powers to liquidate the independence of our country.

During the next few years Nazi pressure on Austria tightened. With bombs and assassinations, radio and illegal leaflets they tried to intimidate the government and people of Austria. The Nazi underground movement grew; a new greeting emerged: "Eighty-eight" replaced the forbidden "Heil Hitler". However, all this did not dampen my ambition to become a singer and actress. My grandmother managed to get me an audition with the famous tenor, Richard Tauber. He listened to my singing of Mozart's *Wiegenlied* and found my voice and execution excellent. He asked my grandmother to enrol me in the *Schauspiel Schule.* Little did I realize that in a few years' time, I would have to act for my life . . . only the stage setting was to be by a man called Adolph Hitler.

Nearly all the male Trillers served under the Hapsburgs and so gallantly did they distinguish themselves that the highest awards were bestowed on them. My father's cousin, Major F. Triller, was considered worthy of a monument in the centre of Mureck, the town of his birth.

Adding their fame to the Triller family were the women. Wealthy industrialists like Prisching, Grosschaedl and Frankl chose their wives from the Triller line. One of these exceedingly attractive girls was Rosa and her turbulent love-life caused uproars around 1898, when two Imperial Staff Officers duelled with deadly weapons to decide a private quarrel over her integrity. Although when I first met her she was a widow, her vibrant beauty captivated the richest butcher in Graz. Disregarding his marriage he laid before Rosa all his wealth and became her slave in every sense. When his much older wife died in 1934 he tried to shoot Rosa because of her refusal to marry him. After this incident, she scandalized our family by driving in open carriages through the city of Graz and once halting my mother's half-sister's chauffeur-driven Daimler, forcing Frau Sossich to greet her. Her own nieces, Olga, Josefine and Hannerl Sauruck, whose mother was also a Triller, followed in her footsteps. Sensational love affairs, breach of promise cases, and more, rocked the foundation of our family.

The beautiful, elfin faced Josefine sued a prominent surgeon by the name of Dr Gnas. The fiery girl, then aged twenty-eight, attended Court surrounded by pressmen and supported by her entire family of eleven, including her father, Erhard Sauruck, a giant and well-known personality. During the hearing, scenes never before witnessed took place. The Judge, needing protection, ran with the crucifix in his hand along the corridor, chased by Erhard Sauruck, who again was followed by the police called in to deal with the situation. Finally Josefine stormed from the witness box and slapped the face of Dr Gnas who had called her a liar. She then flung the one carat solitaire engagement ring out of the open window, which produced a rush of people hurrying downstairs to search for the valuable gem. Whoever found it kept it a secret but the speculation continued.

At this time I attended the Convent school at the Schlossbergkai in Graz, exclusive as it was expensive. Princess Liechtenstein and Countess Meran, a descendant of the Grandduke Johann of Austria, were friends of mine and I was privileged to spend weekends at various castles. However, the newspapers were full of spicy details of the Josefine Sauruck affair and I was in great demand by my class mates for information of the latest developments. 'Not to-night Josefine' became a classic and the Sister Superior requested my removal for the time being, which was granted. Three weeks later, I was back at school, and my cousin Josefine enjoying herself at St Moritz.

This sensational case was soon forgotten however, for soon

our beloved Austria was overrun by the Germans. I was fifteen years old and wide awake. A regime of hatred and terror began and although I was too young to realize the full consequences, my instinct told me that friends suddenly became foes and could no longer be trusted.

The Convent was closed by the Nazis in 1938. It was good-bye to childhood and the awful realization dawned that dreams can vanish in a moment. The cult to worship the flesh became predominant, and motherhood the supreme aim for every girl old enough to have a child, although rather incongruously, she could not marry at all until eighteen and needed parental consent until twenty-one. Looks could be equally vital to people with no ear-lobes, as they were under suspicion of being Jewish. One of my aunts, Professor Gustl Bolzano, a brilliant music teacher, was fired from the College and in order to get another post she wore heavy gold earrings to cover half her ears.

My mother warned me not to speak to strangers about her views regarding the new regime – "Traitors and hired ruffians, who will terrorize all freedom loving people." Her warnings became reality. The Austrian Nazis, by now all highly honoured for selling out Austria to the Germans, thus to enlarge Hitler's dream of his Thousand-Year-Reich, ruled the country with an iron fist. Dr Goebbels said "Propaganda is the strongest weapon", so why should not I try it against our conquerors. In 1938, this was sheer madness, but I did.

Soon after the annexation on March 13, 1938, Austria was named the Ostmark and divided into *Gaue* (counties) and every Nazi coveted the title of *Fuehrer,* thus we had *Gaufuehrers, Ortsgruppenfuehrers* and *Arbeitsfuehrers* galore. The Gendarmerie and Police were placed under the authorities of the illegal Nazi-members, most of them freshly released from jails, and the Gestapo, imported from Germany, saw to it that all of them kept in line.

In this sinister set-up one could hardly breathe or think, least of all dare to take counter-action.

However, my dislike for these bullying methods became of paramount importance and when the first orders of flagging houses, two flags with schwastikas in the middle per window were demanded, my mother and I displayed only half of them. Little did we know that the son of the Nazi Doctor Kloss was driving up and down the streets to register the missing ones, thus our first brush with the local Law was at hand. Amongst all this intimidation and hatred I encountered the first innovation to determine the cause of my life in the person of a young handsome Gendarmerie officer, Peter Steinegger. This tall Austrian often called at my home during his patrols of the area and cast more than a friendly eye on me. Girl-like I teased him, placing my late father's officer's cap on his head, and flattered his looks, to which he would reply: "When you've finished with me, I don't know whether I am coming or going."

Now the jokes were over and he came to warn me of impending danger, urging us to put all the flags on display, as the *Gaufuehrer* was due to inspect the houses in the afternoon. He also stressed that if anyone knew of his intervention, he would be in serious trouble.

After his departure mother placed the required flags, plus Hitler's picture in the window and said: "I'm glad your father is not alive to see our humiliation, he would have never given in, they would have had to shoot him first."

One week later we were supplied with a Government radio, so that we should listen to our 'master's voice' and all the propaganda Goebbels could dish out. At the same time I was told my Convent School was closed down and that I did not need to register for my next term. I usually looked forward to Easter, but this time it hung over us like an avalanche ready to crush us. Our friends called, but they seemed very frightened to talk and we heard of mass-arrests in Stainz. Also the word torture was mentioned and I asked: "What is TORTURE mother?" "To inflict extreme physical pain to extort a confession," she said.

Easter Saturday 1938. Leaflets instructing us to line up by the local school to receive GIFTS from the Fuehrer were handed out and we had to obey. Once arrived there we had our names taken and then lined up in several queues, rather embarrassed, looking at each other. Suddenly, a van drove up with men taking pictures of us standing there like beggars. Grotesquely, next to us stood Frau Kathe Totz, one of the richest ladies in the district. She was not only a great personality, but also a fierce anti-Nazi. She whispered to my mother that this 'show' was staged by the Nazis to prove the necessity for our liberation by the Germans. I began to laugh which brought me a sharp rebuke from both.

Alas, our turn to be introduced to the Nazi Hierarchy came and we were greeted with Hitler salutes and then given four tins of peas and beans each. Unable to comprehend the purpose and the pittance we were holding, we left for home. Once we felt safe, Frau Totz flung the tins in the nearby ditch exclaiming: "I own hundreds of acres with my food-stock never better and here I am forced to accept such nonsense." The same really applied to us, for our larder was full of ham and delicious butter, not to mention that my mother had close on a hundred hens.

A few days after I had an idea to get even with this clumsily prepared hand-out and I formed a plan to ridicule the Nazis by thanking them in a poem and to post it at night at the school-house. The place was only fifteen minutes' walk from our house and was the focal point of many meetings, also the Headquarters of the most feared Nazi, the Ortsgruppen-fuehrer Karl Ortner.

Making myself a wooden pen, I wrote in two inch block-letters, the following Poem:

Wir danken unserem Fuehrer . . .
Fuer seine gute Tat . . .
Die er uns am Karsamstag . . .
Mit Linsen, Erbsen, Brot . . .
So reich bescheret hat . . .
Die Wurst die gute fiel zur Seit' . . .
Fuer seine Protektionsleut . . .

Wir danken dem Herrn Ortner . . .
Der uns in Reihen stellt . . .
Damit wir uns nicht irren . . .
Wie komisch ist die Welt . . .

Wir danken unsern Befreiern . . .
Nun haben wir Grund zum feiern . . .
Der Hitler verspricht uns Blumengarten . . .
Oesterreich erwache!! wir sind verraten!!!

As soon as it was dark enough, I dressed in men's clothing and made for my destination to post my approximately 2ft x 4ft POEM, pinning it on the outside school-board usually reserved for important notices. All went well and back home I hid a copy of my work behind the Fuehrer's picture – I thought this to be the best place.

Around 11 a.m., the following day Frau Wiesberger, our very good friend and neighbour, called . . . but she was in tears and despair: "They arrested my husband," she cried, explaining that they believed he had hung up an anti-Nazi poster. "Please help me," she begged and I promised to do so.

That same night I posted the second poem at the chapel-door. Of course, I did not want to be heroic and get caught, but simply to prove that Wiesberger, now in jail, could not be the offender, or at least he was not the only one protesting against the betrayal of Austria.

Once more my friend Steinegger raced to my home, urging me to destroy the evidence . . . if there was any . . . but it was too late already, for two Brownshirt Nazis invaded us some half an hour later, taking our place apart. Handcuffed they marched me some 5 km to the Gendarmerie H.Q. at St. Stefan near Stainz, where I was confronted with the Commandant Herr Benko. Rather odd, his wife Ani was the local photographer and had taken my picture on my fifteenth birthday.

I stared at the Commandant, thinking of what my mother had told me recently . . . they would have to kill your father to silence him . . . and I said very firmly: "Charge me . . . or let me free." "You are at the wrong side to dictate the terms," he answered sarcastically, but I repeated my demand. Suddenly, he got hold of me and locked me in the adjoining room, leaving me there some three hours to cool off, as he laughingly stated.

After this period I was marched back into the Commandant's office, told to sit down, and given a paper and pen. "Write your poem in bold block letters," the Gestapo officer demanded, but I refused telling him I did not know what he had in mind. Angrily, he began to dictate the content, deliberately leaving out some words and of course hoping that subconsciously I would write them down. However, his hopes did not come true and he told me to stop writing. Inspector Benko looked up, guessing the officer's intention and said: "She is only fifteen and should be dealt with by the Juvenile Court."

"Oh you think so," was the snappy reply and he added: "In a few years, or shall I say months, she will be a potential man-trap, how are we going to catch her then?"

Fancy putting this idea in my mind, I thought surveying my foes, whilst the Gestapo officer formerly charged me with insulting behaviour against the Fuehrer and his officers. Picking up Hitler's *Mein Kampf* from the desk, he pronounced the sentence: "Fifteen strokes of the birch, one for each year of your life."

I stood upright, motionless repeating the sentence in my mind.

The two Brownshirts took me into another room, whilst one forcefully removed my blouse, yet amongst all this goings-on, I felt proud in the knowledge I had hurt the Nazis sufficiently to make them take such cruel revenge.

The Gestapo officer brought a whip and began lashing over my back, counting the strokes. The pain was nothing compared to the inferno in my brain and whilst bending under the birching, I shouted: "I hate you you beast, I shall never forgive you for this." After some ten lashes I fell to my knees, for the pain on my right shoulder was unbearable and I saw blood running down my arm. Obviously the skin had burst open. At last the punishment was over and I just lay face down on the floor with someone throwing my blouse over me and telling me to go home. Slowly I lifted myself up and staggered into the other room where Steinegger was sitting behind the desk. He buried his face with his hands and said: "Please believe me, I had nothing to do with this, but if ever I should have a girl, I shall name her Burgi after you." Bewildered I gazed at him, for at that moment I hated all men, for little was I to know that one day he would be the father of a daughter (and a son who became one of the greatest International Skiing-jumpers) to uphold his promise.

Trembling I signed my release papers and left without looking up.

It was nearly 8 p.m. and getting dusky as I made my

homeward journey. The swelling on my back was getting bigger, yet my greatest worry was would I be scarred for ever and how would my mother react at seeing me like this? However, the most important thing was that I had made my impact on the Nazis and that from now on they had better watch out for I was growing up so fast and the same men who were condemning me to death would soon be grovelling, vieing for my favours, and the list of the contenders was in my head. Somehow all this wishful thinking was like a drug to ease my pain and to shorten my two hours' walk.

The Nazi police showed me how they dealt with 'criminals' like myself . . . the thrashing they gave me left weals on my back. My mother was shocked, and I swore never to forget. I had been an objector, now I was the enemy of the Germans. The hatred born that day was to be nourished by the cruelty I witnessed in the following months.

Systematically I set about the Nazis, listing every name recorded in reports on various functions in the newspapers, hoping with all my young heart that one day I would bring about the downfall of the owner.

In February 1940 my eighty-year-old grandmother received a Court order to appear in connection with the *Ahnenpass*, a family tree search ordered by the S.S. Chief Heinrich Himmler. I telephoned our Solicitor, Dr Brown, but he was completely stunned by this action and asked me to accompany my grandmother to Court, where he would meet us. Before leaving her home at No.8 Moserhofgasse, Graz, she held my hand and said: "I am sorry Burgi, but the truth will have to be told."

I wondered what it was all about.

The proceedings were very formal, and my grandmother was sworn in. As she removed her glove, I noticed a diamond and ruby ring which glittered and dazzled me. Why had I never seen it before? With impatience I awaited the hearing.

The Judge requested my grandmother to stand before his table, which she did, but retaliated immediately by placing her large handbag on it, demanding to know why she had been summoned.

Startled by grandmother's action, he removed her bag. "I ask the questions!" he stormed. My grandmother was not intimidated. "In my days gentlemen never shouted at ladies, she retorted indignantly.

I wanted to go forward and comfort her, but the Judge had begun to speak and I listened as if glued to my seat.

"It is known to this Court that you, Luise Ortner *née* Kern, gave birth to a child by the name of Margaretha who was adopted by your late sister Josefa Krenn. We also know that this girl born, June 6, 1885 is not the child of your husband Franz Ortner."

Grandmother interrupted and said: "How could she be his daughter, I did not meet Ortner until 1890."

Angrily the Judge told her to be silent and went on: "What we want to know Frau Ortner is the truth. By whom was this child fathered?"

Grandmother swayed a little and Dr Brown rushed forward to help her compose herself. "Herr Richter, Your Honour, Margaretha's father was not a Jew, if that is what you are searching for, but if he was one I should be the first person to admit it."

The silence in Court was unreal and I was glad when she spoke again: "It all happened in 1884, when the rich were rich and the poor were poor, but I was neither. I was considered very beautiful and the Czech, Notar Johan Brauer, fell in love with me. We married and Margaretha was our only child." The Judge waved her to go on talking, when she suddenly said: "I still fail to see what it has got to do with this *Anstreicher*, what I have done nearly sixty years ago?"

At this moment I trembled for Grandmother who meant of course the Fuehrer, who at one time had been a house-painter *(Anstreicher)* and I feared serious consequences for insulting Hitler. Dr Brown and I looked at the Judge's face and it seemed like a hostile mask watching the reaction of the few people in Court. At last he spoke in a rasping tone, calling my grandmother a silly old woman who had been caught out. Obviously he enjoyed belittling her, but abstained from ordering further punishment. Greatly relieved, I glanced at our solicitor who nodded to me as if to indicate the ordeal was over. The Judge, however, did not think so, and urged my grandmother to tell him the rest of her story. In my humble opinion he did it for curiosity only.

As the old lady was still standing, I asked for a chair to be put for her. Indignantly, she pushed it away, arranged her hat and, taking her time, said: "If Herr Hitler is so interested to know what I did in 1884, he shall have the truth and nothing but the truth. I was twenty-two years, young and different from the local girls in Wartenberg (Brauer's residence), a little wicked perhaps. My dresses covered me up but never obstructed the view. Soon I discovered that Shani Brauer, who, by the way, came from a Judge's family, relished to look at me . . ." she paused, then went on: "He was no oil painting, rather sloppy shoulders, but good cloth and money can cover up a lot of faults." Even the Judge smiled at this remark and Grandmother at once took advantage of this by saying: "Sir, I notice you've got a sense of humour." Continuing with her own story: "Shani fell desperately in love with me, we married, had the child, but unfortunately I never deserved so much love, nor did I know what to do with it then." Wiping the tears from her eyes, she said: "Brauer gave me the stars and the moon, but his stupid jealousy drove me away from him, thus I left, taking the girl with me. My childless elder sister was only too pleased to adopt her, once more proving that money talks by buying for the child her husband's name of Krenn." Grandmother turned towards me asking my forgiveness and said: "Your grandfather I told that your mother had died, so he would leave me alone. Soon afterwards Brauer divorced me and I married Ortner." Once more she faced the Judge and finished nostalgically: "I often wished I had a magic wand to bring back dear Shani, but it must be Herr Hitler who's got one, otherwise how could he have known about Margaretha and that she was not Ortner's child?"

The Judge told the Clerk of the Court to bring the papers to sign. He placed them before my grandmother. Dr Brown came forward and showed her where to sign. Once more she erupted and demanded to know what further declaration they needed to believe her story. Exhausted with anxiety for her safety, I pleaded with her to do as Dr Brown said as the Judge was 'walking out in disgust' as he put it. Despite all this Grandmother was a pillar of strength and put us all to shame, upholding her dignity as a lady under the most strenuous circumstances.

At last we could depart from the Courtroom. For me it was like getting out safely from a house on fire and Dr Brown agreed with this comparison. However, Grandmother was in the best of moods and requested to be taken to the Café Kaiserhof for a strong cognac. We all felt better and were about to leave when calmly my grandmother removed from her finger the diamond and ruby ring, given to her by my own grandfather, Johann Brauer, and handed it to me. She said nothing, but I understood.

On February 3, 1942, Luise Ortner, née Kern, formerly Brauer, died alone in one small room, where she had been placed after the Court hearing. Her large flat was taken over by Nazis. Major Heinrich Kern, her brother, a *Maria Theresan Ritter,* which made him the equivalent of a British Knight, was deeply grieved by her death and protested before and after to the Military Authorities regarding the treatment his sister had received, but to no avail. In order to express his own disgust for the Nazis he removed the word "Major K.u.K" from his name-shield on his door. Although he was ordered to replace it or face imprisonment, he stood firm, thus personifying the Kern spirit.

The Nazis Motto "Who is not for us, is against us, and the ones against us we shall wipe out" came true. With perfect clarity I saw the state my country was in. On reflection, I am glad that Hitler expressed his views so very blatantly, for it made the choice to fight him all the way an easy and honourable one. In deadly seriousness I directed all my efforts towards undermining the Nazis and their regime of horror.

CHAPTER 2

CONFRONTATION WITH EVIL

Everything seemed to be happening at once. For thousands of Austrians the life they had built up over many years was smashed to pieces on March 13, 1938, when Hitler's might occupied my country. My family was on the black list. My 'Klan' number was 305074 and to get it I had to dig up the past back to 1750. A correspondence rush set in which covered several countries and was very costly. The object . . . to establish *Arische Abstammung* . . . (free of Jewish blood). People were suddenly confronted with a past of which they knew little or nothing and were victimised. In addition to this they were examined for proof of mental weakness, tuberculosis or epilepsy. Sterilization was ordered and sometimes cold-blooded murder in a General Hospital. I was lucky indeed as my entire family was healthy and had served Austria in one way or another. My only snag was, my family had married into Jewish families. Of course that would not do as far as the Nazis were concerned.

The local *Gauleiter* (equal to a Mayor), Karl Ortner, was one of the 'witch hunters' singling out the undesirables. He made all his public threats come true – those who opposed him were imprisoned. Soon after my sentence of fifteen strokes of the birch for ridiculing Hitler, my mother was ordered to appear before Ortner. Full of arrogance he received her at his office at the local school. He pointed out that she had failed to discipline me and finally instructed her to keep me away from my Jewish uncle, Professor Benno

Bolzano, who had changed his name from Mayer. He gave her a further list of names of people I should not see. She was amazed, but was equally determined to get her own back on this impertinent Nazi. As one cannot reason with a bully, she used the medicine prescribed by his master, Hitler. My mother informed Ortner that she had good reason to believe that we were related through her own mother's marriage to a man by the name of Franz Ortner. Further that his only sister Helene gave birth to a crippled son, the same illness from which my mother's half-brother, Franz Ortner junior, suffered. As he realized the implications, the *Gauleiter's*face changed from red to purple. The Nazis had to be *pure* and of *sound* stock. If this 'illness' of which my mother spoke leaked out, the *Gauleiter's* post would soon be vacant. Adding a touch of sarcasm, my mother told Ortner that she was not *née* Ortner, but that she was *née* Brauer by her mother's first marriage to a Czech Notar who died as Cavalry Captain in the first world war. When Mother got back and related the story to me, I laughed my head off, but also sensed that a man like Ortner would not take this lying down. I was right!

An order from the local Labour Exchange instructed me to start work with a family called Anton Fritz in Graz (twenty-five kilometres from where we lived). The strange co-incidence was the fact that the family lived at the same address, No. 41 Grillparzerstrasse, as my relative Admiral Albin Munzer, (retired). It was May 1939 and I started work on a Monday. Ringing the door bell opposite where it said "Munzer", I smiled to myself. To my amzement a Nazi in brown uniform answered. "Heil Hitler!" he shouted. It took my breath away, but I had no doubts, this was Herr Fritz all right. I walked inside and he briskly introduced me to his wife, then left us alone. Frau Fritz was a rather frail woman and explained to me the duties for the day, in particular pointing out that at all times I was to hold a soft duster in my hand when touching the highly polished furniture.

The Fritz family left, taking the small girl with them. Once alone in the rather elegant flat I began to look around. There were three rooms, a kitchen, bathroom and bedroom leading off the dining-room, all tastefully furnished and very clean. However, as I began to work, foul odours coming from one of the rooms next to the kitchen made me suspicious. I investigated, but found the door locked. Above the door were two small windows, I fetched a ladder. What I saw took my breath away. An old white-haired woman was sitting on a heap of rags delousing herself like an ape. She was bowed with despair, grovelling about in her squalor, pulling her hair and scratching her skin which showed patches of festering sores.

With my bare hand, I smashed the little window. The stench that met me was appalling and I realized that the woman was beyond caring, for she never looked up. Frantically I spoke to her, asking her questions, but she went on playing with her body-waste and I felt sick with despair. It was clear to me, only a sadist like Fritz would imprison a human being, watching her dying slowly. I decided to get help and hurried across the corridor to where Admiral Munzer lived, and rang the doorbell. My injured hand was bleeding badly. On seeing me, my uncle looked shocked and pulled me inside, but I implored him to come at once and see what I had just witnessed. The experienced old officer agreed that no one could now help this woman. Horrified we returned to his flat and he explained that the woman was Jewish and previously owned the flat now occupied by Fritz, who had mentioned to the Admiral in 1938 that he would "do away with the Jewess" as soon as possible. This, of course, was the cheapest way of disposing of helpless old women, and no matter how horrified we all were, the facts spoke for themselves.

One thing was certain, I could not work another minute for Nazis like Fritz, and decided to leave this house of horror which I had entered only two hours ago. I went into the kitchen and wrote two notes. One read: "God will punish you for this crime". The second one I pinned on the dirty baby-nappies awaiting my services: "You can wash them yourself."

I asked Admiral Munzer to come with me to the police to support my statement about this woman, and to request she should be removed at once into a hospital. The Officer looked at me in amazement, but said they would investigate the matter. Indeed they did so! Only the outcome was to boomerang on me. Back home at my grandmother's, I had to lie down for I felt sick. I explained why I had returned home and said that I would *never* go back to work for Fritz. Of course my grandmother was deeply moved by my story but explained to me for the first time that Nazi policy was to kill all Jews. In the afternoon, two men from the Gestapo arrived and insisted on speaking with me. They showed me the two notes I left for Fritz and called me "an impertinent girl." After they had left, I cried my heart out, feeling the reaction and the hopelessness in which I found myself.

"You are only sixteen, you will forget about it in time," said my grandmother.

How could one ever forget a crime like this?

I was given permission to go home to my mother's place in the country for the next three weeks. The Labour officials said to 'clear' my mind, but the more I tried to forget the incident, the more I kept thinking about it.

Then came a new post, again in Graz, and I wondered what monster it would be this time. Luckily my fears were unfounded, for the people were Civil Servants, and not open Nazis, also the little girl liked me instantly.

I had been working for two days at this place, when one morning at about midday the door bell rang and a woman from an Insurance Company asked to see Herr Urschitz, my employer. He and his wife were not due in before one o'clock, but she decided to wait. She followed me into the kitchen where I was cutting onions for a *Gulasch.* We talked of how I liked this job, and of my mother who lived in the country. Suddenly I remembered Uschi, the little girl, and excused myself to see if she was still asleep. When I returned the woman informed me that she would make another call and come back. I remember telling her how strong the onions were, and how they made me cry, but she laughed and departed.

Somehow, as I stirred the *Gulasch,* I felt very dizzy and sick, but could not explain it. The next thing I knew was finding myself on the floor surrounded by onlookers. I faintly heard a woman say that she heard a bang above her and investigated. She smelled gas, so her husband broke open the door. Before long the ambulance arrived and took me to the General Hospital. A doctor and two policemen came with me. Once there, I was put in a room alone and they pumped out my stomach. All the time I noticed two men in civilian clothes watching, whilst the doctor told me not to worry. Slowly what had happened in the last few hours began to make sense, and I reconstructed the events to the man who told me not to worry, and his sensitive face bent over me as he listened. Although I did not know if I could trust him, I simply had to tell my story to release my anxiety.

The Insurance woman must have turned on the gas whilst I was seeing to the child, for the oven-jet was full on. The very strong smell of the onions confused me, and by the time she departed, I was swaying about incapable of realizing what was wrong. As I fell to the floor I brought down the radio, making such a noise that the people below were alarmed. "Why? Why?" hammered my brain, until the picture became crystal clear. "Gestapo . . . gruesome . . . evil . . . sadistic . . . terrifying . . . appalling . . . pitiless . . . ogres!" I spelled it out for the doctor who was watching me, motionless. I told him of my suspicions, because I had reported a crime against a Jewish woman whom I had seen rotting away in Graz. "Of course you made things worse for yourself by calling it a crime," he said rather desperately. Nearly hysterical I shouted at him: "You have sworn to save lives, not to destroy them, doctor." He put his hand over my mouth to silence me, but I kept on crying. Suddenly the nurse came in with a sedative, which the doctor took from her at once, saying: "We will let her have a good cry, sometimes it works wonders." Brushing my hair off my face, they both left my room.

A little later the doctor came by himself and to my surprise said: "You can trust me, I am no Nazi, take these tablets and go to sleep." I did, with some apprehension, for sleep and peace of mind were all I craved for.

When I awoke some hours later, the doctor came in smilingly and said: "Feeling better now? I am Armin Torggler, your friend remember." He felt my pulse. While looking at his watch he said: "It would be better if you felt mine, Fraulein Triller." Of course I understood, but I wanted no entanglements, no complications now that I had time to think what was foremost in my heart. To fight the Nazis every inch of the way. Much too long Dr Torggler bent over my hand and kissed it, leaving a tingle, a spark, which, if fanned, could erupt to the real thing. We both knew it was the wrong time and the wrong place, yet nature cannot be surpressed and he whispered: "I have a Jewish grandmother my friend and if they find out, I shall be getting the needle with the right serum." "Oh no Armin," I replied as if it was a dreadful discovery and kissed him on the lips, closing my eyes . . . with him retorting; *"Jetzt koennte die Welt versinken und Du und ich wir bleiben allein"* . . . (now for all I care the world could be sinking, with you and I together).

The following morning an Officer of the Gestapo came and questioned me. Obviously they made a blunder, for my employer insisted that they had no Insurance Company whose representative would call on them. Further, two women living in the house made a sworn statement that they had seen a woman in her thirties leaving the flat of the Urschitz family, thus my story was verified, and to dismiss their agent became impossible. The Gestapo had to think fast and concoct a plot for the newspapers. Dr Torggler brought me the morning edition and laughed. On page three it read: ATTRACTIVE YOUNG GIRL FOUND IN GAS-FILLED KITCHEN . . . The story hinted of the jealous older woman versus the younger girl, even mentioning a young man called Schweiger whom I casually had referred to in my conversation with the 'strange woman'. However, the Gestapo made another error as I never disclosed that name to any of the people who questioned me, only the Gestapo agent could have told them; the woman they said had disappeared into thin air but was wanted for questioning!

Three days later I left the hospital for my mother's home in the country. Dr Torggler visited me as often as he could, and we became good friends. The thirty-six-year-old lung specialist was mine for the asking. His passion loomed before me, whilst he was trying to groom me with a 'U' Certificate. Although I was very fond of him, and found him clever, to fall in love with him was another matter. His philosophy of life had serenity and he abhorred terror. We would sit in my little 'Wendy-house', which was open on three sides, and watch the clouds go by. Armin would hold my hand and say: "Love is the most tremendous thing in the world," and I would listen with an awe-inspired manner, befitting my sixteen years of age. Nevertheless, I had really never been at peace with myself since the Nazis made black into white and night into day, yet the company of this mature man worked wonders.

During one of his visits it rained for days. As he approached our house I went to meet him on horse-back . . . when suddenly my mare sneezed violently. Dr Torggler was so startled that he slipped and fell to the ground, breaking his glasses. I laughed my head off, despite the poor man's plight, yet he forgave me, seeing my point of view, and finally we both laughed, sitting on the ground wet as church mice, until my mother arrived, and apologized on my behalf. It was as if we were having our last fling, for this was Torggler's last visit to us – one week later a letter arrived, bearing the stamp of the Karlau-Prison at Graz. Trembling, I opened it. The few lines were written by Dr Torggler, asking me to visit him with the enclosed pass. Fearfully I complied and reached Graz by bus the following day, wondering what went wrong.

I was led to the visiting room and told to wait, whilst a guard fetched Armin. He was handcuffed. "We have only minutes Burgi," he said, "they confronted me to become a member of the Nazi Party, or resign. I refused, then the nurse who attended you in hospital shouted: 'He only refuses because of the Triller girl, I've seen them kissing in the ward and also when she left'."

With tears streaming down my face, I shook my head, stroking his thin brown hair. Suddenly, he put his handcuffed hands over me and kissed me, with me trying to indicate that I was not good for him and his career. He would not listen and whispered: "The only people who are bad for me, you and I know only too well, for they will stop at nothing, even murder." I understood fully and we kissed each other in spite of the guard standing by, as if there was no tomorrow left for us. Defiance and pride were all that we had left, I wanted to boost Armin's morale and this was my only chance to show him my loyalty.

Soon after this visit, I received a letter from Poland. It was from Armin and he told me that his work as a surgeon kept him alive, but that his thoughts were always with me. He reminded me of our song: *"Soviele Sterne am Himmel stehen, soviele Kuesse musst Du mir geben"* . . . (As many stars are in the sky, as many kisses you must give me). I closed my eyes, for the end of my rainbow was not visible.

Events were moving so fast that I had little time to brood over things I could not alter. The imminent problems were right under my nose at home. Suddenly, there seemed never a dull moment in our house as I found myself called-up for National Service – *Reichsarbeits-dienst.* Although I expected my call-up any day, getting the actual order was another matter. Obviously, I had passed my two previous medicals, hence my swift departure to report at the final H.Q., the Castle Deutschlandsberg. Already in residence were hundreds of girls and boys ready to leave for Germany within forty-eight hours. I was given a uniform with the brilliant observation "it fits", despite the fact that the sleeves would have done justice to a gorilla. The skirt was much too long, the blouse and jacket fitted to the point of bursting at the seams, thus bringing me in cat whistles from the boys. A farewell dance was organized by the Nazi Party and we all had to attend. Somehow, I brought with me my evening dress, which was really not allowed but I decided to wear it, even at the prospect of being sent off. Music and laughter filled the air as I entered, bravely knowing I would cause a stir. The slipper satin tea rose coloured gown was tailor made and glistened under the chandeliers. A young man in Nazi uniform was staring at me with delight and I remembered his face from the march past in the morning. "I must have looked a sight," I thought holding his glance and knowing that he was going to ask me to dance. With only seconds to think, between me and the son of the most powerful Nazi, Reinbacher, I formed a plan. I pretended not to know who the arrogant fellow was, and he informed me to the lovely tunes of Johann Strauss. Looking at me victoriously his eyes were saying: "Every girl in the room would give her right arm to be you," while I smiled, testing how good an actress I was.

After his pointless introduction, I made the most of the evening, with him jumping to my wishes, buying me flowers in the nearby foyer and reaching for balloons released from an opening in the ceiling. Rudi Reinbacher was totally bewitched and, to my amazement, told me around midnight that he dreaded the thought of my leaving for Germany. "I only obey the orders of the Fuehrer," I stated and he held me a shade closer. *"Und wenn die Liebe will . . . dann stehn die Sterne still und mein Herz das liegt in Deiner kleinen Hand"* . . . (When love is in command . . . all the stars stand still and my heart lies in your little hand). The orchestra was playing and I knew Rudi Reinbacher was mine for the asking.

After my return to the sleeping quarters, I faced an onslaught of questions from the other girls, who were teasing and taunting me, and I said, without modesty: "The Eagle does not catch flies." The lights in the huge dormitory went out, but in my ears the music was still playing . . . "when love is in command, all the stars stand still . . ." until I went to sleep.

In the morning I was ordered to see the Commanding Officer and rather feared some bad news. However, to my amazement he told me that I was *freigestellt* . . . free to go home to my mother and that I could collect my travel expenses. The unmentionable had happened, feminine mystique had conquered man and I hardly knew how to face the other girls. My final orders were to go to room number eight and I obeyed. There stood Rudi with his father who congratulated me, and although it was too funny for words, I deserved it for pulling off such an achievement. The crowning triumph came when Rudi drove me home in his father's staff car, and delivered me into the arms of my dumbfounded mother. I had passed my debut on the stage of Hitler's war.

It was 1940 and a new purge had begun. The victims – the old, infirm and the crippled – all had to make room for the Super Race Himmler had in mind. All human rights were brushed aside and the reaction of the people involved was one of shock.

A local doctor by the name of Kloss was the first to fall in line with the Nazi policy and set up a register of the 'unwanted'. He had forgotten one of his sisters-in-law was a very good friend of ours and her son Paul a boyfriend of mine. In complete contrast to him, they were most religious people and kindness itself, thus Paul informed me of two names on his uncle's list – Wastel Klinger, the seventy-five-year-old man living in one of our outbuildings, and Gretel Hafner, the seventeen-year-old girl with slightly deformed feet, who helped my mother. As neither of them could read or write they appealed to us for help. My mother and I composed letters to various authorities, but with negative results . . . "The decision rests with Dr Kloss" was the inevitable answer. I could only think of one solution and hoped it would work.

Dr Kloss had one son. His name was Willi and he fancied himself with the girls. Aware of his good looks he would drive up and down the country road in his father's red Mercedes, hooting past our house – he envied his cousin Paul because he was taking me out. As far as girls were concerned Willi's intentions were always dishonourable; I took the chance in both hands and laid the bait for the 'shark' to nibble. At once he accepted my invitation to spend the following afternoon at my home and arrived showily dressed, with an embroidered Swastika on his blue tie. Discreetly, Mother and I had a good laugh. However, it so happened that my best friend, Melanie, the only daughter of a rich solicitor, was also staying with us, thus making up a threesome, much to the dismay of poor Willi.

After lunch we went bathing at the nearby river. Melanie was already dressed in a black swimsuit and lying on the lawn next to Willi, waiting for me to get ready. Taking my time, I put on my new emerald green swimsuit, fish-netted together at the sides with the tiniest of straps and, placing a matching bow in my deep-black hair, I made an entrance like a *prima donna,* whereupon Willi's eyes nearly fell out of his head. Generously he smiled, scrutinizing every inch of my body in slow motion and only someone like myself with a hard head and a target in mind could stand it for that long. However, Melanie did not get my point and excused herself to go for a swim, urging Willi to come along – he rudely declined.

"Will you come with me?" I asked teasingly.

"You look much too gorgeous to get wet," Willi exclaimed

and I sat myself beside him, stroking his back.

"Give a man a chance," he pleaded laughingly and I pushed him over on to the grass, with him retaliating by holding me down, saying quite seriously: "*Grossdeutschland* wants a fit race, not freaks requiring medical aid . . . you've got the perfect hips for bearing children." He could have knocked me down with a feather, but on second thoughts it did not surprise me, coming from Dr Kloss's son, and I asked him: "Who are the freaks you have in mind, Wastel and Gretel?" Blushingly he admitted that it was so but as they were in my mother's employ, he might be able to help me through his father. "The rules can be broken," he said, bending over me and asking me of all things, if I thought he had broad shoulders? Willi obviously tried to stall further questions on what I had foremost in my mind and kept flattering me, amongst promises of help for the 'doomed people'. Suddenly, he exclaimed very definitely: "As the quotation says 'one hand washes the other' so could I be of use, if you . . ." But I interrupted him, countering: "If I married you, Willi?" As if hit by a heavy hammer, he stared at me, but to save his face he agreed with a lump in his throat. I suggested that now we should go for a swim, if only to cool down. Imagining well what went on inside Willi Kloss – the regrets that he was taken by surprise and most of all how to tell his Nazi father of this unthinkable relationship between us – I felt quite confident of getting my own way.

However, my mother was worried, knowing Willi's father's ruthlessness. Nevertheless Willi became a regular visitor, but restricted to being on his best behaviour. I suppose, if ever a girl had taught him a lesson he would not forget, it was I. In the weeks that followed he must have had some idea that I was playing. Rumours of our secret engagement swept the district, with top Nazis, who previously had ignored me, greeting me, and for a while my place in the sun was very acceptable.

Storm-clouds were gathering. Willi's father was furious, and summoned my mother to his surgery. "My heir, my only son and your daughter," he began, "are two opposite poles and live in a different environment. A marriage is unthinkable."

My mother was angry and hurt. She forbade me to see Willi again, but as far as I was concerned the fruit was ripe to pick and pick I did – my own place of confrontation with Dr Kloss. Pushing his chest out, he explained that I was an open anti-Nazi, already tried and convicted before a Nazi Court, thus quite unsuitable for his son. To his astonishment I fully endorsed his views, but told him that love was blind and, as if to add to his agony, informed him that Willi declared his intention to elope with me if necessary. Dr Kloss's face grew purple; he stressed my Jewish connections and said that he would have to resign from the Party, making a full statement of his reason for so doing. Lifting him once more from his depression, I said: "That won't be necessary Dr Kloss, I have an offer to leave for Belgium with Melanie, thus confronting your son with a *fait accompli.*" "Yes, yes," he said "I should be most grateful to you in that case and maybe I can be useful to your mother." Sitting down demurely opposite his desk I told him of how he could assist my mother, by allowing Wastel and Gretel to look after her as they had done since 1936. Glancing at me from the corner of his eyes, he got the message, assuring me not to worry. Dr Kloss did not fool me for one minute and I knew that only if I got it in black and white would he stick to his promise. I demanded an official medical certificate, exempting the two from deportation to a mental home, stating that in his opinion, Wastel Klinger and Gretel Hafner were fit to work and curable. "Now I can only hope it will not boomerang on me," Dr Kloss said as he handed me the signed document. "Of course not," was my reply. "Why should it, all you have to do . . ." "Yes?" he asked anxiously. " . . . is to stick to your considered medical opinion, Dr Kloss," I answered turning on my heels to leave.

The agony of playing the fool with a loaded weapon against me was over at last and my efforts rewarded. Entrusting the vital papers to my mother, I was certain that all would be well and that Dr Kloss would keep his side of the bargain, for more than one reason. Overjoyed, my mother showed Wastel and Gretel the documents; the girl's mother knelt before me in gratitude. Although I found it distressing, I also realized that mother-love was perhaps the greatest in times of stress and despair.

The autumn leaves had fallen and the phoney war was over, with reports coming in of heavy fighting on all fronts. Even my Nazi boy friend Reinbacher could not escape the *Tagesbefehl* of his Fuehrer and was sent to Klagenfurt to await front line service. At this same time Dr Torggler's letters ceased and I guessed what that meant. However, the opportunities were there and I had the will to serve, with no bargains at the leadership counter, only painstaking preparations, high aims, long days and sleepless nights. My biggest fear was of following my girl-friends in falling in love, getting married, settling down in a comfortable rut and accepting Hitler as a necessary evil. At nights I lay awake and came to the conclusion that our thoughts have the power to make or unmake us. I had the weapon of a woman and the strength of will-power, a unified force, and I vowed to use them against Hitler and his men.

The Autumn Fair and the Ball Season had started with invitations from my relatives in Graz. The one from my cousin Hannerl Sauruck I was able to accept. She was five years older than I and had five brothers and two elder sisters. Her father, a giant of a man some six foot six inches tall, with the strength of a bull, was my late father's best friend and looked upon me as his ward. On my arrival at the Sauruck house, a comical thing happened. As I was walking up the wooden steps, a young, partly dressed pilot officer came stumbling down, landing on his bottom. Excitedly he asked my pardon, but I did not know why. I then noticed Herr Sauruck at the head of the stairs, shouting at the top of his voice: "I'll teach you to sneak into my house visiting my daughter and taking off your jacket when I am out, you Gerry *Luftwaffen* pilot. Tell your C.O. to come and collect the rest of your gear, you little bumble bee." Enraged the German shouted back: "Do not forget, *mein Herr,* I am an officer and flyer of Goering's *Luftwaffe* and we will conquer the world." To which the old man replied: "The only flying you have done is down these steps, and if I see you again in my home, you will be incapable of flying for good." Moving past the pilot, I was helpless with laughter, but I am afraid he did not share my sense of humour, and I don't blame him. In spite of this fracas, Hannerl chaperoned me to the Ball, but the question remained: "Who was chaperoning who?"

At this particular time Graz was full of excitement and flags. The reason – the bombing of Coventry.

THE HEART OF ENGLAND IS DESTROYED, the banners read, and from every loudspeaker people were urged to visit the Fair and see the films brought back by the pilots taking part in the raid and the burning of the City of Coventry. The people came and stood in queues to see the horror of destruction. So did I, except that I did not go inside the tents to watch. I only wanted to observe the reaction of the ordinary man and woman in the street. It taught me a lot. The ruthlessness of people drunk with victory. Outside the tent was a large caricature of Winston Churchill digging graves for the Coventry victims, with a small baby lying dead at his feet. In disgust I walked away and last night's Ball was like a curse on my mind. I told the Sauruck family what I had seen but they seemed afraid to talk about it, only Herr Sauruck called the *Luftwaffe* "Pigs in uniforms", bringing him black looks from his youngest son Erhard, who in fact was wearing one. Authoritatively he addressed Erhard, telling him to stand when he spoke to him and Sauruck said: "I trust you will never forget the rules and disgrace yourself, or I shall disown you my boy. I fought with Triller (he meant my father) in Italy, but not against defenceless women and children.

The following morning I decided to leave. About the middle of the night there was a knock at the door and Herr Sauruck went to open up. Hannerl and I watched, full of suspense, from the window. It was Frau Munzer, the seventy year old wife of Admiral Munzer. Whatever was she wanting from the Saurucks? Being her relative I went to investigate and found a woman in great distress to say the least. Hannerl gave her brandy, which she gulped down. Somehow she managed to tell us the most horrible story I've ever heard.

Because of her husband's insistence to the police and authorities that the old Jewish woman at No.41 Grillparzerstrasse (where I had worked for only two hours) needed desperate medical aid, he was arrested by the Gestapo. For days she knew nothing about her husband's fate, until this very day when the bell rang and a large parcel was flung into her hall. By the shape she could see that it contained limbs and to her horror she realized it was Admiral Munzer's cut-up body. First she fainted, then she shouted for help, which brought her a warning from her neighbour Anton Fritz – the Nazi responsible in the first place for both crimes – so she gathered all her remaining strength, and came here. Shivering with cold and fear, Hannerl and I listened; Sauruck's knuckles showed through his skin as he ground his large hands like millstones. I wondered what went through his mind, and I was certain of one thing. If he had been able to get hold of Fritz he would have strangled him with his bare hands and never regretted it. What can one do, what can one think at times like this? Stark horror stared us all in the face. Who would be next in our family? Finally, we managed to put Frau Munzer to bed. She was too exhausted, too desperate, too old to care. It was up to us to take her blows on our shoulders. Sauruck managed to get the 'parcel' out of the house that night and, with the help of a grave-digger, arranged the funeral. Although the Gestapo called on Sauruck the following day, giving orders to keep the burial secret, we made it possible for people personally known to the Admiral to know the truth and, if they wished, to attend the funeral. As my own mother was too upset, I represented her and laid a wreath of water-lilies interwoven in evergreen laurel foliage, befitting a hero. In deadly silence we paid our last respects, unable to express to the widow, the way we felt. The small gathering dispersed with Gestapo agents taking down our names and addresses. Dwelling upon the terrors of this regime I knew if I lived to be a hundred I should never forget this atrocity.

Tuesday, 28 January 1941. The arrival of an unexpected document made me sit up and take stock of myself. It came from the Minister of Labour at Leibnitz and exempted me entirely from National Service – *Arbeitsdienst* – and was dated January, 26 and signed by the *Arbeitsfuehrer* (Minister)

Die Reichsarbeitsdienstpflichtige

Familienname:

T r i l l e r

[illegible]nen:

Notburga

[illegible]atum:

21.1.1922

[illegible]ort:
[illegible]

Graz Stmk.

M[illegible]s-Nr.

323/22/293/1/6

Eigenhändige Unterschrift der [illegible] RAD [illegible]ten:

Triller Notburga

wird hiermit vom Reichsarbeitsdienst

freigestellt.

Grund:

aus gesundheitlichen Gründen

Reichsarbeitsdienst [illegible]
Dienstsiegel
Meldeamt [illegible]

Bock

Arbeitsführer.

Unterschrift des RAD-Meldeamtsleiters

Ort: Leibnitz den 26.1.41.

Exemption Certificate

Dr Bock. Bewildered, I examined this unique document. As it was signed on a Sunday it was obviously done behind closed doors, perhaps even under pressure. After the first initial shock I had a good laugh . . . . Exempted on medical grounds, without actually stating the reason, rather ambiguous, susceptible to two or more meanings. Who were they kidding, or better intimidating? Obviously the doctors, who issued me at the recent examinations with a certificate stating exceptionally healthy.

My mother had joined me in deliberating who could be behind this document and *why*. There was only one logical answer: my exemption was due to the fact that Rudi, the son of a powerful Nazi, desired me, thus had ways and means to enforce his will. High pressure arguments must have preceded to overrule the medical profession responsible at the recruiting centre, and to get the 'top dog' to sign it, thus eliminating vetoes, as I was a known anti-Nazi in the district, thus promoting a *coup d'état* within the local Nazi hierarchy. However, one thing Dr Bock did make sure of – to confuse the file he made me one year older, as most probably only recruits born in the year 1923 came under review and there was no point or necessity in checking the 1922 entries.

Somehow it made me shiver to think to what length they would go in order to get their own way, yet I was equally flattered that my formula, using men as instruments of my policy, worked so well. Perhaps I was able to expose a more profound reality in a world of stupid bestiality, although it sounded shocking and satirical. The fruit hung before me to pick and all I needed was to be myself, as God created me, using my intelligence and determination to defeat a Dictatorship of unprecedented terror . . . by eradication with the strongest weapon – WOMAN.

CHAPTER 3

THE ULTIMATUM

Hurrying along the darkened streets in Leoben, a small town in the heart of Austria, my mind was concentrating on one man – Hugo Michalitsch, a Doctor in Economy and nearly fifty years old. Behind his bespectacled eyes radiated the strange kind of magnetism of a man who knew what he wanted and went all out to get it. He preferred me to call him Dr M –, thus adding an air of mystery. Suddenly I found myself outside his house. I had known him for the past six months, but this was my first visit at his invitation. Whatever my fears – was he an imposter, an informer, a Casanova or a true anti-Nazi – it was too late to go back. I pressed my finger on the bell.

Dr M – opened the door, pulled me swiftly inside, and bolted it. Following him through the hall to the living-room I kept looking about me. Good pieces of furniture were in evidence, and plenty of silverware added an impression of prosperity. I was wondering who kept it so clean as I knew Dr M – lived alone.

Four people were standing in the room as I entered. They looked grave, to put it mildly, and my host made the introductions: a middle-aged surgeon of whom I had heard, a Polish engineer who told me that he worked at the nearby iron and steel works at Donawitz, and an elderly woman resembling a fortune-teller at a fairground. Finally I was introduced to a tall officer wearing the uniform of the *Gebirgsjaeger* (mountain troops). "This is Oberleutnant von

Schindler, my deputy," Dr M – said, observing me closely. Bowing slightly, the Officer countered rather cooly: "So this is the girl who will bluff the Nazis and put us on a progressive path!" Taking a deep breath, I answered one shade cooler: "So far the Nazis have left me haunting memories of terror, murder and blackmail and I have all the intentions of getting even with them."

With waving gestures, Dr M – parted us and continued: "No other girl among the hundreds called up for the *Reichsarbeitsdienst* (National Service) in this area got out of it." Murmurs went through the room and the others wanted to know how it was possible in my case. Dr M – raised his voice and emphasized: "Additionally, I should like to stress that Burgi was on the Nazi's blacklist, and already has been punished for an offence against Hitler, thus making her escape more incredible."

They stared at me as if I was for sale and I could hear my heart beat. At last Dr M – explained how I, at the final recruiting-place, the Castle Deutschlandberg, met, charmed and bamboozled the Nazi Minister's only son, Rudi Reinbacher. How, after the grand farewell dance he found it 'impossible' to let me go and, through his powerful father, obtained a total exemption from National Service. My friends listened with great interest, but Dr M – had not yet finished with his findings of me and said: "Whatever the mysterious charms of a woman may be this girl has them. With them she has achieved this staggering success against the regime." In a strange way, I felt like a painting being offered for auction. However, I wanted to be in the Resistance and realized that its leaders had to be satisfied with my background. After a silence, Dr Helm, the surgeon, asked me to speak for myself and state my ideas.

"I have the will to serve," I began and gave my views for action:

(a) To establish contacts with Nazi victims, for people who have an axe to grind are more willing to assist.
(b) To get information of those with foreign connections.
(c) To make lists of Jewish or partly Jewish people and get them under cover.

(d) To list all dangerous Nazis and their informers, get to know their weaknesses and use them in the struggle to free our own victims.

I ended by declaring that I had no intention of becoming a dead heroine and, as far as I was concerned the end justified the means.

All eyes were on me and Dr Helm stated: "For one so young, you are hard as a flint." To which I retorted in a flash: "I don't suppose you've ever been thrashed with a birch until your skin burst."

Dr M – told us to stop bickering, pulled me towards him and teased me that I was still the *Baby* amongst them. He asked us to be seated in the dimly-lit room and we obeyed. Standing in the middle of the room he said: "For a long time I have toyed with the idea of penetrating the international network of espionage against the Nazis and their Yes-men in occupied countries. Our biggest handicap lies in establishing vital contacts, without the necessary travel papers and stamps from the Nazi authorities." "So what can you do, to alter this situation Dr M –?" Schindler asked; Dr M – had the answer ready: "By sending a girl, attractive and clever enough to fool the authorities. Dr Goebbels and his master's aims are to promote love matches and offspring, thus there are good chances of visiting soldiers in occupied countries." "Very ingenious," Dr Helm countered, and the others added their own ideas and doubts at the top of their voices until Dr M – managed to talk again. Pointing at me he said smilingly: "No one would doubt that she's got a boyfriend crazy enough to want to see her . . ." He paused, ". . . in the North Pole, if necessary." They all laughed as he continued: "The only difference will be that once we have achieved our aims, we will have to 'kill' him off and look for others on various fronts." Oberleutnant von Schindler was dubious: "In my opinion, we can only use this bluff once, if lucky, twice, then the Gestapo will get wise and follow her into the lions' den." A knife-sharp look from Dr M – fell on Schindler as he stated: "If any of you are scared before we get started, you'd better get out now. I am a planner not a dreamer and I demand confidence and loyalty." The Officer turned away for a moment and then faced the table once more. Holding Dr M –'s gaze he stated: "The Gestapo are not fools *meine Herren*, but, for all it is worth, you do have my fullest support in all your actions."

Dr M – had not quite calmed down and insisted that the Gestapo were utter fools where sex was concerned. *Zersetzung der Deutschen Wehrmacht* (undermining the morals of the Forces) he stressed, walking past Schindler and flippantly brushing his hand over the German Eagle and Swastika on his jacket. A faint smile came over Schindler's face and I felt sorry for him. Dr M – fetched a bottle of schnaps and glasses, and offered drinks all around. I declined for I could not take alcohol that strong, and laughter defused the rather tense meeting.

After a while Dr M – made his final bid for leadership and outlined what was really on his mind. Taking a deep breath he began; "Through my nephew, who is at present in Norway, I learned of a man called Dr Schleifinger. He had an affair with a girl at Narvik which resulted in a baby, but this is not what interested me at all, only the fact that her father is, or was, one of the toughest Resistance men in that area." He paused and examined our faces. Mine was aglow with suspense to hear the rest. Dr M – continued: "As Dr Schleifinger is a resident of Graz, I looked up his telephone number and decided to give him a ring. Lucky for him he answered and, when I mentioned mutual friends in Narvik, he agreed at once to see me, providing I did not speak so loud as his wife was standing near him." Dr M – explained the rest of his plan and, at times, we were in fits of laughter as to how, through an indiscretion thousands of miles away, fate stepped in and opened avenues of great possibilities for complete strangers. "The first show-down with the 'master minds' is ours, if we decide to take it," Dr M – exclaimed.

At that very moment I knew Dr M – had a foreign mission in mind and that he was going to ask the leading question. Rather solemnly he rose, turned towards me and said: "Have you got the nerve and necessary acting ability to visit the Nielsens in Oslo, and prove to my 'doubting Thomases' that it can be done and that we are in business?" I was going to shout "Yes" but he sobered me down with his afterthoughts:

"If you don't succeed, the Gestapo will squash you like a cigarette in an ashtray, is that clear?" There was an uproar and comments from all sides. However, the bizarre situation intrigued me and I agreed to go. Dr M – shook my hands and looked straight into my eyes. The mission so full of suspense and danger had been launched and my post as courier established.

All I had so far endured under the Nazis and the terror I had witnessed were not in vain, for I could use my feminine powers to penetrate and play havoc with the Nazis' morale.

A new day had dawned for me. From my humdrum existence I would proceed to a life of great adventure and travel. I longed to get started, to be successful, yet dreaded that I might perish in one of the Gestapo dungeons somewhere in war-torn Europe. Not much of a prospect for an ex-convent girl with an exclusive education and private training to become a singer? Or was it? War is ugly and savage. Millions of people accepted Hitler as a saint or necessary evil, a Caesar of all Europe, but I could not agree.

Dr M – listened to my views with interest and added his secret plans and preparations to my new-found inspiration. He explained how, through his job in the Labour Exchange and his access to files, he knew of many people's movements, which enabled him to get names useful to the Resistance, "And that is how I picked you," he added. Apparently next to my particulars were three crosses, standing for anti-Nazi and undesirable. He was also under orders to get me the worst jobs possible and to report on my activities at work. I laughed at the latter and told him that *now* he had a chance to keep an eye on me, at least as long as the war lasted. "With your musical training I shall send you as a Troop-entertainer to Norway," he stated, "a test for further missions." "But what about the travel-papers?" I asked in amazement. "They are already in my hands," he said, walking over to his desk and bringing them for all to see.

I visualized myself a modern Mata Hari criss-crossing the Continent. Obviously Dr M – had everything prepared – a contact in Oslo and a permit to travel under the name Gitta Herberstein. "Actresses like high sounding names," he declared laughingly. Things began to make sense – the

Nielsen family in Norway, my long journey, and I was convinced that, in an emergency I could even go on stage and sing to prove my part. Only one question remained . . . how could I defend myself if I was attacked? "The only weapon you will need you've got already," was Dr M –'s devastatingly frank answer. Schindler put his arm around me, adding his own brand of humour: "The Germans and patrols will be only looking at her fairy eyes and undulating curves, forgetting all about rules and regulations." "Splendid," Dr M – said at the top of his voice, "I am glad that my deputy has got the message at last."

Around a table the final details were discussed and the briefing began. Dr M – referred to the various countries I should have to cross-travel and pointed out the distances as compared to my own small country of Steiermark. For instance between Klagenfurt (near the Jugoslavian border) and Flensburg (Danish border) are approximately 1000 kilometres and he mentioned that one could travel in and out the many Fjords and it would take the length of 20,000 kilometres. With my heart in my mouth I listened, thrilled and eager to go. "One is only eighteen and tempestuous once and never again," Oberleutnant von Schindler said, and I felt a bang in my heart. Dr M – rebuked Schindler for his 'silly' remark and he apologized to both of us. To me it seemed so formal and unnecessary in the face of our common danger and sacrifices. However, Dr M – ignored it and went on with his lecture on Narvik and the military details, in particular the anti-aircraft guns, No. 88, which were made in my home town of Graz in Austria. Suddenly he asked me on which side of his office the wash-basin stood. "You open your door from left to right and just miss the basin," I answered slightly bemused at his change of subject. Unruffled by my smiles he explained that a photographic memory was worth more than all drawings and notes, for what was in one's head no one could extract by force. "Exactly," Dr Helm said, "it could also work both ways." Dr M – looked angry and replied in a drawl: "You're a good surgeon but a bad physiognomist."

They wished me luck and departed, all except Dr M – and Schindler. It was nearly midnight. The two men went into the kitchen to make coffee, while I stretched myself on the couch, trying to outweigh the doubts in my mind, until the officer entered the room with a tray of good smelling drinks. "They say old Churchill can sleep anywhere and rest," he said jovially and I agreed, yawning in a most unladylike fashion. Schindler knelt down to hand me my cup. I was about to take it when he put it back on the table, held my hand and kissed it. Both our lips trembled until he spoke first: "There is no retreat for you now, Burgi, and at times you will be the loneliest person in a large crowd." Dr M –'s entry saved me from breaking down and crying. He willed me to laugh and be gay, though I thought of the *Few*, including the Battle of Britain pilots, who were taking on Hitler and his might single-handed. Now it was our turn to show what we were made of and win some victory for humanity.

Early in the morning I returned to my mother's home, – my lips sealed and my heart racing. My mind was already *en route:* Leoben-Vienna-Berlin-Warnemuende-Goeteborg-OSLO.

October 24, 1941. As anticipated Oberleutnant von Schindler brought my travel papers and money. With the thoroughness of a solicitor defending a murderer we both examined the documents and had to admit that they were perfect and should fool anyone, providing the bearer out-acted Greta Garbo and outlived the nine lives of a cat. I sincerely hoped to do both. My outward calmness pleased Schindler who called me 'Gitta', to which I did not blink an eyelash. He handed me a small parcel saying: "You are too naked without this, at least you'd have a chance to use it if there should be no other way out." "Thank you," I said, toneless, as I undid the wrappings. I stared at my 'present' – a brand new Luger "38" and he asked me if I knew how to use it. Although I had a vague idea and some knowledge in firearms, this weapon was new to me. Schindler explained every detail, loading and re-loading it until I managed to do it to his satisfaction. He promised to call on me the next afternoon, Saturday 25, October, to do some practise shooting. The 'play' had become serious and I had matured in a strange way.

As promised he came again. Whilst Mother made Schindler some coffee, I went to fetch a document which I believed to be equally useful, if not even better. To the amazement of the officer, I showed him a military diary printed in Oslo 1940 which was sent to me by a friend of an officer who was killed in Norway during the fighting. Schindler was dumbfounded, for documents like these had to be destroyed, but he exclaimed: "What a stroke of luck, girl, this diary gives you a second identity if need be, plus a boyfriend already established in Norway." He was hilarious with joy at our good luck and pencilled in on the map the route I was to take. Rather thoughtfully he remarked: "Whoever said that the written word, the pen, is stronger than the sword was right and you are blessed with looks, luck and ingenuity."

We went into my step-father's stable to try out the revolver. First Schindler fired at bundles of straw, thus muffling the sound and showing me from what height to aim at a man to kill him. I shuddered. He handed the gun to me, told me to hide it under my clothing, and then ordered me to fire, timing me with his stop-watch. After several tries, he considered me good enough to stay alive.

"That will be all for today Gitta," he said and pulled me to a bundle of straw, explaining that he had Slavish blood in his veins and that he was a Baron by birth. With a bitter, yet far-away look in his almond shaped eyes, he continued: "Ever since the Germans raped my native Czechoslovakia, I am seething with hatred, although paradoxically I wear the Fuehrer's uniform," and, squashing a straw, added: "No one helped me to fight them in 1938 so I joined them, thus hoping to have my revenge from a ring-side seat."

Feeling sorry for him and watching his behaviour I had to admit Schindler was a very handsome six-foot man with an intelligent face and I could fall for his charms like a brick. Bemused at my total silence, his rather arrogant mouth smiled in a flirtatious manner and I got up, brushing the straw off my trousers. Schindler followed suit, standing right close to me. "Gitta," he said deliberately, "if I loved you I should never let you go, so you know how I feel." "That leaves me room to manoeuvre," I countered, tossing

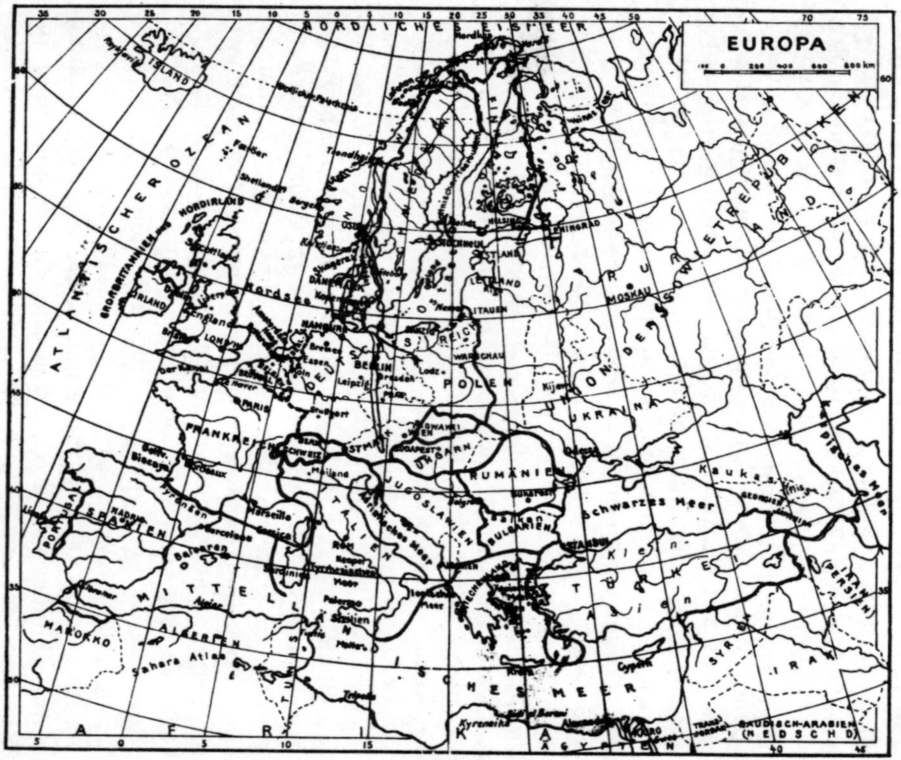
EUROPA
NORDLICHES EISMEER
ISLAND
ATLANTISCHER OZEAN
Färöer
Shetlandin
NORDIRLAND
IRLAND
GROSSBRITANNIEN
England
LONDON
Nordsee
PARIS
FRANKREICH
SPANIEN
PORTUGAL
MADRID
Marseille
Corsica
Barcelona
Balearen
MAROKKO
ALGERIEN
Sahara Atlas
MITTELLÄNDISCHES MEER
ITALIEN
Rom
Neapel
Sardinien
Sizilien
Palermo
Tripolis
Malta
HAMBURG
BERLIN
Leipzig
Dresden
Stuttgart
Bremen
Essen
Köln
OSLO
Trondheim
Bergen
DÄNEMARK
STOCKHOLM
HELSINKI
ESTLAND
LETTLAND
LITAUEN
WARSCHAU
POLEN
Lodz
LENINGRAD
MOSKAU
UKRAINA
Kijew
Odessa
UNGARN
BUDAPEST
SLOWAKEI
WIEN
OSTMARK
SCHWEIZ
Mailand
JUGOSLAWIEN
Belgrad
RUMÄNIEN
Bukarest
BULGARIEN
Balkan
Adriatisches Meer
Tyrrhenisches Meer
Ionisches Meer
GRIECHENLAND
STAMBUL
Schwarzes Meer
Kaukasus
Kaspisches Meer
TÜRKEI
Klein-Asien
Kreta
Cypern
SYRIEN
IRAK
IRAN (PERSIEN)
SAUDISCH-ARABIEN
(NEDSCHD)
ÄGYPTEN
KAIRO
Alexandria
Kyrenaika
AFRIKA
UNION DER SOZIALISTISCHEN SOWJETREPUBLIKEN

back my head and walking off back to the house.

We said good-bye standing in the yard, with Schindler saluting me smartly. Was it the beginning or the end of a beautiful friendship I wondered as I returned to my room deep in thought.

Sunday October 26, 1941. The few things I decided to take were packed in my suitcase and, as far as my mother knew I was off to visit Aunt Jenny in Vienna. I declined being accompanied to the small village station for I wanted to be alone, to think and to prepare myself morally. I was glad Dr M – picked a Sunday as I was less likely to meet people I knew coming and going to work.

Once I was on the train and safely in my compartment, I felt a load lifting off my shoulders, particularly when I had changed over to the express to Vienna. The farther the distance from my home, the better I liked it. Snuggled against my new blue winter coat, only recently bought by my grandmother and the envy of my girl friends, I sat in my corner of the first-class carriage, enjoying the scenery. As expected, I was the only female present and surrounded by men in uniforms. Some talked, others read newspapers and glinted from the corners of their eyes. When I rose to remove my maroon coloured jacket and displayed my white crochet Angora sweater, the monocle of the middle-aged Colonel fell from his eye and he jumped up to assist me. The young officer sitting next to me said to his friend across the seat, loud enough for me to hear it: "We may have youth and looks, but the old boy got rank." Demurely, I sat down again, smiling to all, challenging my criticiser to speak, which he did rather embarassingly. However, he seemed right, for the Colonel at once took over and monopolized my company. He huffed and he puffed and he nearly blew the train down. His zest for the military genius of the Fuehrer knew no bounds and if it was not so utterly funny, he would have bored me to death. My only way out was to get my book and read. However, it did surprise me how calmly he took this open affront and excused himself to go for a drink. Fortunately, for the younger officers, he did not notice their giggles and comments, but my target was still too far away to become pert or complacent, thus I continued reading *Das Haus des Michael Senn* with great interest. It also put me in another frame of mind, for it was given to me by the first man who saved my life, Dr Torggler. He was partly Jewish and loved me deeply without my really knowing it until it was too late and he on his way to a punishment camp in Russia. I closed my eyes and remembered what he said when presenting me with this book. "You will find lots of parallels between you and the heroine, Rosa Senn, you both exude sex with a capital S, yet reject to acknowledge your volcanic passions and ferment in inner struggles."

By now, no one talked, only the rattling of the train's wheels reminded me of movement and I read on until my eyes hurt and I had to put my book away. We neared Vienna and people prepared to get off, except the Colonel who by now had told me that his destination was also Oslo, of all places. In a way, I was relieved, for it is better the devil you know than the one you might meet.

Different officers changed over, but my seemingly endless journey continued as scheduled and I had no option but to make the best of it. I tried to be pleasant, entertaining my illustrious company and I wondered how long my luck could possibly last. Fortunately for me most of the men in uniform lived in an ivory tower, inspired by *Blitzkrieg* and victories, never doubting the invincibility of their *Wehrmacht* and the never ending magical powers of the Fuehrer. They would have scoffed at the very idea that a slip of a girl could do them any real harm, what with Europe under their heels and their *Luftwaffe* bombing British towns and British shipping from Murmansk to Scotland – who would dare to challenge this supremacy? I had a go at it and I was very, proud of this fact. Various military patrols came by checking and rechecking my travel papers. At moments like these my heart stood still until their *Heil Hitlers* and smiles (in that order) indicated that all was well and that I was safe for the next few hours. Louis Pasteur's quotation "Chance favours the prepared mind" seemed appropriate, for my biggest enemy was the lack of sleep, and the tiredness which overcomes all people. I could not allow any flaws in my conversation, fearing to drift into the past of reality, perhaps disclosing names, and at times I had to pull out every ounce of my reserve strength to hold my own with some of my much older and wiser companions. If cross-examined and cornered I pretended to play the fool, the flirtatious 'hussy' and, to my amazement, it worked wonders, chalking off the hours until the new day. The challenge of tomorrow was closest on my mind.

October 31, 1941. Oslo was only two hours away when great consternation on the train set in. What was the matter? Hastily I went to the toilet, splashed my face with cold water and wrapped my revolver in my nightie, pushing it into my well-filled suitcase. Suddenly the train halted. I glanced through the curtains but noticed nothing of importance. Was it an ambush by Norway's heroic partisans? What a thought indeed. I smiled and walked back to my compartment. The Colonel was dressed to perfection, standing to attention and exclaiming at the top of his voice: "General Dietl, the hero of Norway, is on the train," adding, "the Fuehrer has specially mentioned him in his *Tagesbefehl.*" There was no time to comment for the clicking of heels was heard and there facing the entrance, stood the General and his aides. The Colonel made his report, attended by two other officers, and one nurse in uniform, and we all stood with awe, like Christmas trees, for the final inspection. However, my 'friend' went one step further and introduced me as a troop entertainer Fräulein Gitta Herberstein. General Dietl looked at me closely; my seeming calm belied the terror that gripped me. Could this be the end of my mission – so soon? "Splendid," he said. "I understand the Wehrmachts Theatre will play at Narvik for Christmas, these boys deserve some fun, or they forget what a girl looks like." "*Jawohl Ihre* Excellency, I fully endorse your views," I countered quietly. He smiled and retorted: "You must be an Austrian to call me Excellency and I must say it sounds better, but the Germans call me Herr General." My knees nearly gave way. I recalled my own grandfather's rank, a General under the Habsburgs , thus my familiarity with the word 'Excellency'. Wishing us all a good stay in Norway and shaking hands, General Dietl departed with his escort.

The emotional *crescendo* was over and I knew that Oslo was mine to view in an hour or so and all this with the blessing of the Fuehrer. My big gamble had paid off.

As expected Mr and Mrs Nielsen were at the station and took me straight to their flat which was in an American type building on the west side of the town called Kirkeveien. They were surprised to see such a young girl, but when I told them of my experiences on this journey they laughed and it seemed to me as if I boosted their morale. Mr Nielsen who was in his fifties was exactly as Dr M – described, rugged and tough. His wife had clear blue eyes and a most charming smile, but best of all she spoke German, or *Deutsch,* the language of my native Austria. As I was very tired Mrs Nielsen put me to bed with a warm cup of milk, still marvelling how young I was, until I drifted into a long and relaxing sleep.

When I awoke I realized that I was not dreaming, but thousands of kilometres from my own country and that my freedom and life depended on the sincerity of the Nielsens. After a good meal of fish and various vegetables we talked and Mrs Nielsen stated: "We Norwegians are idealists and realists, we are proud and we like to be free," adding with a deep sigh, "nevertheless we do have many Quislings in the pay of the Germans." I expressed my own views regarding my native country, pointing out that according to Hitler's *Volksabstimmung* (Polls) in 1938, ninety-nine per cent voted for him. Of course they were faked figures, but even the real ones were frightening to say the least. Mrs Nielsen agreed and changed the subject to her husband's former marriage which was blessed by a daughter. Little did she realize that I already knew what had happened to her but had no option but to listen. She told me of her husband's fury when he found out that it was a German who gave her a child and he threatened to kill him. However, the consequences, as in most cases of hostages being killed deterred him in the end. In a way I felt awful handing her the correspondence given to me by Schindler before my departure, knowing the unhappiness connected with this name. However, as I did not know the contents, it was my duty to carry out my orders, thus I gave the letter to Mrs Nielsen. Sadly, she took it and left the room, obviously to give it to her husband. I could hear loud voices and her faint crying and I wished that I had never come at all. War brought hatred and unhappiness to all parts of the globe and we were only a nutshell in a torrent of sea. Whatever my personal thoughts I had to make the best of my short stay and extract any information useful to the Resistance and assist their aims to grind Hitler's war machine to a standstill. However, to me the end seemed an eternity away. My repertoire of human knowledge increased as the hours passed erratically, and led to a profound attachment to Norway and its people.

By the following evening I felt quite at home with the Nielsens. We discussed the strength of the German Forces and they told me of the humiliating retreat of the British Forces from Norway, and of their heroic fight around Namsos-Grong and Drontheim. I requested to go sight-seeing and they obliged, but they seemed a little frightened. However, they showed me the University Library at Solli-Platz, the Artindustry Museum (Ullevalsein 5), and the Nation Gallery with collections from Norway's great artists. What amazed me was the fact that one did not have to pay to enter the above mentioned places. Also the periphery of Oslo was wonderful, with little trains leading everywhere. The one I went on was the *Holmenkollbanen* leading to a place of the same name and to the famous Skieng jump from where Norway's skiers first showed the world the fine art of skiiing. Afterwards, we visited the *Skie* Museum with its unique collection and I saw *skies* more than a thousand years old.

The next day we went to the half island of Bygdoy, which we reached from Pipervika. On this island is another Museum, an open-air one called *Folkemusset,*which houses famous ships such as *Fram* which was used by the daring explorers Nansen and Amundsen to penetrate the secrets of the eternal ice. All this left a deep impression on me and for hours I forgot that there was a war on and thousands dying. However, Mrs Nielsen was most concerned for my safe return, she believed I had risked enough by coming. Not so her husband who said: "We need human pigeons and you are made of the right material to get through. All other methods are far too risky." He outlined what happened to the patriot who morsed the signal telling the British Admiralty where the fiercely hunted battleship *Bismarck* was hiding . . . his name was Olaf Fjeld, he came from Spitzbergen, and he was found riddled with bullets in a barn. Despite his gruesome story I asked Herr Nielsen if he had any military details useful to the Resistance, emphasizing: "The weapons which do not arrive here, won't be killing your men and we know where they are loaded and dispatched." The man's face lit up and he banged me on my back so that I nearly fell over as he shouted: "That's the stuff Gitta, disrupt communications, bomb them, blast them, just stop them getting to the occupied countries and we have the Germans licked in no time." I never expected an outburst of this kind from the rather cool Norwegian. A few minutes later he went into the next room and brought back some drawings which he put before me. "German positions," he said and put his finger right on Banak, adding, "from there the *Stukas* operate and attack the British convoys." He told me of anti-aircraft guns, believed to come from Austria, which were very successful. I nodded, for I knew they were made in Graz.

My three days' stay was up and I had to disappear from the scene, or register with the German police, which, of course, was impossible. After a modest farewell party I packed my things and prepared to leave. Greta Nielsen was very sad to see me go. "You are so young and full of life. Who has the right to take it from you? I always wished I had a daughter of my own, but since I've seen what the Gestapo did to a family with three small children, I thank God that I have none." She began to cry and I understood perfectly, holding her close to me, thanking her for their hospitality. "I shall look into the fjord's dark waters and search for your bittersweet face, my child," she said under tears, "and know that you are safe. Remember our Nordish saying: "The same God who makes us wet, will make us dry and if it was never dark, one would not know of the stars." Mr Nielsen just stood there grimly and wished me a safe journey, asking: "If you had to explain your sudden return to Vienna, what will you say?" "I found the man I hoped to wed already married, thus I could not go on and decided to offer my talents to another Front Theatre," I replied flippantly. "And the best of luck to you my girl, I'll fight them to the very end," he drawled, dipping his hat to me and opening the door. My heart saluted their courage and shared his vision that the down-trodden people of Norway would be free again.

November 3, 1941. Freshly inspired with confidence I boarded the train for Austria. My thoughts were lingering with the Nielsens, the lovely view, and the full train, but most of all I was confident in my ability to succeed in getting back, the same way I had managed to come.

At lunch time I went to the dining-car and found myself a table. Whilst looking at the menu card I noticed a very tall man sitting opposite me. He smiled and I responded . . . why, I did not quite know. Perhaps it was his civilian suit amongst so many uniforms. He asked in German, rather hiding his accent, if he could have the menu card. I handed it to him in silence. As he studied it, I pretended to look out of the window, but kept glancing at him. He was very blond, with eyes as blue as the midsummer's sky. Suddenly he returned my glance and held it. His opening words were interrupted by the waiter bringing the soup. We began to eat, but his eyes x-rayed me. The other courses followed but I had the feeling both of us were glad to finish our meal. He looks an ambitious and successful man, I thought, and arranged my jacket, which did not go unnoticed. Like a relief signal he handed me his visiting card. On it was written in gold letters: Count Harald-Wedel-Jarlsberg. I managed to hide my surprise. "Gitta Herberstein," I said. He paused and asked me to join him for a glass of wine, but I told him that I was not a connoisseur and he laughed heartily. The train was racing along and I noticed the passing scenery less and less with Jarlsberg monopolizing every moment of my time. I made him laugh with anecdotes from my past. He seemed so interested in all my views and looked at me in sheer amazement when I stated that to marry a poor man one was young enough at forty years of age. "Your honesty does you justice, but I believe love must come first, it's the only thing which still makes sense," he said with great emphasis. The dining-car began to empty, and we were alone in the long waggon which seemed like a banquet hall without the candelabras. We drank to each other with shining eyes, yet my womanly instinct told me to beware for I was up against a man at least ten years my senior, a character of mysterious behaviour, so I turned off the charm. However, the Count neither wished nor cared to take notice and was as engaging as from the onset. At last, when Jarlsberg had paid all bills, and left a large tip for the waiter, we each went to our own compartment.

I relaxed, but my mind focused on the Count. He hardly mentioned his personal life except that he was single and on his way to Vienna to take up a new post. He had not asked me for my reason for visiting Norway, and the more I kept thinking, the stranger and more unaccountable his position seemed. Use my own judgment, Dr M – had said and I did, but not very successfully. In remarkable order the Count reappeared just before reaching the Swedish border and offered to help with my documents. It gave me a jolt for an instant, but having passed all official customs, my slight nervousness disappeared and a rather relieved looking Count Jarlsberg escorted me to my compartment. He placed his coat on the empty seat next to me, told me that he was going to join me for the rest of our journey, and went to fetch his luggage. Was this my chance to secure a new agent? I had high hopes of inducing him.

Jarlsberg returned in a few minutes and made himself comfortable. I was soon to discover that he loved music and drama, his knowledge of which was remarkable. When one is up against a dazzling and clever personality one listens, and I always remembered my upbringing. However, the Count gave me little opportunity to explore my own intentions, thus a dangerous enchantment was born. I was never afraid of facts, but my loyalty lay with my cause. By the time we reached Goteburg in Sweden I initiated the talk to my own liking, but realized that the thing unsaid dominated the situation. The Count responded by simply looking at me demurely and expressing an occasional "hmm".

November 8, 1941. Vienna was within sight, with an elusive rainbow hovering above my head, although I tried to dismiss my feelings as utter nonsense. In a crowded gangway we prepared to get off, rather nervously fondling the luggage and saying "good-bye". Jarlsberg took the initiative, coming dangerously close to my lips and said: "Remember to telephone me as soon as you get to Baroness Haan's." Then with the fingertips of his right hand he outlined the shape of my mouth and gave a deep sigh, at which I whispered: "One week ago I did not know that you existed," and the Count replied: "Existed yes, but I was not alive." Soldiers were pushing past us and we had to part. We waved to each other until we were out of sight.

I managed to get a taxi and arrived in the afternoon at my aunt's place which is situated in the best part of Vienna. Aunt Jenny was more than surprised at my visit, but Nelly, my thirty years older cousin, suspected that I had been 'up' to something. She was a good friend of mine and could read me like a book. Before going to bed I telephoned the Count as promised. He answered the call himself and we arranged a rendezvous at the Opera Café for the next afternoon at three-thirty.

I got there on time, but Jarlsberg beat me to it. The Café was filled with well dressed and well off people. He began to talk and tell me that he missed me and I searched his face for the truth. The radio was playing marches, when suddenly there were fanfares with an announcement from the OKW, the H.Q. of the German 'Might'. The sinking of British ships and the losses were given in cold figures. Some people jumped to their feet shouting: *"Sieg Heil . . . Sieg Heil . . . Sieg Heil . . ."* followed by the singing of the song: *"Denn wir fahren, denn wir fahren gegen Engeland."* Count Jarlsberg made no comments. We only looked at each other. Suddenly he broke the silence saying: "All that matters is you and I, for I am in love with you." Rather bewildered I accepted his statement. He told me about his family in Norway and of their prominent position, referring to books on the history of his country. I was convinced that he told me the truth, but was more concerned with his present living conditions, to which he made no reference. All I could do was to bide my time and hope that soon we could talk freely.

Before leaving the Café he invited me to spend a short

holiday with him at the Liechtenstein Hunting Lodge, belonging to Prince Liechtenstein. It was near my home in Leoben and, to my surprise, I said 'yes' at once. We were to have a guide, thus making it a threesome and morally acceptable. The Count promised to make all necessary bookings and to keep me informed. With the remark: "I shall be counting the hours until we meet again," we said *Auf Wiedersehn.*

I did not see Jarlsberg again before my final return journey to Leoben. Of course, I was looking forward to my report at Dr M –'s and the reunion with my mother. She was amazed to learn that, in fact, I went to Oslo and not Vienna, and expressed her deep concern for my safety. After my first night's sleep in my own bed once more I felt my old self and started singing before breakfast. However, Mother did not share my feelings and asked me to tell Dr M – to stay away from me. I knew only too well who was behind this request. My future step-father, Herr Joachim Oberleitner, as he resented my stay in more than one way. Sad as it was true, I longed to get away from it all and my mind focused on Count Jarlsberg. Somehow I also wanted to find the answer – was he really in love with me or was it a trap?

The days and weeks passed but no letter from Jarlsberg, only two telephone calls, intercepted by Herr Oberleitner, so I decided to ring him and he assured me that everything was booked at the Lodge and that he expected me on the twelve-thirty p.m. train, on December 1, in Wald. With my home life wretched, it was the only thing to look forward to and I packed and repacked my skiing outfits, trying on various caps and liking, or disliking, what I saw in the mirror.

At last the day came and the twenty-five minute journey from my home, St. Stefan to Wald, seemed endless. However, upon my arrival I saw the Count waiting for me smiling all over his face. He embraced me in front of the crowd, told me how my red-white wool cap suited me, and ushered me to the horse-drawn sleigh which he had obviously engaged to take us part of the way. The winter scenery was glorious and serene as we drove along the small winding roads. Jarlsberg reached for my hands, the driver discreetly turned his head. "I missed you terribly, Gitta," he kept saying. One hour later we halted at a *Gasthaus,* had some warm lunch and picked up Toni, our guide. He was a strong young man, but partly deaf, so was exempted from military service. We set off as soon as we had eaten, as snow began to fall very heavily. Toni and Jarlsberg carried most of the equipment, all I had were my skies, however, they seemed a ton-weight when struggling through two and three feet of snow, mostly uphill. I asked for a pause, but the guide urged us to go on because of the dangerous mountain fog, and we went, hardly speaking one word.

The last efforts towards the Liechtenstein Lodge began. We had already nearly two hours of walking behind us, although from the point of heavenly views it was worth every

Prince Liechtenstein's Hunting Lodge

effort. It was so still that we could hear our own breathing and I couldn't help feeling that surely God must live right up there. Suddenly, like a sleeping beauty among masses of snow, the Lodge appeared, lonely and peaceful. "A jewel imprisoned by winter's magic," I said and my escort nodded and smiled.

The Count unlocked the heavy oak door and we walked into the house, jokingly bowing to each other. Toni made for the kitchen, for he knew the place well, unpacked our foodstock and prepared some hot drink. Jarlsberg and I walked into the living-room immediately facing us. It was the first time since we had met that we were all alone and each glance betrayed our thoughts. He held me close, but I excused myself to explore the rest of the Lodge. It was comfortably furnished, clean, and the beds had warm sheets and beautiful woollen blankets. Beside each bed was a large lambskin rug. I looked through the small gitter barred windows and admired the work of the timeless Creator. Was it only an elusive dream or reality? Here I was protected by this perfect seclusion, away from the merciless war. As I lingered with my thoughts, the Count appeared in the doorway, reminding me to check the kitchen activities or we should starve to death surrounded by so much beauty. Laughingly, we went to inspect the goings on in the kitchen but Toni had already laid the table and dished up omelettes with jam, followed by Russian tea with rum. It all tasted wonderful and we ate with great appetite.

After the meal Toni lit the fire in the open hearth of the living-room, whilst I played an old gramophone. Evening was falling fast and Toni retired to his room. For us the night was still young and full of mystery. We began to dance. The paraffin lamp flickered over our heads while soft romantic music filled the air. Jarlsberg kept holding me tighter and his dancing became more of a love-making; conquest was written on his face and he informed me that temptation was no sin, to which I replied: "I always believed the Nordic race to be cool and reserved, but you are like an iceberg full of fire." He laughed heartily, explaining that underneath, all people are very much the same. I disagreed and he whispered ardently: "I am almost drunk with the desire to love you. I may be a bad *wolf* but you could change me into a *sheep.*" When I pushed him firmly from me he still refused to accept defeat and gaily stated; "Perhaps that is the reason why I'm in love, because you make me fight for you. For a girl of eighteen your sharp logic intrigues me and makes me wonder how many women live inside of you." A slight tremble went through my body but I knew what he meant. Reassuringly he pulled me on his knees and made it clear he wished to marry me, if I accepted his proposal. I was dazed. What could I say to this offer? We decided to leave before the weekend to see my mother, and Jarlsberg read in this suggestion my firm, 'yes'. He seemed very happy again, put on a suitable record: "Love is the greatest secret," and we danced, oblivious of the world and its events. At this hour I seemed to owe everything to a man who looked exceptionally good, was wealthy and whose love enveloped me like a dream. It was so obvious that he would accept my real identity, my secret, and I made up my mind to tell him in the presence of my mother.

The dance was over and we sat down. Gently he laid my head against his shoulder, stroking my hair. "Your jet-black hair will cause a furore amongst the girls in Norway," he said spontaneously, and I agreed, remembering how blonde they were. Jarlsberg lit a cigarette and I excused myself to get some snapshots of my family which were with my things in the bedroom. "Please don't be long," he said, blowing me kisses like a child, and I promised to hurry.

A small paraffin lamp was alight in the hall and I noticed it needed turning lower, which I did, still thinking about the startling turn this brief holiday had taken, when suddenly I saw some papers and a leather wallet beside the Count's rucksack. They must have fallen out and I decided to put them back. Sheer womanly curiosity made me look at his photograph, partly displayed from his identity card. I examined his birthdates and signature and my eyes began to swim in mist and tears. I steadied myself at the table with my brain repeating what was stamped on the card:

Geheime Staatspolizei, Staatspolizeileitstelle

WIEN

– G E S T A P O –

Cold perspiration stood on my forehead and my feet seemed so heavy, yet my heart was pulsating like mad. What was I to do? What could I possibly do in this situation? A drama began to unfold, stranger than fiction, and to escape by myself, imprisoned by ice and snow, miles from the village was impossible.

I pushed the card into the first pocket of the rucksack, and braced myself for my return to Jarlsberg. Fortunately, the light in the room was not too bright and, with the soft music adding an air of romance, the Count did not see the expression on my face. I told him that I could not find my photos, but would show them to him at Mother's. He put his arms around me but now they felt like chains. Nevertheless, my only chance of survival was to act, replacing my heart with the Luger I had left at home. On the record the deep voice of Pola Negri was singing:

Nur eine Stunde, die dank' ich Dir,
Nur die allein gehoerte mir . . .

Only one hour, I belonged to you
And for this hour, I'm thanking you.
You talked of love and happiness
And we both believed in fate
But this hour was to be our last.

If ever words were written to suit an event, Pola Negri sang them for us. However, Jarlsberg noticed no difference between the woman who left the room and the stranger who returned. He was in a state of blissful happiness, thus giving me some borrowed time to work matters out.

The log fire was burning brightly and I kept thinking how utterly impossible our affair really was. I would rather die than turn coat against all the principles I stood and fought for. We suddenly became enemies as we danced. At last he noticed how tired I looked and advised me to go to bed. Grateful for his understanding, I said "good-night" and disappeared into my bedroom, double locking my door. For seconds I pressed my body against the cool wood, quietly saying: "Never, never . . ." I prayed that sleep would relieve my tortured mind, but it took a long time to squash the doubts. I believed that we cannot alter by promises of heavenly love and earthly passion basically what we are and we have to live with our conscience, right and wrong.

The following morning was so beautiful and I wished that nature would not be so lavish with its gifts, giving them to good and bad alike. Toni and the Count had already prepared breakfast and teased me for being late. Afterwards they went for skiing exercise and I was glad to be alone – if only to think things out. In the back of my mind I still hoped for a way out, but how? As soon as I knew they were far enough from the Lodge, I began to search through Jarlsberg's luggage. I hated every moment of it but it was the only action I could think of. Well wrapped in waterproof cloth lay his automatic revolver and dark plans crossed my mind.

Suddenly, the Count stood in the doorway . . . like a giant towering over my kneeling figure.

He pulled me up, slammed the door with his foot, and, within seconds, he was holding the revolver in his hand and pointing it directly at my head. "What are you looking for Gitta, or should I say Burgi?"

My knees felt like jelly. Jarlsberg knew who I was and had perhaps known all the time. He pushed me with the weapon to a chair and continued to question me as to my identity, relentlessly digging into my past. "Did you truly think that I should come with any girl who fancied me for a holiday, without knowing who she was?" he said angrily and went on: "Once we reached Vienna it was easy to trace you, when you mentioned your aunt. What intrigued me most was the fact that, whilst I was chasing you as an officer of the Gestapo, I was falling in love with you as a man. Somehow it seemed odd, but since I've met you I could not stop wanting to possess you." Realizing that I was completely at his mercy and that he could shoot me without a trial, I played for time to live. Jarlsberg was tough and I did not underestimate his arrogance, but most of all I knew that he was still in love with me and that was the crux of the matter. As long as we talked he would not shoot me. I asked him how he, as a gentleman from Norway, visualized his life under Hitler, how much he truly had in common with this gang of Nazis and cold-blooded killers. I appealed to his better self, to examine his conscience, but he refused to listen. He explained the Fuehrer's genius, his love for the Nordic nations, in particular, as they were free of Jewish blood. I could clearly see that Jarlsberg meant what he said, thus giving me little hope of survival. The minutes dragged on without any compromise in sight, only Jarlsberg's demand that I come over to his side of the fence, or be damned. I reminded him to study the maps of the world and see if it was humanly possible for Germany to win this war and told him that a question like this sentenced my half-uncle of Jewish origin to a punishment centre and probably certain death. The Count became more furious and shouted: "Jewish pigs like him poisoned your mind in the first place and I trust he will get what he deserves."

The harder I tried to reason with Jarlsberg, the worse it got. Walking up and down in front of me like a caged tiger, he insisted that I hear him out: A further microscopic study of Hitler, as seen by Dr Goebbels! Jarlsberg tried another tactic to wear me down, or to make me see sense, as he called it, saying: "Suppose the Allies do win this war, what do you expect they will give you for services rendered? Three cheers?" He laughed uproariously, telling me to get hold of myself and to turn tragedy into *triumph*. Angered by his outbursts, I retorted sharply: "One Quisling in the room is enough, I could never betray my own country and my own people. Don't forget I had an Austrian father, who was a hundred per cent invalid and died for his country. I have a Czech mother, whose relatives are still suffering under the Germans. Do you call this a triumph?"

A gulf had opened between us, too wide and too deep to fill. Suddenly, he turned towards me brandishing his revolver, saying: "You have exactly one hour to make up your mind, whether you wish to live or die and, make no mistake, I mean this." Count Jarlsberg came closer. His eyes narrowed as in a distorted voice, breathing heavily, he said: "Sixty minutes is all you've got my girl, or I will blast your heart out, so it won't be hurting anyone else." He left the room turning the key from the outside.

Might and conscience clashed head on. Of course I was afraid of dying, but to live with a betrayal of that kind was even worse. I have known people who had been executed under the Nazis, hang for their belief in freedom and one was a woman of nearly sixty. At least I could die with dignity! I folded my hands in prayer, for I had no more illusions as far as Jarlsberg was concerned. Last night's kisses lay like a curse on my lips and I wanted to meet my executioner with fortitude. Time was now unimportant. I just lay on my bed and stared at the ceiling hoping that the Count was a good shot. At last he came, strutting into my room, ordering me to get up. We looked at each other like true enemies: "Your answer is written all over your face, Burgi," he said rather sadly, but I was beyond caring and told him to get on with it. His face muscles twitched and a faint smile came over his lips. "When I first met you in Norway, I suspected that you were up to something, but you tempted me biologically. I have known women before, but you were so exciting, a mixture of all of them rolled into one. My passion for you grew with every hour and I refused to accept that one could be such an utter fool. I was crazy enough to believe what you told me, although I knew better, but by then I was desperately in love with you." Jarlsberg turned his back and I could hear the release of the safety catch. The suspense was unbearable but my heart was still. Covering my face with both hands I moved towards the wall, trying to keep upright. Two shots rang out, but I was still standing on my feet, feeling towards my heart. Suddenly, Jarlsberg got hold of me saying: "It even takes courage to be a coward. My head told me to kill you, but my heart would not let me. You are free to leave." The Count walked past me, leaving traces of fear and unfulfilled passions. I left the Lodge immediately with Toni escorting me to the *Gasthaus* from which we had started. I was free again. Relieved and shocked I returned home to Mother, but decided not to alarm her in any way. My only confession was to Dr M –, but he was confident that I was relatively safe, as a report of this kind to the Gestapo H.Q. at Vienna could only boomerang on the Count, thus costing him his career, if not his head. As for my own life, I acquired new wisdom . . . that we cannot escape each other . . . and that Dr M –'s views had paid off so far.

JUGOSLAVIA

OPERATION RUDOLF

1941 was nearing its end and I was lucky to be alive. However new plans were in the air and a visit by Baron Schindler could only have one reason: a new Mission. Schindler came straight to the point and handed me an open letter addressed to me. With it was a photograph of a German Officer, a Second Lieutenant, covered with medals. I read the letter:

My Darling Burgi,

In three weeks I shall be posted to the Front. My only wish is to see you again and if possible to marry you. I have applied for the necessary papers, so now it is up to you to get the permit and come as soon as possible. I love and miss you very much.

Please excuse the shortness of this letter but I have a lot to do. Nevertheless, you are always on my mind and in my heart.

My Dearest, until we meet in Zagreb, all my love,

Ever yours,

Rudolf.

Putting the letter down, I looked at the photograph and it seemed as if Rudolf's eyes were following me as I turned towards Schindler and said: "What are my orders? I fully understand the situation." For a while my second in command searched my face and answered: "It should not be difficult pretending to be his girl friend," and he pointed to the photograph, "but you will need his letter to get your travel permission." Schindler ordered me to reply to Rudolf's letter and dictated part of it, leaving the rest of it to "my romantic nature," as he said. I then handed my letter and a photograph of myself to the Baron, who hastily placed it in his brief-case.

I was glad when Schindler left, so that I could examine my prospective boy friend's picture. It tantalized me, like some unattainable object. Dark eyes full of smouldering fire invited me to an adventure I dreaded – his mouth was hard, uncompromising, though fascinating. On the back of the photograph was written: "With all my love, Rudolf."

The masquerade was bold and daring! Now it was up to me to get there and take the message, the size of a stamp, as Schindler described it, with the contents which were none of my business. The following day I made an appointment with the Nazi Burgermaster and German Commandant. As they had little to do they saw me at once, read my letter from Rudolf Koroschetz, examined the stamp of the Censor and, most of all, the medals on Rudolf's chest. I was relieved, to say the least, when they found it in order. The Commandant stretched himself, sighed and said: "So much love must be rewarded and I sincerely trust that you can get wed in the short time available." I gave him the dates of my intended departure and he duly signed all papers for February 5, 1942. My audience was over and, as I reached the door, he shouted: "Just one moment, Fräulein Triller." For seconds I trembled, had he become suspicious? but he said: "If it's a boy I will be the godfather." Nonplussed at this remark, I gave the Hitler salute and felt the occasion warranted it.

Twenty-four hours later, I reported to Dr M – in Leoben, and showed him my travel papers. He was very pleased and asked me to bring him my best snowboots, as the message would be sewn between the leather lining. Regarding my Mission, he simply outlined the trains and, for the action, I would have to rely on my sixth sense, 'crossing the bridges' when I got there. Apparently Rudolf was fully informed and knew what to do after my arrival at the Post Hotel in Zagreb, Jugoslavia. As scheduled I left Leoben very early in the afternoon on February 5 with Schindler escorting me to the station. It snowed mercilessly and now and then the Baron brushed the flakes from my fur cap, lingering with his hands on my shoulders, but my mind strangely was in Zagreb with Rudolf. Two men, both risking their lives for the Resistance, and yet the one who was so far away was the closest on my mind. By now I knew that Schindler felt more for me than Dr M – would permit and loyalty replaced the word 'love'.

I boarded my train and, standing on the first step, I was the exact height of the Baron, who looked sad and suddenly exclaimed: "I salute you, so that I shall not kiss you." At last, the train began to move, putting a distance between me and the slender young man whom Mother called my Svengali! Born in 1919 in Czechoslovakia, he was now serving as an officer at the Leoben Gebirgsjager Barracks, cleverly dividing his services between the German Army and the Resistance.

The train was crowded but I found a compartment, where I was the only girl among seven soldiers of various ranks. Naturally they were delighted and a puzzle started – who should sit next, and opposite me. They rearranged themselves, whilst I laughed and joked. Suddenly the door opened and a man in a long grey leather coat came in. With some awe we all looked at him. He was rude and pushed us together. Starting to hold an inquest, he asked for our names and destinations and whether married or single, and finally declared: "Thanks to the Fuehrer we can travel all over the parts of Europe conquered by the German Army." A young Sergeant shouted *"Sieg Heil, Sieg Heil,"* and most of them stood to attention. Luckily for me, in their great excitement they did not notice my expression and smiles. Encouraged by so much patriotism, the strange man continued, predicting that the war would be won in six months, all Jews would be exterminated, and all traitors hanged. "The rest of the world will be glad to lick our boots for mercy," he exclaimed. By now he had all the soldiers on his side, shouting *"Heil* Hitler" and *"Heil unserem grossen Fuehrer."* As I had to be most careful, I dared not laugh, but one had to see this crowd to appreciate how funny they really were. If any of these Nazis had any idea who I was and where I was heading for, plus the note in my boots, they would have gladly cut my throat from one end to the other.

Counting the stations to my first stop kept me sane and hopeful of escaping this mob. At last Selztal, the rail-junction came into sight. I alighted as the train drew into the station, and hurried along to the nearby Station Hotel to get a room for the night. The place was poorly lit and an elderly porter answered my call, but he was not at all pleased to give me a room for only one night. Grudgingly, he handed me key No. 5 and I walked up the wooden stairs until I came to my number which was barely visible. It was bitterly cold and I could hardly open the door. Inside the room was a cold stove with wood lying beside it. After putting my small case down, I went to the toilet, asking the porter once more where it was. When I came back I had the feeling that someone was in my room, but dismissed my thoughts at once. As it was too cold to go to bed I decided to make a fire. I found some matches, opened the stove and noticed some brown paper tied in a bundle. I pushed it back but it felt heavy. Was it a bomb? An explosive? The wildest ideas crossed my mind, but I pulled it out carefully. I listened and shook it. It made noises as if the contents were broken. Hurriedly I took it downstairs and handed it to the man I had registered with upon my arrival. He examined the parcel, picked up the telephone and rang the police. The very word made me uneasy but all I could do was wait and see.

Sitting in the entrance hall was an old woman, hiding her face. I walked past her and heard footsteps coming down the landing. My pulse went faster as I recognized the man in 'grey' from the train. He bumped into the gesticulating porter without an apology and sent him reeling. When he learned who had found the parcel he said in a moderate tone: "But how did it get into the *Fräulein's* room?" I was amazed at this question! How did *he* know it was in my room, I could have found it anywhere.

Soon the local police arrived with two officers. My travel companion showed his papers and the atmosphere became electric. My very strong suspicion that he was a Gestapo officer increased, as he took over the case and opened the parcel. The contents consisted of gold watches, rings and gold teeth. Full of suspense I watched as the old woman now pushed up against me. She smelled of beer and I moved away. However, my 'friend' called me back, asking me questions as to my travelling plans, but all I could think about was these gruesome rings and teeth. We in the Resistance had heard of how the SS looted their victims before sending them to their death camps and this man obviously was no exception. I began to understand why this attempt to implicate me was staged. He needed an alibi to search my room to look for his goods, perhaps even trying to impress me with his gold articles and secure my arrest.

These men were human devils indeed.

After a telephone call to my home village to cross check my identity I was cleared of any suspicion and we all went back to our rooms. Although it was midnight I did not bother to undress for I was freezing cold. I could hear the creaking of the old floors and the footsteps along the corridors, but most of all I feared the man in grey.

At six thirty a bell rang. I got up, washed a little and went downstairs for my breakfast. The room was already half full of uniformed men, but all I saw was my 'shadow' getting up and coming towards me. Of course his invitation was a command and I had to accept. It was the first time that I had a good look at him. He stood over six feet tall, with very narrow shoulders, no hips and a pale complexion. Somehow we both sized each other up, with him watching me from the corner of his watery grey eyes. A waitress brought the breakfast of stale bread, some margarine, and jam. The coffee smelled ghastly and had saccharin for a sweetner. Oblivious to these starvation rations, my 'friend' said: "We are still much better off than the British." I could hardly wait to finish my breakfast at 'Tiffany's', paid my bill and left in a hurry.

The train for Zagreb was already there and I managed to find a non-smoker compartment to myself. Whilst taking off my coat and emptying out my pockets, I found a note on a small piece of paper: THIS TRAIN WILL GO UP. Cold fear possessed me. Was it a hoax or a trap to reveal myself? If I had anything to hide, I would obviously get off this train as fast as possible – or so the writer of this note must have thought. Being heroic sounds all right in books but is far from reality. Awkwardly busying myself with my luggage my brain explored all pros and cons, when suddenly I felt someone behind me. Outlining my contours with his gloved hands, he said: "I should say you are five foot three inches and 36-24-36, an explosive affair." Of course I knew who this voice belonged to and with philosophical calmness answered: "How right you are, *mein Herr,* but my fiancé would not approve the fact . . . that you are flirting with me." Nudging me with his arm he assured me that I was in the best of hands and safe. I shuddered to think of this prospect. However, I decided to play it cool and never underestimate his cunning. He sat himself opposite me, kissing my hands as a sort of peace gesture.

The train began to move out of Selztal and I realized that my mind had been made up for me. I also knew that this man was an officer of the dreaded Gestapo and that flattery was my only chance of survival. But he went one step further. "I am an incurable romantic," he said out of the blue, and his grey, grey eyes pierced me. He took hold of me by the waist and I tried to get out of the door, but he held it. Desire was written all over him and I felt sick at the thought of it. My only weapon was talking, so I asked him for his name: "Egon," he said. "Do you know there is a song about your name?" and pushing him from me I began to sing:

> *Egon aus lauter lauter Liebe zu Dir bin ich so tief gesunken.*
> Egon because I love you so much, I've surrendered completely.

Luckily, he found it amusing and the first tricky situation was under control. Complimenting me on my singing, he pointed out that I should do well on a stage. I countered that there was only room for a few at the top and that I never fancied myself playing the maid of *Countess Maritza.* "Poor *Fräulein,"* he said, "I agree you are much too exciting for such small parts." As we passed through picturesque scenery I suddenly realized that he was still holding me in his arms –

fortunately we stopped at a station. We sat down, still playing 'cat and mouse' in a deadly game. Every question was tricky and had a double meaning, and Egon was like a spider trying to engulf me.

As the journey continued I was unable to see a solution to my dilemma. This man was here to shadow me and in all probability this train would blow up. Inspired by an iron determination not to break down I created an illusion of no real danger, but my mental faculties became impaired and my speech slower.

I glanced at my watch . . . it was 3.15 p.m. As if someone had fired a gun, the train stopped and everything happened at once. I was flung to the floor as bits and pieces flew about in the air. The door seemed suddenly on top of me and my companion was flung to one side of the compartment. People were shouting for help. Like an exploding flash-bulb the Gestapo officer reached for his revolver and crawled out through the window. "No one leaves this train!" he ordered.

Sounds of distress came from everywhere. I had to make my own decision and make it quickly. I was still in one piece, so, having made sure of that, I gathered all my strength and my little case, and scrambled through the open window. The train was lying on its left side and I had to let myself down some six feet into the cold snow. Impelled by a combination of fear and will power, I made it. My legs seemed propelled by some unseen force as I progressed alongside the upturned waggons until I reached the last one. I dragged myself along the main road, sitting down now and then to recover from my exhaustion. At last I was offered a lift, on a military lorry going to Zagreb five kilometres ahead. Was this the long arm of coincidence or sheer luck? The driver, a Corporal, was a kind sort of fellow but a bit simple. He asked me for a date and I left the answer until we had reached Zagreb. When he began raising his voice, I made it clear that I was on my way to be married, thus putting before him a *fait accompli,* and we continued the journey in silence.

I was in no mood for jokes and went straight to the Post Hotel. The place was warm and clean. A fat man at the desk with whom I registered ushered me personally to my room.

He seemed shocked at how tired I looked and informed me that some food would be sent up to me, for which I thanked him in advance. As soon as he left, I looked in the mirror and saw what a mess my shoulder length hair was in. As I was brushing it there was a heavy knock at the door. At once I reached for my Luger, and hid it under my sweater. It was only a waiter with the food. What a sight met my eyes — delicious meat with rice and salad, and two large pieces of cake. I could hardly believe my luck. I forgot all about danger and my appearance and began to eat and eat. After I had finished my meal I tasted the tea with rum, or should I say, rum with tea? Having been exposed to the cold weather for the last two hours, I forgot the soporific effect of a strong drink. All I could think about was being safe and well after the train crash. The room began to sway, I lay on the bed and slipped into a sound sleep, my revolver still next to my body.

There was banging on my door — the porter telling me that the time was 5.30 p.m. and that I was wanted on the telephone. Before I could get downstairs, it rang off and I realized that someone had checked on me. Who could it be? I looked at my watch, two and a quarter hours had elapsed since the train was derailed and there I was sleeping my head off. I realized that my train should have arrived at Zagreb at 4.45 p.m. and that my orders were to proceed after this telephone call. The route was pencilled over in my letter.

It was six o'clock and nearly dark when I left the hotel. Proceeding along the cobbled square I came to a road winding uphill. Trees and bushes were bending under loads of snow. As I hurried along clutching my case and hugging my fear suddenly I knew that I was no longer alone. The footsteps came closer and closer and I began to walk faster without turning around. I could not bear it any longer and at the next bend I glanced back. My heart stood still, for I recognized Egon, the man from the train. All the ideas in the world could not help me now, only bold and direct action. I counted the bends on the hill and according to my arithmetic this should be the last one where Rudolf was to meet me between 6.30 and 7 p.m. Desperately I looked at my watch. I was on time, but where was Rudolf? Was it all a trap? The telephone call came to my mind, but Rudolf was nowhere. The only certainty . . . the Gestapo right on my heels. Like a drowning woman, I clutched at a straw. There in the twilight, I saw a figure – it was Rudolf, at last. Running towards him I flung myself into his open arms whispering "Gestapo right behind me." Holding me firmly he turned me around saying: "There is no one, Burgi, it's all been taken care of." My eyes were searching the road but all I could see were snowy branches moving. I looked at Rudolf's black eyes and they were full of expression. His face was triumphant and he said quietly: "You have just witnessed the vanishing of our enemy without a sound," and indicated with his hand that they had cut his throat.

Rudolf and I walked towards the stone house where he lived. I was still shaken, thus he half carried me inside to the laughter of the men sitting around. All of them were armed and I wondered if they had expected an ambush. Rudolf helped me out of my coat and took my suitcase into the next room. As soon as he returned he asked me for the message and I pointed to my right boot. However, thoroughly shaken and with my hands frozen, I was in no state to take them off, so Rudolf did it for me. The men's laughter increased when they noticed my big toe peeping through my sock. In fury Rudolf jumped to his feet telling them to get out fast before he threw them out one by one. "Please forgive these idiots," he said, adding: "None of them would have the guts to travel as far as you did by themselves." This was the first time Rudolf and I had been alone and I had to admit to myself that he was far more dashing than his photograph could ever convey. "I am here safely and that is all that matters," I said. As if guessing my thoughts he replied: "Women have no place in my life, my heart has ceased to exist since the Germans occupied us." Looking at him firmly, I answered: "Don't worry Rudolf, I have no heart at all, only vanity left." "Good, so we understand each other from the beginning," he said promptly.

The first meeting with my 'fiancé' was over, brief and to the point. I was told where my room was and that my food was available and ready in the kitchen. That was what one calls making no fuss, I thought and smiled at the departing

Rudolf as I entered my own room which was very spartan but clean and had iron bars on the windows. The floor was bare and cold. Tired and amazed at sheer human endurance, I went to bed and slept like a log.

Early in the morning a girl about twenty years of age brought me coffee and bread with butter. She just put the tray down and left. All my life I suffered from these first impression feelings and I thought, with *her* around, who needs enemies? Half an hour later she returned and told me where I could wash and where the toilet facilities were – outside of course. Everything was primitive – only Rudolf did not fit into this set up. He was far too well spoken and his hands showed very little sign of work. I was still engrossed with my thoughts when there was a knock and Rudolf came to wish me 'Good morning'. He was smiling, showing teeth like pearls. In a way it was a wicked smile! He thanked me for the message, which was decoded and, as he said, of great value to Tito. It was the first time I had heard that name mentioned. "Please tell me about this man called Tito," I pleaded and he obliged: "He is our Leader, wily as a fox, here, there and everywhere to direct actions and he dictates the battleground for the Germans to fight us. Their savagry is only matched by our heroism." Rudolf's face lit up when he told me of Tito's strategy and his personal plans to lead a double life until victory was ours. The latter he stressed, reaching for my hands. "They are so small," he observed, holding them against his heart. Temptation stared right at us, our lips were only an inch apart, our bodies trembling, but gently he sat me down on a chair and left the room without uttering one single word.

Alone with my thoughts, I analysed the people around me and considered what strange fate united them. There was the woman, Eva, how much was she involved? Rudolf alone held the key to this puzzle and how much of *man* was still left in him as far as the opposite sex was concerned? One thing was certain, as long as Rudolf was their leader, they could never be pinned down and destroyed by the Germans. He was truly incorruptible, the master-mind of his Partisans. In the midst of my 'reasoning', Rudolf came back and asked me to go for a walk through the surrounding woods. I asked him if he was not afraid of being seen. He laughed and said: "Of course I am, who in my position is not, only a fool walks carefree, but the Germans would need ten men for each one of us, thus I stand a fair chance."

Before leaving, he armed himself with grenades, an automatic revolver, plus a long sharp knife which he pushed down his black boots.

We set off. It was a lovely clear day and, in the distance we saw German soldiers, some of them walking about with girls. I held his arm as we stepped over tree stumps and brushed past branches partly covered in snow. Deeper and deeper we went into the forest. The stillness was unreal, but the man beside me was not. We glanced at each other, our unanswered questions dying on our lips; in a cruel way it was perfect. On our way back I fell down; Rudolf lifted me up and I realized that I was the weaker of the two, for I wanted him to kiss me. All he said was: "If I kissed you, we would both explode with all the ammunition I've got on me and that would never do, would it?" "How ingenious," I thought, he eliminated a situation too dangerous for both of us, reversing the motto that 'fools rush in where angels fear to tread'. Briskly we walked back home, shyly exchanging glances, with Rudolf now and then touching my fingertips. An unknown radiance went through my body, it seemed almost wicked in a world of terror to experience such stolen moments of bliss. Zagreb, February 7, 1942, was a day to remember.

After a frugal meal of onion soup and Gulasch with brown bread, Rudolf changed his clothing to go out for the night. Two other men arrived in leather jackets and heavy boots armed to the teeth and speaking in Slovenish. I could hear them arguing in the next room. My ears were pressed against the communication door and I could understand what Rudolf said. He called for Eva, telling her to take care of me. I felt a pang in my heart, for I visualized the worst. At last Rudolf sent for me, telling the others to leave us alone. Standing by the window he outlined their operation for this very night and assured me that Eva would see me safe whatever else happened. "If I do not return, say a prayer for me." I nodded, amazed at his calmness. We stood there for a few minutes, just facing each other, until Rudolf walked past me, blowing a kiss from the open door. I was glad that he exhibited a little human frailty if only for a single instance and a strange happiness flowed into me. Rudolf had dropped his disguise for one moment. Soon after that all the men left the house. The silence was frightening, but being alone with Eva was worse than the fear of a German ambush.

Without knocking, Eva entered my room. She brought her machine gun and ammunition and placed them noisily under the table. Infuriated by my smile she asked me if I was afraid of her weapon. "Not in the least," I said "but I doubt very much if your gun would have got you through all check-posts, some two hundred kilometres from Leoben to Zagreb." She looked at me bewildered as I continued and told her that women have only one weapon to fight with – their hearts. Hysterical, her eyes glowing like torches, she charged at me with a long sharp knife, forcing me back to my bed. I held her right wrist with all my power, but the blade came closer and closer to my chest. Mad with jealousy she meant to kill me. I managed to pull my Luger from under my pillow. We struggled on until I was on top of her and held my gun at her heart. Feeling the cold steel she dropped her knife, put up both hands, and shouted at me: "You are after Rudolf you bitch, you have conquered him." How could I reason with her? I simply asked her to leave and pushed her to the door. She departed, raving and cursing me.

I tried to calm down by lying still, but to regain peace of mind was impossible. Holding my revolver tightly I thought . . . what a life, what an existence, but who was to blame? Love can have so many faces and this was one of them. The realization that Rudolf could possibly look at me was too much for poor Eva. I smiled to myself and remembered when she first touched my soft woollen sweater, yearning to possess it, to beguile Rudolf. The paradox of it all! We fought the same enemy, though we belonged in different worlds. Eva, earthy, uneducated, the female animal, attractive but showy. I, brought up amongst the ex-Habsburg aristocracy, taught in the best private schools, had glimpsed the highlights of life in another society. How possibly could we be compatible? Eva and I . . . Eva and I . . . sleep relieved my tortured mind.

Heavy footsteps aroused me and I expected another blast from Eva. I looked at my watch on my arm – it was 2.30 a.m. I struggled to get my revolver, which had fallen down at the side of my bed, and held it facing the door. However, it was Rudolf who knocked on the wall to indicate that he was back. As he kept walking around I sensed that something was wrong. I heard excited voices and Eva arguing. Rudolf told me to come to his room. I obeyed, flinging my coat over my shoulders, expecting a showdown with Eva. Rudolf stood by the window, blowing the smoke from his cigar slowly into the air. Two of the three men I had previously met were with him. They stared at me strangely. Suddenly Rudolf turned around, violently stamping out his cigar under his boot. With great emotion he said: "They got Janoc and killed him." In that simple statement lay all the bitterness and sorrow. Rudolf went on: "One has no bargaining power with the Gestapo and death is preferable to questioning." He said this, as if to soften the blow from which he could not escape. At that moment my heart reached out for him, but he did not even look at me, only stared back out of the window into the darkness. One by one we left, indicating our sorrow, but all Rudolf did was to stand there motionless, a lonely figure in a turbulent world.

A few hours' sleep eased my troubled mind. Somehow I wished that I would not have to see Rudolf in the morning, for what could I possibly say to him after that dramatic night? To my surprise, at breakfast Rudolf emerged as confident as ever. Only his look was harder when he told me to take back a coded letter to Austria. "When do I leave?" I asked, and he answered, "It all depends on what happens today. In our position we never know from one moment to the next *who* or *what* has priority."

Rudolf went to fetch a bottle of wine and two glasses. We toasted each other and the Resistance. Rudolf was in his element and said: "At the moment we are only a few hundred, but the people will rise and join our ranks; for every one they kill, ten will fill the gap. They will come in thousands from the mountains, challenging the Germans to battle where they decide, not as now being contented with ambushes and sabotage." Changing the subject he said smilingly: "I understand from Eva that you had a little misunderstanding." "Yes," I stammered, blushing all over my face, "but you've only got her version of the incident, I believe you ought to know mine as well." He laughed, showing again those tiger-like teeth of his, and waved me not to bother, saying: "I can well imagine the two of you having a fight, but I am really not worth it – I who am walking daily to my execution, without seeing it." Reprimanding him for being so callous, I asked him not to treat Eva as if she was a slave, but to praise her now and then, thus gaining her respect. Rudolf flew into a rage and answered coldly: "You don't understand how we live here, if I gave her my little finger she would expect the whole hand." Again the terror of living showed in the face of the man sitting opposite me and I realized how mistrustful he was of human encounters. The 'fortress' Rudolf was still full of mysteries. Suddenly he begged: "Tell me all about you, your friends and your life." He listened carefully and I wondered how much he would remember after I had gone home. When I finished with the hope that we might meet again after this war was over, he took my hand and said slowly: "Nothing is impossible, Burgi, nothing." Rather abruptly he left, requesting me to be ready at ten next morning.

I was alone, looking at myself in the mirror thinking: What really mattered? The result of my mission! Not Rudolf or I! Aggressors must be stopped, but personal feelings can be controlled, discarded if necessary. Part of my mind accepted all this, only the heart, the complex emotional one, could not be pinned down with a few adjectives. One thing was certain, I had come to the end of my short stay in Jugoslavia, with nothing but my thoughts to fill my waiting time of some eighteen hours.

The house was so still, although Eva was working in the kitchen preparing our lunch. I dreaded to sit with her at the same table, but had little choice, save starving. In fact it was Rudolf who came and told me that the food was ready. The three of us avoided looking at each other, as if hiding a guilty secret. Only Eva's noisy eating made me look up. I had the feeling that she did it deliberately, for it stopped when I excused myself from the table.

With Rudolf's voice still booming in my ear, I shut the door. Obviously he told her off, but she laughed loudly. Soon I heard his footsteps in the room next to mine, pacing up and down. The communication door was the only barrier between us and when he ceased walking, I wondered if he was listening to what I was doing. In an odd way, I found it amusing, but on second thoughts, he was clearly avoiding me. Why? At last he left and all was quiet. I did not see him again until eight o'clock the following morning when he told me to be ready to leave in fifteen minutes. Reminding him that the day before he told me we would leave at 10 a.m., he snapped: "That was yesterday and I'll want you out of here before the Germans pay us a visit." I obeyed, collected my few things together and was ready when Rudolf came into the room. He hesitated, pushed a letter into my handbag whilst I picked up my small suitcase, then rather slowly he took my coat, which had a large white fur collar, in his hands. He pressed the soft fur against his cheeks saying: "Please don't move for a moment, just stand there, for I want to behold these minutes for ever." Rudolf's face was dead-set, like someone knowing it was good-bye for ever. He helped me into the coat, fidgeting with my collar, then stood back and opened the door to ask his two friends and Eva in. One by one they lined up and Rudolf gave the order to stand to attention. I said this was too much honour but he would not hear of it and we all, except Eva, shook hands, saying the normal farewells. Eva stared at me with her lips pressed tightly and I felt truly sorry for her. Rudolf walked past, ignoring her blatant affront and led me to the waiting 'bakery van'. I got in and he shut the door. Suddenly, he stood to attention and saluted, his dark eyes penetrating into my heart. The unbearable tension was at last eased when the driver drove off briskly.

Zagreb's station came into sight, but my mind was still with Rudolf and I felt the weight of my responsibilities, perhaps for the first time. "How lucky I am," I thought, "to be *me* in the world at this time." I boarded the train for Austria and knew that even reality can be magical and that regrets and happiness go together. Looking out of the window I noticed what a clear fine day it was and I suddenly found myself crying. Perhaps the realization was still too much for me? Opening my handbag to get my handkerchief I noticed the letter. Odd, I thought, it was open! I hurriedly disappeared into the toilet to hide it in my clothing. Suddenly, I began to read. It was Rudolf's handwriting.

"Beloved Burgi,

Ever since I received your photograph I was looking forward to meeting you . . . and when you came you exceeded all my expectations.

I believed to have finished with girls, but your nearness made me tremble. I wanted ecstasy in which the earth moves and the fireworks go off, but the overpowering thing in my life is the fight for the freedom of my country. I cannot have both so I had to send you away.

If I had held you in my arms and kissed you, I could never let you go from me.

Rudolf."

Eva was right after all. I was in a dream, beautiful and cruel. Reality lay at the other end of my journey, but the memory of Rudolf would linger on, for always. When I was safely back in Leoben, Baron Schindler's entry in his diary read: "Mission accomplished."

It was rather extraordinary that Schindler kept a diary on my movements. Was it personal, audacious or careless? I shall never know!

CHAPTER 5

RAIL–JUNCTION ST. MICHAEL

At the end of May 1942, Dr M – spread the message that my 'fiancé', Rudolf Koroschetz had been killed in action and that I was eligible once more for possible suitors. Secretly I felt sorry to have to use grief in preparation for a further Mission. At the same time my mother informed me that she intended to marry Herrn Joachim Oberleitner. He was a bachelor of fifty-five, an expert in horses and the former trainer at Baron Rothchield's Estate in Fronleiten. Rather amazed, I accepted her decision, wishing her luck. My new stepfather was tall and good-looking. He soon found himself involved with the German *Wehrmacht* and was placed in charge of a stud of some one hundred and twenty pedigree fillies, supplied with a house, two veterinary surgeons, and two French prisoners of war. Everything went according to plan, with visits from officials, military experts, and Nazis dislocating their arms with giving the Hitler salute. The only thing pleasant for me was that there were lovely horses galloping outside my window, giving me the chance to ride again to my heart's delight. However, the Leoben Labour Exchange had other plans for my future entertainment and sent me an official card, ordering me to present myself. To my great consternation, I was given a post as Material Clerk at the H.Q. of the Rail-Junction, St. Michael. How my appointment came about, I shall never know, for Dr M –, an official at this Exchange, disclaimed any knowledge regarding this job which gave me a unique opportunity to note down

St. Michael – 5. Mai 1943

B e s c h e i n i g u n g .

das: B u r g i   S c h a i l e   geb. am 21.1.1922 im Dienste der Deutschen Reichsbahn steht und bei der Bahnmeisterei, als Kanzleikraft tätig ist.

Employment Certificate of H.Q. St. Michael

military transports and goods trains loaded with heavy armour and ammunition. Dr M – in his wisdom declared it must have been the decision of a blithering idiot – or a genius – to place a cat in a fish-shop!

"Raeder muessen rollen fuer den Sieg", read the Nazi slogan. My eyes lingered on the huge writing and I thought perhaps the wheels of fate were rolling my way at last, for I dreaded the quietness and serenity at home, particularly now that I had to share my mother with a strange man.

Fitted out with the necessary documents, I started my job during the first week in June. Already informed at the Labour Exchange of the status of my co-workers, my arrival was odd, to put it mildly. Dressed in an exotic patterned silk gown, I entered to the total unconcern of the staff, wondering how Cleopatra felt when her tigers refused to take notice. My 'tigers' consisted of three men and two women who all shouted "*Heil* Hitler" and pointed to the only empty chair for me to sit down. I looked about me. There was the No.1, the *Bahnmeister*, his deputy a senior Inspector and finally, my own superior, an Inspector of Rail Materials. The first two were assisted by a chain-smoking woman in her mid-thirties and the latter by a rather dandily dressed girl, who seemed badly ignored. Opposite me sat my boss whose name-shield read: "Inspector H.M. Moser". I soon saw that he had a glass eye and was bursting with laughter. Giving me some paperwork to copy-type he indicated that talking was forbidden; glancing at his watch, he whispered: "Coffee break is at ten to eleven *Fräulein.*" At last the bell rang and all got up staring at me as if they had just discovered a mermaid. Bewildered, I rose, with Moser pushing me through the door, chiming "*Heil* Hitler". Stumbling along the rail lines we began to laugh, relaxing from the stiff atmosphere of the office while I called Moser 'His Majesty', to which he replied "You're joking . . . H.M. in my case stands for help me!"

As we drank our coffee in the restaurant, Moser sighed and said: "Who on earth has sent you to our outfit! I always had my doubts of our winning this war . . . now I am certain we won't." Pointing to his glass eye and telling me of his war injury in 1918, he added: "Miss Triller, you will be as useful as this with regard to materials, our H.Q. is a madhouse, with orders to drive the sane insane and we are directly responsible to the Minister for Productivity, Herr Albert Speer, who in turn is assuring the Fuehrer of victory." "What a mouthful," I answered laughingly and apologized for joking, not quite knowing how seriously to take Moser. However, he enjoyed my humour and in no time I had him in fits of laughter, describing the rest of the H.Q. Staff, the way I saw them, while noticing that my twenty-five-year older friend had forgotten to drink his coffee. Back at the office, muffled coughs and shuffling feet indicated their disapproval of our new friendship. If the women's looks could kill I would have dropped dead instantly!

One week had gone by and June, with all its loveliness, was here. The calendar read June 10, 1942. The radio announced the liquidation of Lidice in Czechoslovakia, because the Czech Resistance had killed the S.S. Chief Heidrich. Mother and I were stunned, for we had close relatives in that area.

Four days later a depressed looking Schindler, came to see me. He told me of the massacre, the indiscriminate slaughter of all men and fifty-six women at Lidice. Horrified I listened, shaking my head in disbelief, yet Schindler went on and on and told me that his only sister, Maria and her husband were two of the victims. "The Germans are very thorough in documenting matters," he said bitterly "they informed me so that I could disassociate myself, as an officer, from my family." Although I was ablaze with fury at this outrage, there was not much I could say to my friend to ease his hurt, except to reassure him of my will to fight the Nazis more uncompromisingly than ever.

Somehow, I was glad to go to work, if only to forget, and soon one month had passed. To the dismay of Inspector Moser, I had not made much progress in my knowledge of screws, bolts and nuts. The latter I felt also applied to the rest of the staff, with the exception of my boss, who assisted me in every manner. However, the constant shouting of "*Heil* Hitler" and "*Sieg Heil*", in German (*Heil* meaning slippery) made the office 'unsafe' to walk in, in many ways. By now Moser and I had become good friends, sharing our ideas and our dwindling food rations to the obvious dislike of our fellow workers. Unfortunately, our air-raid warden, Herr Kemp, did not approve of my friendship with Moser and gave us a stiff warning, with my step-father endorsing his own disapproval. I remember it was the first argument my mother and he had had since their marriage and of course I played a big part in it. "Your daughter will get us all in trouble," he kept on saying until Mother started to cry. Gavin, the elder of our French P.O.Ws., realizing that something was up, asked me, before I left for work, what was wrong? To distract from the real issue, I gave him the newspaper with the account of the massacre of Lidice and he hurried into the outdoor lavatory, obviously to read it. By now I had become thick skinned, although the mental agony was far from over, with the bickerings at my H.Q. reaching boiling point. Willing my watch to go faster for 5.30 p.m. to come, I counted the hours before I could get home again and be on my own to read, or write some of my first novel *Erster Fruehling* (First Spring). Perhaps the material stemmed from the desire to be loved in a natural way, without any sinister implications, although there was no happy ending.

June 14 1942. When I got home, my mother gave me a letter which was registered and bore the stamp of the Gestapo H.Q. at Leoben. Hastily, I opened it and read that I had to go and see them the following morning. I did, unaware of the implications. They were rather too polite, until a sharp question hit my ear: "Why, did you give the French P.O.W. a newspaper to read?" There was no point in tormenting myself as to who saw me in the first place, or who told them; they expected an answer and it had better be good. Trying to look innocent was of no use either, as the Chief hinted, so I made a complete denial. As if wild horses had broken loose from a waggon, two of the men took hold of me, each in turn slapping my face so hard that the combs from my hair flew against the wall. "Now then let's have the truth," the reddish-faced officer said, pushing me to the chair, shouting to another man to bring in the "two women witnesses". The door opened and in came Frau Judmaier and her old mother, stating as one that they had seen me, and adding that I had also given the men food in the kitchen.

Although I explained the latter as a necessity to keep them fit and working, this still left the matter of the newspaper unexplained. Realizing that the Gestapo were deadly serious in matters of co-operating with a former enemy, even a prisoner, I had no choice but to make a joke of this very serious situation and requested the woman to tell me where she saw the P.O.W. standing when I gave him the paper? "By the lavatory," she stated truthfully and the look of the two Gestapo officers changed immediately to a broad grin, thus saving me my explanation. Although the women were dismissed, I had to stay and sign some papers, putting me on three month's probation for good behaviour. The Chief advised me to settle down and get married to the first man who would have me. Leaving the place I felt awful with part of my face swollen from the slapping, yet I went back home fortified with a plan, a plan that made me shudder from myself. My only way of survival was to get closer to the enemy, to protect myself from within.

All night I lay awake promoting ideas and dismissing them. I knew, if need be, Schindler would marry me, yet he was too valuable to lose as a contact, thus it had to be a stranger, a man who knew nothing about my activities. The following week my mother was called to the Gestapo and told of the consequences if I did not alter.

One afternoon, Moser and I were ordered to walk to Goess, some five kilometres along the rail lines, to sort out the defective parts and make a report. My job was to walk behind Moser, whom I now called "Moses", and take notes of the items he shouted back to me. To the best of my ability I had done so, but luckily for me he cross-checked my list. Apparently I wrote down all the material in urgent need of replacement under 'A' and those in good condition under 'B', whereas the reverse was intended. The consequences of this mistake might have been interpreted as sabotage, although I did it from sheer ignorance. To counteract my shock, Inspector Moser invited me to 'dine' with him at the Goess Restaurant, and sacrificed two days' meat coupons. The 'feast' consisted of *Gulasch* (I was sure it was horse meat) and one glass of beer. I dare not think what Inspector Wulser would have called me if he had heard of this 'orgy'! Moser and I became good friends, and gestures, like the meal, helped me to overcome the hostile atmosphere at the office.

My secret hope that one of the women would befriend me did not materialize. Mrs Schweiger who worked for seven years with Wulser kept loyally on his side of the fence. They both talked about the victories of the Nazis. Slogans like 'Wheels must turn for Victory' and 'Think before you Travel' inspired them. However, one day I plucked up courage and said to Frau Schweiger: "If I was thinking at all, I would not travel to work here at six thirty in the morning whilst my mother works herself to a standstill without any help at home." Indignantly she said: "Our work has priority, for without us the troops could not reach the Fronts to fight and ensure Victory."

Moser was the only man I could trust and we became staunch allies, daring to taunt Wulser and his gang. Our methods were such that the almighty Nazis could not really harm us. For example, one morning Wulser repeated a speech from Reichsmarschall Herman Goering who had said: "The Royal Air Force has ceased to exist." He was immensely inspired by that statement and recited Goering's speech line-by-line. "Now then you defeatists," he said to Moser and myself, looking at us gleefully and expecting some downcast eyes. Moser's one good eye looked straight through him as he replied calmly: "But the German O.K.W., *Wehrmachtsbericht,* announced this morning that Bomber Squadrons of the Royal Air Force bombed the Rhineland." Wulser's face went purple as he replied: "So what? They scraped together a few more planes, but our *Luftwaffe* shot down thirty or . . ." and he was about to enlarge upon this figure, when I intervened: "Or was it *three* aeroplanes?" Wulser was livid and pointed to his heart saying: "One day I will collapse, working with people like you."

Incidents like these became daily routine. The next one to upset poor Wulser was when I refused to carry my heavy typewriter to the air-raid shelter some fifteen minutes run over rail lines. This new order was to prevent damage in the event of an air raid. I can still see him putting up the notice in the office with the word "Order" written in red ink. His was a nasty mind – to get at people who could or would not defend themselves and it gave him great satisfaction. I just had to clip his wings somehow and my mind was working hard to find an answer. As flattery would get me nowhere with him, the alternative had better be good and effective. Looking through some newspapers, I read one of Hitler's latest speeches and my plan was born. Next morning I confronted Wulser with 'His Master's Voice': "Machinery, bombs, grenades, aeroplanes are replaceable, but my people are not." To stress my point I laid the newspaper with the Fuehrer's words on his desk, and told him that I considered myself one of the non-replaceable 'People' Hitler spoke about. Wulser was too flabbergasted and had no alternative but to see it my way, or disagree with his beloved Fuehrer. This, of course, would have been treason according to Nazi law. Secretly I laughed at my 'performance' which took Wulser by complete surprise.

Further shocks were to come! One afternoon Moser told me to go to change a light bulb in the store close by, as he intended to sort out materials. Anything was better than working at the office, so I went at once. Singing and whistling, I arrived at the shed, unlocked it and went in, picked up the first chair in my way and stood it on top of a box, directly under the dangling wire. Suddenly I was like a sinking boat and crash, bang, off went some detonators below me. The lower I sank, the worse the bangs, so I began to examine my position and found the cause of the explosions – I was standing on top of a cardboard box, filled with new light bulbs and as the legs of my chair went farther down, new bangs filled the air, and all I could do was laugh. People were shouting and running about – someone in the office must have pressed the alarm bell – and the guards with their dogs arrived. The dogs barked and the guards brandished their rifles until the 'mystery' was cleared up, to the amusement of the assembled railway-officials. All other bystanders, with the exception of Wulser, who looked as black as the darkest storm clouds, began to roar with laughter. In no time news of the incident spread all over the area, carrying rumours of sabotage at our *Bahnmeisterei* (Headquarters).

Imagining Wulser's palpitations when hearing the first explosions I felt unable to come back into the office and asked leave to go home, but Moser insisted that I saw the *Bahnmeister* first. Pulling myself together, I entered his office by the back door. Judging by the look on his face, he did not share my humour and he reprimanded me severely, adding: "There are plenty of ammunition factories if you don't like it here." This sober statement made me think twice and I apologized for any embarrassment I may have caused. However my chief did think it advisable to withdraw me from the others' view if only for the afternoon, and sent me home.

In desperation Mother pleaded with me to stop meeting Schindler and Dr M – in case the Gestapo got wise to us. Taking her advice, I asked my boss for an early holiday date starting on July 1, which was granted. This was my ultimate aim to extricate myself from the present entanglements, thus reaching a basis of peaceful co-existence between my parents and the obviously suspicious Gestapo. Rather accommodatingly, my cousin Hannerl, who by now was married to an SS Officer, triggered off a line of action familiar to my way of thinking over the past few weeks. She invited me to attend the SS Ball at the *Puntigam Brauhaus* in Graz and I accepted. Dressed in a scarlet chiffon dress, with a ribbon of the same material flattering my raven-black coiffeur, I arrived at the Ball flanked by my very good looking cousin and her handsome husband. A few eye-brows were raised at my solo arrival, but this was soon to be rectified — I was introduced to Waffenmeister G. Schaile. He was just holding court at his table, when my cousin's husband called him away. Laying down his large cigar, he bowed, clicked his heels and asked me to dance and be his guest at his table. I had the immediate feeling that he enjoyed my company and agreed. We danced, made polite conversation, and sipped the best wine. Hannerl was delighted to see me so sensible, as she called it, and Schaile was attentive, paid compliments, and we made a date for the following weekend. He told me of his background and his French origin, which interested me at once. Nevertheless, he wore the uniform I detested most and any liking was purely physical. His resemblance to the film star, Ray Milland, was outstanding, but when I told him so, he shook his head and laughed. However, there was no doubt that Schaile was distinguished with his well-built figure, black hair and contrasting grey-blue eyes, and immaculate teeth. Suddenly, he asked me: "Why is a girl looking like you not married?" "No one has ever made an offer," I countered untruthfully, to which he jokingly exclaimed: "If I get promoted during my three weeks' stay in Graz, I shall take you up on this." We both had a good laugh and got ready to leave. It was nearly midnight, and as Schaile escorted me home we made small talk and held hands.

The next afternoon we went to the pictures, after which I left by train for St. Stefan, with Schaile promising to visit us the coming Saturday. Back home, I told Mother of my new SS friend, she was startled, and warned me not to be too bold and to hold my horses. I knew what she meant, for she could read me like a book. As if adding weight to my plan, my mother informed me of the sad news that her youngest brother, Julius, was under arrest for an offence against the *Reichsmarschall,* Herman Goering. Apparently Julius was with a crowd of people obstructing the car and booing. Feeling sad was no use, my only chance was to secure a new lease of life, by staying out of jail and working for the Resistance in a more ingenious way – by getting married to an outsider, for the enemy within is much more dangerous and effective. The more I thought about it, the better I liked it and my mind was made up, if Schaile should ask me to marry him, I would accept. Mother's worried look told me to be patient, yet I could not afford to let this opportunity slip through my fingers. I was tired of fighting without protection and, if I was not very much mistaken, the iron was hot to strike now. After four years of Nazi terror, one needed a touch of genius or the devil to survive and I decided to preside over my destiny as long as I was still breathing, In this frame of mind, I declared to my astounded mother: "All our troubles are over once I've married this man Schaile. This time I intend to play both ends against the middle and win."

"Don't be too sure," mother warned, for a start he will never get a permit to marry YOU!"

"We shall see who is right," I answered emphatically.

Soon everything began to make sense. Schaile turned up as I had predicted and my mother's doubtful looks turned to amazement. Rather businesslike, he expressed his desire to marry me, explaining how long it might take to get permission. This however, he added would give me time to explore my true feelings for him. I could have told him the answer on the spot, but this would have been the end perhaps of both my mother's freedom and mine. In logical phrases we discussed our lives, the advantages of being married to an SS Officer and all it entailed. Suddenly, Mother said: "I believe you ought to know that Burgi is in dead trouble with the Gestapo in Leoben." As she explained how it came about Schaile listened carefully, then promised to see the *Herren* of the Gestapo the next morning and told me not to worry about it. I still did, until he returned from his 'visit' to inform me that he had managed to iron out my difficulties and vouch for my future behaviour. In point of fact the afternoon brought more surprises and with it the Gestapo officer who had punched my face not so long ago. He apologized for his error of judgment and for believing the two women witnesses. Words failed me. I could not express my own feelings towards this coward, for it stood out a mile that he was afraid of being reported by Schaile to the SS Amt in Berlin, who would replace him with a Front Officer, as was often done in cases like this. Now that I was mixing with the *Herren* race, I was suddenly welcome at the oddest places and my announcement of our engagement was followed by a flood of well-wishers and presents. My return after Schaile's departure to the Russian Front, to my H.Q. office, confirmed only too well how fickle people can be, as my female staff proved. They showered me with congratulations and offered to help me where they could; only Moser sensed that something was wrong. In fear I withdrew into a shell.

In September the second half of my leave was due and I decided to travel to Stuttgart and visit my future in-laws. They were farmers and well off. My mother-in-law-to-be was a widow, being cared for by her eldest daughter, Maria, a statuesque woman in her late thirties. Although we had nothing in common, they accepted me and I helped in bringing in the harvest and wrote dutiful letters to my fiancé at the Front.

Two days before returning to Austria I received, to my great shock, a letter in a familiar greyish-green envelope. It was from the Gestapo, ordering me to appear before the Stuttgart Court at 11 a.m. on September 16. Wisely or not, I showed it to Schaile's sister, who, rather bewildered, agreed to come with me, but asked me not to mention it to her mother. We set off by bus the following morning and arrived dead on time in Court, where two men were already looking for me. At once I was ushered into a large room to face a judge and court officials. The judge was in a black robe and read out my particulars, becoming increasingly angry as he stated that, on February 5 of this year I had visited an officer by the name of Rudolf Koroschetz and that to obtain my travelling papers I declared myself to be his fiancé. Banging the table with his fist he shouted at me: "Why, Fräulein Triller, did you terminate this relationship?" "Because he was killed your Honour," I whispered. "Not yet my girl," the judge exclaimed, "but we've got him all in one piece and his sentence is death by hanging," he added breathlessly. Feeling the floor rotating, I closed my eyes. All I could think about was Rudolf. My torturer exclaimed at the top of his voice: "You loved him, you slept with him didn't you, admit it." "Yes, yes," I shouted back with sudden emotion, "I did love him and I wished to God I had slept with him." "Get her out of my way", the Judge demanded, "and bring in Maria Schaile." At this time nothing on earth mattered, only the knowledge that they had captured Rudolf and caged him in like a wild animal and here was I giving evidence against him. Maria passed me leaving the courtroom and she was crying. Obviously she must have heard what was said, as she told me not to worry. After five minutes or so, she returned, looking white and shaken and we left in a hurry. Sitting in the bus all I could think about was Rudolf and how embarrassingly he held my fur collar against his face whilst saying 'good-bye'. His black eyes were still haunting me, exposing a heart which I had maintained was non-existent. Two days later I was on my way back home to Austria, with the 'sword of Damocles' still dangling above my head. One thing was certain – now I had to marry Schaile, for the pistols were right at my temples.

December 23 1942. Schaile's mother arrived to attend the wedding, planned for the twenty-ninth at a Registry Office at Graz.

December 24. My parents and friends left for Graz. My grandmother insisted that I stay with her alone, thus giving us a chance to talk things over. Mina Bolzano was very thorough at everything, in fact she arranged the wedding, the reception, my outfit, and paid the bills, but most of all she knew the tragedy behind it.

December 29. By eleven a.m. I was dressed in an off-white satin gown and helped into a fabulous white fur coat, a gift from my grandmother, and made from an Icelandic bear. Benno, her son, who happened to be on leave, was my best man, for I could think of no better person to give me away. Hunted by the Gestapo, like myself, for being a half-Jew, forced to serve as a common private, we aligned ourselves more than ever on this my wedding day. It was like a public demonstration that two unwanted people were determined to stay alive, one way or the other.

Eleven thirty a.m. Georg Schaile arrived with his best man, a Major, and presented me as was usual, with my bride's bouquet. It consisted of nineteen roses, representing the years of my age. My fiancé jokingly remarked that if we had waited until January, he would have had to pay for twenty. How well spoken I thought, and we all proceeded to leave for the ceremony at the Town Hall. During it I trembled like a leaf in the wind, sometimes leaning, on the verge of collapse, against my uncle Benno. Upon leaving, hundreds of people lined the stately staircase along the corridors, shouting 'good luck' and I recognized their faces from my schooldays. Outside the carriages waited, headed by two white horses rearing to go. Amongst shaking hands and blowing kisses we lead the procession of six Landaus to the Grand Hotel and our reception. Toasts and speeches followed, until at last we left around 4 p.m. for my home in St. Stefan. There more celebrations were in store for us and, by the time we were alone, it was two in the morning.

The Christmas tree still glistened in the corner by my grand piano, with bottles of champagne flanked at a table. My husband proposed to open one, but I declined, so he pulled me close to kiss me. At this moment my whole world fell to pieces before my eyes and I could go on no longer. I confronted him with the cruel statement that I was not in love with him and if he was claiming his rights my answer was that being a Catholic one had to be married in church – thus our civil contract was void. Running his fingers through his hair as if to awaken from a nightmare, he gripped my right arm and said: "You knew from the onset that I could not marry you in church, but I can wait, I don't like obedient animals," adding, "in a way I've asked for this treatment, yet I do love you most sincerely." What an awful mess I was in, yet the rights and the wrongs did not matter and if this was evil, this was me at this time of my life. Too many were herded into concentration camps and perished, but I had just signed a contract with the SS Chief Himmler (who had given permission for this marriage to take place) to stay alive – for the time being anyway.

January 6, 1943. It was almost a relief when a telegram marked 'urgent' arrived for Schaile. It read: "Return to unit at once". Somehow, I felt sorry for my husband, for he was flesh and blood and big and strong, yet he never fought back the way I would have done in his place. Rather complacent up to his last hours with me, he kept taking photographs of me in the snow and advising me of my financial position, now that I was married with a monthly income twice the amount of my step-father's. At near midnight, his train was due to leave and Mother and I packed some sandwiches. Looking guiltily at her, I said: "Now you can tell your husband he won't have to keep me any longer."

Georg asked me not to come to the station, and made a startling confession: "Now that we are parting, I must tell you that the laugh is really on me, for I told the SS Council, to further my permission to marry, that you were pregnant." As I looked bewildered and worried stiff, thinking of the possible implications, he laughingly advised me to play them up for a while, to get preferential treatment and then inform them of the mistake. Now both of us laughed and I knew that Schaile was in love with me, although I did not deserve it. The whys in my life began adding up, yet only the men who loved me knew the answer. Unbeknown to him I cut off some twigs from the Christmas tree and lay them on the table by the entrance. "Please forgive me . . . *auf Wiedersehn,*" I said.

Georg Schaile had gone out of my life as silently as he came in and all that reminded me of him were the photographs, presents and letters. 1943 also saw some fierce fighting on the Eastern Front and the newspapers were filled with notices of death. Two of my best friends' husbands were terribly wounded, having lost one arm and one leg each. Another, Paula Vesligy, was widowed at the age of twenty-two, with one child aged three and one expected in June. Grief-stricken, I heard the news and read the advert in the paper: *"In unsagbarem Schmerz gebe ich die traurige Nachricht, das mein geliebter Mann und Vater meiner Kinder im Osten gefallen ist."* Paula simply expressed the awful pain and hurt at the loss of her husband and I decided to go and see her. I found her father looking after the little child. Tearfully he explained that his daughter was being questioned by the Gestapo because she omitted to add that Paul had died for his "beloved Fuehrer". Startled and furious I heard the old man's lament, thinking how dare they treat a war widow in such a way and how little life really meant to the Nazis. However, Paula did return home, a shadow of her former self, with two fatherless children to bring up. It was at times like these that I knew what I was fighting for: women who suffered many injustices and could not retaliate in a world ruled by heartless men manifesting to fight for our freedom, only to enslave us in their sinister plan to conquer the weak and helpless. My emotions had surfaced once more and I was alive with ideas and plans to bring about the fall of Hitler, however silly it sounded. Though riding a wave of popularity, I was convinced that he could never win – if he did there was no God at all. 'Onward Christian Soldiers', the British sang, and I believed in it every hour of the day.

The winter made way for the spring and my work at H.Q. St. Michael increased, whilst the letters from my husband became more irregular. The third week in March a letter arrived with an official stamp and before opening it, I guessed the contents . . . Missing, presumed dead . . . . As I stood staring across the blank wall I felt I was being stoned to death. I decided at once to go and see our local priest Father Edelsbrunner and he received me with great dignity. To my amazement he told me that he had a letter from my husband, asking him how to become a member of the Catholic Church, thus gaining my love and respect.

"I have answered him immediately my child" the elderly priest said.

"You know what you have done," was my angry reply . . . "You have signed his death-warrant."

Edelsbrunner swayed and sat down, murmuring: "I did not realize, Hitler has replaced GOD completely."

Bewildered, I left his office to go home. Now my ultimate goal was my march against Hitler and all he stood for, but I had no right to feel sorry. "The damned don't cry", they say . . . . . or should it have been the godly daredevils?

Two weeks later my suspicion became reality, for Father Edelsbrunner was arrested and the people in the village asked WHY?

I could have told them, but I dared not; this was another secret I would have to bear . . . . . until victory . . . or . . . death.

CHAPTER 6

ROSES FROM THE *LUFTWAFFE*

Life for me had never lacked colour or excitement. I had experienced the depths of sadness and the heights of gaiety. But there was no incentive at the Headquarters Rail Junction. However, Dr M – believed that observations were vital to our cause and would eventually lead to results. He visualized an International Network of Resistance Groups liasing with us, but all I was sure of was the fact that it was the month of June and Nature was at her best and most beautiful. The weather was glorious and the air filled with the perfume of flowers, rather treacherously enhancing a young girl's dream, whilst a senseless horror swept the world. Despite the latter, the birds united, singing triumphantly, and one could feel the magic of Johann Strauss waltzes sweeping through the trees and bushes. How could one possibly wish to destroy so much beauty and loveliness?

Looking forward to my lunch break, I made my way to the nearby station hotel where the food was as drab as its dirty grey walls. Jumping over the rail lines, imagining the most delicious dishes my mother used to make before Hitler's war put an end to it, I noticed amongst hundreds of soldiers on the platform, a *Luftwaffen* officer arranging his cap smilingly and beckoning me to come his way. Although used to these sort of overtures due to working at a busy rail junction, I suddenly found myself tidying my hair and observing this man. Somehow I knew he was an Austrian, for he lacked the German's aggressiveness in wearing a uniform, and smilingly came closer. The sun was sizzling down on my bare head and we were less than three feet apart, when he said: "I saw you crossing the lines and hoped you would be heading my way." "Very funny, but not very original," I replied, annoyed with the banal approach, and walked past him. However, he begged me to have lunch with him and the prospect of a free meal was tempting enough to brush aside personal views and dislikes – this would mean saving my precious food coupons for an extra day. I accepted his invitation and he introduced himself as Pilot Officer Franz Schlager, adding, "Austrian by birth." He also told me that he was starting his leave of fourteen days.

We walked into the station restaurant, owned by Frau Ladentrog, one of the truly tough woman Nazis in the district. The waiter, Otto Kovaschitz, a midget, was a good friend of mine, found us a corner table, and pointed out the food still available. To pass the time until our lunch was ready, I told Schlager to watch Frau Ladentrog turn up like an Indian smoke signal to cross-check poor Otto and make sure he had taken the full amount of coupons. I explained how she recently caught the midget serving me but not taking any meat stamps and how she shouted at him regardless of the many other customers, calling him a "creature" who should be exterminated, and finally stated, "On second thoughts, Otto, I will keep you for a laugh, to amuse the soldiers." My host listened fearfully in case someone overheard my story and told me to calm down. "I suppose you call yourself a Christian," I said, ignoring his plea as he nodded. I added, "Yes you cannot bear to hear the truth." "Of course, I should like to," he answered, "but not in a public place like here for instance." Holding his look, I smiled and said: "Not here or anywhere else, Herr Pilot Officer, it takes courage to be different, but I do see your point as well." Suddenly, Frau Ladentrog came by. Ignoring me, she addressed Schlager, asking him how much longer we would have to wait for total victory, adding flippantly: "After all, the only country we have to conquer is this silly little island, England."

"The Fuehrer decided," he began, "not to invade England, for why risk German lives, if we can bomb them into submission." Frau Ladentrog was pleased with the answer, whilst Otto arrived with our food, wished us *Guten Appetit,* smiled at me, having heard part of the conversation and knowing how I felt towards the Nazis. At last we began to eat and the owner left, giving me a further black look. Schlager was puzzled by this animosity so I told him the rest of my story about poor Otto, how on that day in question I got up and flung my half full plate of the *Gulasch* at Frau Ladentrog's feet to the great amusement of most soldiers, and made my exit. "Of course one can see," Schlager said, "why she has never forgiven you for this." "The feeling is mutual," I countered, finishing my dessert.

As my lunch time was nearly up, we decided to go for a brisk walk. We both seemed to size each other up until my friend suddenly asked me to describe him. "Not very tall, rather broad shoulders, fairish thin hair and grey-blue eyes." "Oh," he replied, "nothing else," pulling me towards him. "Oh yes," was my answer "your mouth is generous and betrays your apparent coolness." We began laughing and I insisted on his version of me, which he summed up in one sentence: "You make me wish that there were only nights, wine and roses to live for."

Walking back to my office and arranging our rendezvous for the next day, which was a Saturday, Schlager kept reaching for my hand, when Moser passed us, jokingly waving his finger at me. "And who is this elderly gentleman?" Schlager asked with a tone of ridicule as I countered: "The man in the moon and believe it or not he works at H.Q. under my direction." That was the end of my conversation with Schlager; he kissed my hand, rather amateurishly, and retreated across the rail lines.

June 14 1943. Our rendezvous was five kilometers from St. Michael. Franz, looking very smart, was already waiting for me at one thirty. With my eyes still on the Iron Cross lst class, I asked him how he got it. He told me how some Me 109s, including his own, attacked a British Squadron, and although outnumbered, shot down five planes, and returned to their base in Banak without loss. As I listened, I watched his face . . . if this was his mirror it was hiding a cracked heart that had never loved for his statement was stilted and repressed. Schlager must have realized what I was thinking and that I was anti-Nazi, for he added that the Germans in general looked upon the Austrians as Trottels, the equivalent of simpletons. I nearly laughed but said: "We must be Trottels to fight and die for them; after all what possible interest could there be for a small country of not seven million people to go to war with any other nation?" He looked at me astonished and answered: "Luckily you've said this to me and not to a Nazi; they lock people up for less than that." I laughed – perhaps it was nervousness – and thought: "What a way to start our friendship."

We sat down underneath a beautifully shaped chestnut tree. It was so peaceful that even to talk seemed wasteful. I laid my head on the soft grass, stared at the sky, and Franz followed suit. Absorbed in our thoughts we lay there for nearly one hour. He looked at his watch and broke the silence: "I never knew that a girl could be so quiet for so long." Little did he realize that I preferred the stillness of this lovely summer day to any conversation about the *Luftwaffe*. As I did not answer, he said: "The German girls are too militant and here I am, still solo." I wondered if it was a complaint or a challenge to me and smiled at him. He bent over me, outlining my nose with a grass, saying: "You've got the nicest upturned nose, people with that kind of nose can be very loving." Removing his arms from my neck, I made no secret that I was not that sort of girl. If he was looking for a cheap adventure, he had better look somewhere else. Schlager was dumbfounded by my reactions and apologized for any 'silly' remarks he may have made. "Time on my hands and you in my arms – what else would I be thinking?" he asked. I suggested that he walked me home where my mother would make us coffee. By the time we got there our friendship was restored to normal. In the next two hours I knew all about him. His past and his present job as a pilot-instructor, but no matter how he described his daily duties, the emptiness of his life was apparent. The world the Nazis tried to create for him seemed without purpose. When Franz Schlager left our house he begged me to see him again. However, my mother observed with great misgivings my liking for this young man and considered my explanation of trying to change him a complete waste of time.

When we met again we discovered a slender cord . . . a tension that was somehow binding. Although he knew how my mother felt about him, he was determined to prove her wrong, thus creating a double problem. I had to inform Dr M – of this new friendship. Fearing an avalanch of vetoes I was surprised he accepted my news like a gift from heaven. "On the contrary," he said, "this man could be very useful to our cause – he has first-hand knowledge of the latest fighter planes." Wrestling with the logic of the man to whom I had promised allegiance in the fight for freedom, I saw myself cornered and involved with a new mission – to obtain information which might be useful to the Resistance.

My next meeting with Franz was a few days later at his parents' farm. They were most friendly people and lived the busy life of farmers. From a conversation with his mother, I gathered that Franz was the apple of her eye. His sister, a very attractive girl, was engaged to one of Franz's best friends, and she looked upon her brother with great pride. The father, who had the last word in this family, and I don't mean it to be a compliment, adored his son and forecast a great career for him. I was glad when the visit was over. I had gathered a new picture of Franz Schlager, yet my head told me to proceed in my disguise to detect the real man behind the 'drumbeating'. However, the harder I tried to explain him to my mother, the worse it got, and she said: "I shall never trust this man, he is far too deep for my liking." "All he needs is inspiration," I countered, but her reply was devastating: "What he really needs is a bomb under his bottom." Dr M – agreed with me, and told me to proceed with our friendship cautiously.

The days passed quickly and Franz had to rejoin his Squadron stationed at Boeblingen near Stuttgart. Before leaving he came to ask me to marry him. I managed to dissuade him from talking to my mother, as she was in no mood to entertain another war-time marriage as far as I was concerned. "But this is a risk thousands of girls are taking now," Franz countered, trying to make his point. "The truth of the matter is," I replied with conviction, "I would never share my husband with Hitler." He had already guessed my reason for refusing his offer. "If only I had more time, I could make you change your mind," he said. How little he really knew me, I thought, holding his disappointed look as long as I dared. The interlude was over, yet I wished it had ended on a happier note. Nevertheless, this off-beat meeting with him, nourished a great ambition in Dr M –'s strategy, in fact he considered it my big scoop. Explaining the desirability to exploit this situation, he urged me to visit Boeblingen soon. I wrote to Schlager inviting his consent for me to see him again, and, as expected, I received a reply by return giving me a watertight case for the Nazi authorities and my travel papers.

July 14, 1943. Once more I left for Stuttgart, crammed with memories. The approximately five hundred kilometer journey went smoothly, although some of my fellow passengers predicted air raids. At last the boot was on the other foot and Dr Goebbels got the total war he had been advocating for so long. With Stuttgart in sight, I prepared to change trains, for Boeblingen was another nine kilometers away. A charming lady sitting opposite me wished me good luck, with a twinkle in her eyes. I certainly needed it. However, as everything else in my life turned up unexpectedly, so it happened this time. As I walked up the steps at the Rail Station, many people hurried by, most of them in uniforms. Suddenly, I noticed a man resembling Schlager, but dismissed the idea, for he was awaiting me at Boeblingen, and I proceeded upstairs. At the second half of the last turning the same man caught my eye, although he had his back to me and I shouted "Franz!" to satisfy my curiosity. As though hit by a stone the man stopped, turned around slowly, and, of all people, it was Franz Schlager coming towards me in sheer amazement. Disregarding the crowd, he took me in his arms. We were oblivious to the obstruction we were causing. The sun shone warmly on us; then, as he kissed me, he dropped his briefcase on my foot. Apologizing profusely he knelt to inspect the damage. There were many black looks from passengers as they tried to pass us – there were also a few nostalgic and understanding glances. A military policeman arrived and moved us on, to the amusement of some of the other soldiers, one of whom said: "That saved me going to the pictures today, I haven't enjoyed myself so much for a long time." Franz did not think it funny at all but I buried my face under the large brim of my sun hat.

Twenty-five minutes later we were in Boeblingen, heading for the house of Frau Brandl. A scruffy looking woman in a dressing-gown asked us in and I found out, whether I liked it or not, that this was Frau Brandl. The place matched the owner's appearance, although she explained that this, of course, was due to the British 'gangster' raids, and I was glad when she showed me to my room. The three of us marched upstairs with Frau Brandl leading the way. Opening a door wide, she exclaimed: "I am giving you my best room in the house, for I liked your boyfriend from the moment I saw him." There we stood looking at a room empty except for a bed in the centre – a monstrosity – a four-poster made of heavy oak. Frau Brandl assured me it was most comfortable, once it was made up, and offered to fetch the bedding from the air-raid shelter. Off she went, smoking all the time, while I jokingly remarked to Franz: "I could see smoke coming from her ears," but he squeezed my arm, signalling me to wait until she was out of sight. I sat on the bed and laughed – this was humour and pathos rolled into one. Franz bent over to kiss me, when – bang – I hit my head on the big wooden knob, ruining his effort at being romantic. "First my foot and now my head," I said to him, adding, "this is no way to seduce a lady." He started apologizing most sincerely, unable to grasp the fun I was having, but I was in my element, telling him to name the bed 'Giant', and saying: "I don't suppose Frau Brandl will move it into her shelter, unless she chops it up for firewood first." "You're right," Franz replied, "but for a start it spoiled my plans."

Still holding my sore head, I got up to have a look at the view, when seeing that the window had no glass panes, I began laughing once more. Suddenly Franz and I glanced at each other and he guessed what I was thinking. The Royal Air Force was very much in evidence, leaving their visiting cards at the doorstep of Boeblingen's *Luftwaffe* Fighter Squadron. Seriously he exclaimed: "We shall get the upper hand again, don't worry." Placing my arms around his neck, I countered: "All I want for you and millions of others is to stay alive and to enjoy yourselves the way you think fit . . . let's love and not kill each other." "Looking at your ideals from close quarters, I'll agree," Franz answered. As if putting off the evil day he left and we agreed to meet between five thirty and six at this same place, providing there was no air-raid warning. I fully understood the situation – meal time in Germany now depended on the sirens.

Once alone I realized my tense position. The background for playing 'Delilah' was drab indeed for there was not even a mirror to see how I looked. I ventured downstairs to see where the lady of the house was and found her still in the same old dressing-gown, smoking fast and furiously. Hanging on to her skirt were three young children in need of a good wash. If that is how victory looked to the Germans in 1943, what would it be like in one year from now? I requested a mirror and coathangers, dangling before her some cigarettes, which she eagerly reached for. At once she agreed to fetch me these and remarked: "What a nice, quiet boyfriend you've got, the first day he called he hardly spoke at all." She was obviously fishing for information as to our affair, so I excused myself to get ready for the evening. My choice was an ice-blue taffeta dress with silver belt and shoes to match. At five-thirty I was awaiting Franz on the doorstep. He looked startled, seeing me so dressed up. "What a contradiction you are, elegant and earthy," he exclaimed in admiration.

We left immediately for the Restaurant which stood upon a hill some ten minutes' walk away. The place was nearly full and, a pianist was playing Liszt's *Liebestraum*. A waitress ushered us to a corner table with a 'Reserved' ticket on it. Some people looked up, others, knowing Franz, waved. I was a new face indeed. After a plain but plentiful dinner, we left. I was far too relaxed either to go back to my lodgings, or to come to the point of my visit, so I suggested a walk. However, Franz suggested outside the airfield, and I agreed. The night was clear and I could see the fighter planes standing about. As Franz and I walked past the instruments of destruction I wondered how much of a hero he was. Life is full of joy yet we can miss it all by not understanding each other. Too soon our first evening was over and Franz had to return to his Squadron. The following evening he called again. The same restaurant, the same little walk, the same routine, but I felt there was something very wrong and I asked him the reason for his silence. "I am not supposed to be out at all," he said, "the C.O. stopped my pass because I was late last night. Five silly minutes late." Firmly he began to tell me what happened, explaining that, like a recruit he was brought before his C.O. and told off (a) for being late and (b) for not saluting his C.O. at the Restaurant where we dined. Franz protested to these charges that (a) it was only a matter of five minutes and (b) that he did not see him in time to salute. Finally, the C.O., called Schlager sloppy and typical of the Austrian race – "Wine, women and song," he shouted, and ended by calling him a *Trottel* who had to be taught German discipline.

Suddenly I felt this Commanding Officer had prepared my own battleground, thus, in a strange way, he had helped my cause and I began expressing my own views to a dumfounded Schlager. Firstly that he should have reminded his C.O. that the Austrian upstart and Arch-*Trottel*, Hitler, who did not know a *pas de deux* from a pint of beer, was his great Fuehrer and next, that although we spoke a similar language we were *not* Germans and that Vienna was a Congress town when Berlin was still a fishing port. Agitated, we began to discuss the Nazis and how we Austrians had got involved in this dreadful war, and how Hitler could possibly say that he accepted full responsibility for killing millions of innocent people. Franz agreed to all that I said but mentioned the fact that if he had called Hitler what I had, he would have been put against the wall and shot. To calm me down he put his arm around my shoulders exclaiming: "Darling, please be sensible, there is nothing you and I can do to alter the situation, no matter how much we would like to." "Surely there must be" I replied, "why should we blindly obey Hitler without being able to say what happens to our country?" Franz was worried that someone might overhear us, although we were alone, but for me it was now or never and I continued: "This regime has made us into cowards, we are afraid to talk and think without the permission of this madman who decides when we are to be blown to bits." Franz pleaded with me desperately to stop talking like this, even threatening that he would go back to his base, so I shouted at him: "Go, you moral weakling, go back to your German Squadron and lick the boots of your C.O." Franz looked bewildered and I thought for one moment that he would slap my face, but instead he put his arm around me and walked me firmly back to the house. We went straight to my room. Franz looked drawn and anxious.

There was no way out for us now. Summoning all my strength, I was determined that Schlager must see things my way . . . how tenuous is the thread that holds our thoughts together . . . how much could I trust him? The age old battle *à la femme fatale versus man* was on. Lying across the bed, I asked him to pour me a drink from the bottle of wine we had brought back from the Restaurant. He did so but as I reached for the glass he suddenly took it from me and put it on the chair. His eyes flickered passionately and, with his lips half open, he came closer, so dangerously close that either I must let him kiss me, or reject him. I did the latter. Like a wounded tiger, Franz got hold of me, pulling me into the middle of the room. He sounded furious: "What game is this, Burgi, you know I will give everything I have in the world for you." For me it was now all or nothing: "I am working for the Resistance and I need technical details of the Me 109/110, its maximum speed, altitude, fuel supply and your group's formation tactics."

I felt as though I were on a flying trapeze with no one on the other side to catch me. Franz just stood there, pale, but controlled like the perfectly trained soldier he was. I thought he was never going to speak. Then it came: "Details of a highly technical nature, meticulous factual information, for someone as lovely and human as you? . . . I am indeed between the devil and the deep blue sea . . . Hitler being the devil and you the sea luring me in, to drown in your kisses."

As if to escape the climax, I moved back towards the wall, but Franz came after me and I could see he was yielding to my challenge. He insisted that I smile at him "That's my girl, you or no one else," he repeated as he took me in his arms, dismissing all doubts with his kisses, assuring me that all would be well in the end.

He promised to bring me drawings and details of the latest type Me 110 the day I was leaving, thus avoiding the risk of having papers of this nature at Frau Brandl's.

I understood and thanked him. It was all so simple!

We spent the rest of the evening reflecting on our lives and the split second timing at the Stuttgart Station and, of course, our love. However, in the back of our minds we both knew of the dangers which now lay between us and that, if we got caught, the penalty was death. There we lay on this gigantic bed holding hands, talking of love and the enemy. Franz told me of the vanity of Luftmarschall H. Goering and that some of the men in his Squadron were making paper medals, as Hitler had exhausted his stock of decorations for Goering. When I described him as a 'toad-in-the-hole' pinned down by the Royal Air Force, Franz laughed heartily. Suddenly, the sirens sounded – Allied Bombers were on their way into Germany. Franz got up to leave but said, with a hint of irony: "If I get killed this night the world will still be at war and go on living, but it would be poetic justice." I reached for him and he embraced me, holding my face right under the glaring light of the naked bulb. "How can one woman monopolize so much beauty and temptation and how can I step in that cock-pit, fight, and forget you?" He turned and left the room briskly. Fully dressed, I lay on my bed, my mind lingering with Franz and hoping for his safe return. Was he one hundred per cent on the level? Would he keep his promise? All I wanted was defiance against the Nazis and their terror. I did not bother to go into the cellar, although Frau Brandl urged me to. My battle was won, that was all I could think about, until sleep took advantage of me.

The following morning Frau Brandl brought my breakfast and, for the first time, I had a good look at her. She was only five years older than me, but all traces of youth had gone. If that was what war and worry did to us women, then why not stop it?

An hour later Franz arrived, his briefcase tucked under his arm. Hastily he handed me a small parcel and suggested that I left at noon for Austria. We were convinced that no one could possibly guess anything and his explanation for my sudden departure was my mother's illness. He advised me to keep calm as if nothing had happened. My train was to leave Boeblingen, near Stuttgart, at twelve fifteen. Franz carried my suitcase and a bunch of twelve yellow roses. Being superstitious, I said that yellow roses were unlucky, to which he replied: "Nonsense, *Liebling*, I shall bring you luck." The minutes ticked away and the train came in sight. We stood in silence. Franz got out his handkerchief to dab a tear he said was in my eye, but I assured him that it was not so. "Don't be ashamed of your feelings," he said, "if you could see inside me you would think I was being tortured." With passionate intensity he held me close, disregarding the many people on the platform, poking fun at himself until I smilingly said: "A sense of humour can be a great help in times of stress, or is it our outrageous defiance against the society we live with." Franz looked at me humbly and replied: "My rebellion came with you, the day you walked over those rail lines in St. Michael, utterly flirtatious but with a directness that captivated my heart." I boarded the train with Franz kissing my hand and wishing me a safe journey. Once inside, I moved to the open window blowing him kisses and hoping that I remained faceless until I reached home. As the train moved out of the station Franz waved until I was out of sight.

Settling myself cosily in the corner, I closed my eyes. Were my logical ideas about the Resistance and my emotional convictions about love compatible? Or were they enemies destroying each other? The scientist observes and experiments, discarding risks, whilst I was expected to follow orders without questioning the outcome . . . the human pigeon in action. Although a difficult objective had been achieved, had it produced the feeling of conviction? How long could one be impregnable and calculative, working out the rights and wrongs of another human being and make him conform to a pattern, however justified? All's fair in love and war – I had watched men's frailties and exploited them for our cause. Nearly all surrendered, curiously wanting to taste the lips that promised all and nothing. Somehow it was sensuality transmitted to men which never failed to seduce. How much longer could I live up to this demand? Whatever my thoughts and deliberations on this home bound journey, the massive responsibility of the documents I had acquired would have to be placed into other channels once I had reached Leoben.

Twenty-four hours later I was there. Immediately I went to Dr M –'s flat and showed him the drawings. He considered them vital, but hurriedly copied with minor errors. He also pointed out that we must get rid of these as soon as possible, mentioning a contact in France, which, in rational terms, meant another mission for me. Pondering over the events of the past few days, Dr M –'s plans did not inspire me. His ethics in dealing with people disturbed me. "People are not puppets, they may be good or bad, but they have feelings, like you and me and sometimes I hate what I am doing." "This sounds all very well at normal times," he countered. "Remember, we are fighting the most ruthless regime in the world and they will not hesitate to murder a few more millions in the name of the Fuehrer." I had to admit Dr M – talked sense, and avoided a further discussion. As I picked up my roses he smilingly said: "This is your highly personal affair, Burgi, but if you become soft, I'll have to take over and give you moral guidance." Facing him squarely, I asked: "And what kind of God should I believe in, Dr M –? "Your own integrity," he answered, showing me to the door. My own integrity, I asked myself, on my way home, but who gave it to me in the first place?

A few days later Baron von Schindler visited me to see if I was all right, and to congratulate me on another successful mission. The first petals of Schlager's roses were falling and Schindler picked them off my little table. With his back to me he remarked: "They are like the tears you pretend you never cry." At moments like these I glimpsed behind the man von Schindler tried to hide in order to be tough, driving himself to the limit in a world which had no use for weaklings and no time for pity. Rather forlornly Schindler walked past me, said good-bye, and deposited the rose petals in an ashtray on his way out. I realized we both had become so absorbed in our job and its execution that our views were like nails which, when hammered in, caused sparks to fly. However, over cautious people are never creative either in thought or action, nor profoundly stirred by the sufferings of others. With that idea to comfort me, I felt Schlager was just one more stepping stone against the forces of evil.

CHAPTER 7

FRANCE – STRASBOURG

August 1943. The weather was glorious. The Royal Air Force was getting on top of the *Luftwaffe*, and so fortifying faith in the Resistance.

My strong determination to fight on, until we had beaten the Nazis, increased. Once more I switched off my private life and all it encompassed to step into the arena of dangers. Confronted with a new order, I was given forty-eight hours to get ready. My task – to bring the drawings and photographs of the Me 110 to Strasbourg and hand these to an agent of the French Resistance. His code-name was Valentine, because he was born on February 14 and he worked at the Ice Café next to the station. As I pretended to visit Schlager again and the *Luftwaffe* had priority, I got my travel papers from my home town. My forged papers related to visiting my 'wounded brother' in Strasbourg, thus from Stuttgart onwards I would have to rely on these entirely.

All was set and my journey began on August 3, 1943. It was swelteringly hot. To add to this discomfort the train was full to bursting with soldiers going on leave. Every compartment told its own story, and, as always, an attractive girl was a welcome passenger. One had to be full of understanding and indifferent to foul mouthed individuals. By now, after a total of some eight thousand kilometres, I considered myself a seasoned traveller. When I reached Salzburg, more troops, some of them in tropical uniforms, boarded my train, and the one empty seat opposite me was filled in seconds. One officer was bringing in luggage as if he was moving house, and I had to duck my head to avoid collisions. Nevertheless, he looked so helpless that I offered to assist. He thanked me and explained that this was the last box. Sitting himself down he remarked: "As far as I am concerned, the war is over." A careless joke for an officer, I thought and smiled at him encouragingly. In return he introduced himself as Lieutenant Walter Borg, and clicked his heels. "Pleased to meet you," I answered, "my name is Burgi Triller and I am on my way to Strasbourg to visit my wounded brother." Now that I had told my story, I felt relieved and hoped that Borg would not make an issue of it. I was right, the Lieutenant was very tactful indeed and left it to me to select the conversation. I chose films, but Borg's frown told me that he was not interested. "Let's talk about you, you are much prettier than most film stars, if I may say so." "You may," I answered smilingly. Rather contradictorily he went on talking: "Ilse Werner (one of the most popular stars at this time) visited our unit some time ago and I had the honour of being introduced to her." Borg paused for a while, shaking his head and continued: "All she's got is a large bottom lip and false eyelashes, the rest of her face one could not see through all the heavy make up." I laughingly answered: "Her lip may be due to kissing too many *Luftwaffen* boys." "You're so right, Miss Triller," he replied, "I've heard she likes them, especially those with lots of medals." Borg looked down at his own chest, without decorations, making his point. "Your logic inspires me, Lieutenant," I said, "but it would be wiser if you were to tell me the secret of the blanket which you are nursing." "This is a surprise," he countered. At that moment a waiter came past, asking for orders and I heard Borg request a saucer of milk. The man looked startled. What, an Officer drinking from a saucer? But he answered "Yes, sir," and left. I chuckled with laughter as I began to realize that, inside the blanket he obviously had an animal. As he untangled the parcel out came a large tortoise. He explained how he found it in Africa and decided to bring it to his sister who lived in Munich. "Has it got a name?" I asked. "Oh, yes, I call it Baby." The waiter returned and, seeing the animal, put the milk on the floor. Borg gave him a rather large tip, for which the man thanked him gratefully. "He can tell you have had little opportunity to spend your money," I said, and we both laughed.

I began to study Lieutenant Borg closer, and found him inescapably charming rather than good looking. He was slim with wavy fair hair and a little mischief in his green brown eyes. As the journey continued, we accepted each other's company with delight. I felt genuinely sorry that I had to lie to him about the wounded brother. The time went so fast, I hardly noticed the stations at which the train had stopped until another officer in the compartment declared that we were not far from Munich. Suddenly the train began to slow down, then stopped altogether. People began running about to find out what was the matter. We soon discovered that there was an air-raid alarm – "Allied bombers imminent" – although the train had already reached the outskirts of the town. Normally there was an advance warning, but this time the Royal Air Force was quicker. Borg was calm and collected his luggage. Luckily for him, I had only one suitcase, so I could help him to carry some of his goods. We certainly looked an odd couple – I was loaded like a soldier and Borg clutched a rolled-up blanket. As we got off the train, pushing our way through the crowds on the dark pavements, I could not help laughing, which brought me some nasty remarks from some of the people.

Now that the air raids boomeranged on the Germans, they shouted 'gangsterism'. Where was Goering's *Luftwaffe?* Only a short while ago he publicly declared that his name would be *Maier,* if one British plane ever crossed the German frontiers. I wondered what some of the population, after a devastating air raid, would call him now?

Milling along with the crowd from the train, Borg saw a white painted arrow pointing the way to a building, which seemed to me to be very low indeed. Borg led me down some steps as we heard voices below urging us to "come this way." The place was lit by one candle and all I could see were a few figures sitting wrapped in blankets. The blast from the anti-aircraft guns was in full swing and it seemed as if, at each blast, bits and pieces in this shelter kept falling down. We sat on our luggage and I kept whispering to Borg: "Let's go into the open air, I don't want to be buried alive." The first bombs were dropping and the explosions rocked the whole place. Lieutenant Borg put his arm around me protectively. It was my first serious air raid and I was afraid of dying. Trying to shelter me with his understanding, Borg said: "If it is any comfort to you Fräulein Burgi, I am sharing this moment with you." What a wonderful philosophy I thought, pulling myself together. Suddenly, the tortoise slipped down to the floor and escaped into the darkness. Borg began to search at once, when an elderly woman asked: "What have you lost?" "My baby," he replied, sounding very anxious. Great consternation followed. I began to laugh, knowing what Borg meant and what the people were thinking. Several shadows started moving about, searching the place up and down, but I could not stop laughing and the harder I tried to control myself, the worse it got. To me, they all looked like the dwarfs in *Snow White* shuffling to and fro. From out of the darkness a woman came towards me, accusingly pointing her finger right under my nose, saying: "A fine mother you are, there is your poor husband on his hands and knees, whilst you are treating it as a joke." Another person said "disgraceful woman", meaning me of course, thus the whole situation became hilarious. By now I was unable to explain anything for tears of laughter were running down my face. The woman most hostile towards me literally ordered her husband to go upstairs and fetch a bottle of milk. He obeyed and came back in a few minutes. "There is some milk," he said to Borg who tried to make himself heard for a change, but it was too late for any explanations. He had found the animal and shone his torch on it. The old man was staring at it as if he had seen a ghost. "It is a tortoise, Mama," he exclaimed to his wife, who came waddling along to see for herself. "So it is," she replied in a tone of indignation. "What did you think it was," enquired Borg, "a gnome?" Before I could intervene, the two started to argue, with her husband chiming in. Poor Walter Borg, there I was nearly paralysed with laughter, unable to assist him in any way. Only the 'all clear' ended the quarrel. We got hold of our goods and left in a hurry. As Borg and I were walking up the steps, I heard a woman say: "Calm down, Amalia, calm down, these two are from a circus." Walter glanced at me, realizing that I would start to laugh again, and half carried me up the rest of the stairs, until we came to the main road. This time it was Borg who was loaded like a donkey, and supporting me. I dared not look at him . . . then he too began to laugh.

As we walked through the crowds who were coming from all directions, Borg spotted a military vehicle, driven by an old friend. He signalled him to stop. The two men exchanged handshakes and were so delighted to see each other that Borg forgot to introduce me. However, the other man asked if we wanted transport and Walter asked to be driven to his sister's place. "This girl is coming with me," he said and, to the amazement of the driver, we kept on laughing and got in. Borg's sister's house was on the outskirts of Munich and stood in a well cultivated garden. Walter asked his friend to come inside, so that he could explain, but the friend declined, obviously thinking that we had had one too many. Borg rang the door bell and a lady in her early thirties opened it. Brother and sister embraced each other, with me standing back, again holding nearly all the luggage. Only Baby was covered up, lying on the steps. The lady of the house became aware that I was obviously with Walter. He apologized and introduced me to his sister. The three of us then began to carry in the luggage, and I could not help noticing how very clean the place was, and laid out with good carpets. Borg's sister was the wife of an Army Surgeon and they seemed to be comfortably off. "Call me Hilda," she said, and I had the feeling that she liked me instantly. I was really thankful that Walter had so kindly brought me along. A little rest would do me good. Frau Hilda showed me the bathroom, which was lavishly furnished and smelled of lilac perfume. "My favourite," I exclaimed and thanked her for having me as a guest. She smiled contentedly like one who enjoyed giving pleasure, and left me.

This heavenly bathroom had black and white tiles, with rugs to match, and mirrors, mirrors everywhere. I ran the bath water, scented it, undressed, and lowered myself into the relaxing liquid. It was like a dream, and all this I owed to Walter Borg and his charming sister, neither of whom I had known twenty-four hours ago. My lucky star was certainly with me. After my bath I put on my summer housecoat, which was of pure green silk with water lilies scattered all over it. I headed for the kitchen, where I could hear Hilda's voice. "You do look a different person now," she said, with Walter giving me a pinch on the cheek. They both ushered me to the dining-room. The table was already laid with delicious food, which made my mouth water. We all sat down and began to eat while I stuffed myself like a duck, Hilda and Walter, however, tactfully overlooked this fact. Hilda explained that Walter had told her of our adventures, and that she found them exhilarating as she too deplored the lack of humour left in the Germans since the British had intensified their raids. "God only knows how it will end," she sighed and looked at me sadly. I noticed how much like her brother she was. The same fine cut features, the same half-disguised smile.

Frau Hilda began to tell us that, in a recent letter her husband had indicated that the *Lazarets* were filled to the brink. She asked Walter for a cigarette, which she took and lit instantly. "I am amazed you are smoking, Hilda," he remarked. "Well, one does a lot of things when one is lonely," she replied, with a hint of anger, as she got up and removed the dishes on to a tray. "Walter," it was the first time I had called him by this name, "I hope you have not upset your sister." "She's all right," was the answer. A typical reply from a man.

Sitting on the couch we relaxed into the wonderfully soft cushions. Walter looked at me with eyes that shone, but my mind was occupied with my travelling plans for Strasbourg and I asked him for the time-tables. "You are going to have at least one day's rest," he said. "We will send a telegram to your brother, so that he won't worry himself over your delay." Walter was one step ahead of me and I had to think fast. "There is no real hurry," I said, "I will get there somehow, in any case I have not even told my brother that I am coming, only the doctor knows." Walter looked surprised, but assured me to leave it all to him. A little apprehensively I enquired what arrangements he had in mind. "After coffee we will go to the station and find which is the best train to Strasbourg," he explained, leaving me a little more time to think.

The coffee was served from a silver pot, in cups of finest porcelain. Frau Hilda was the perfect housewife and obviously enjoyed entertaining. After coffee, I excused myself and went to get dressed. My bedroom was one of the guest rooms and was as tastefully furnished as the rest of the house. However, my choice of gowns was easy, as I only had two dresses with me. I decided to wear the primrose yellow linen dress. Frau Hilda liked the dress and made no secret of her admiration. "Look Walter how lovely she looks," turning me around. "I wish I had your dark hair, Burgi," she said, "but I suppose the compliments should come from Walter," and she poked him in the ribs. In my view he did not need much encouragement. A little while later, Walter and I left for the town, and decided to walk, rather than take the tram. He seemed to know Munich very well, and began to tell me about his boyhood. Unfortunately I was not listening at all. My mind was focused on Strasbourg . . . the papers in my possession were burning a hole in my conscience. Added to this, was the worry of the stricter control system at the railways, which I had only noticed since reaching Munich. The *Wehrmacht-Police* were tougher and had been doubled. One error in giving the right explanation as to the whereabouts of my 'brother' would mean the end of my mission. An idea developed in the back of my mind – Walter Borg. There was no safer way than to travel with an officer. A happy couple *en route* to visit a relative wounded in battle. We arrived at Munich station and Walter commented on my silence during our walk. "I am sorry," I said, "but you see I was thinking how sad I shall be to leave, perhaps never to see you and your sister again." Walter stopped, turned towards me and said: "So shall I miss you in every way, I never had a girl friend before, at least not one like you, Burgi." "Oh Walter," I replied, "why don't you come with me to Strasbourg?" "Of course I will *Liebling,*" he answered, holding my waist. Walter was such a nice boy and I felt sorry to take advantage of his obvious feelings for me, but the alternative – getting caught – was unthinkable. After all I made him happy if only for hours and this knowledge partly eased my conscience.

The necessary enquiries at the station showed that there was not a through train that evening and I could see how this pleased Walter. We walked back to his home through the park where everything was in full bloom, where love's young dream could blossom, but only I knew the heartache it would bring in the end. Walter's summer madness had just begun and he showed it with every look, with every gesture. Quietly we spent the evening with his sister, and, as if the angels were smiling on us, there was no alarm to interrupt the serenity. We simply sat there holding hands and letting the rest of the world go by.

The following morning we left for Strasbourg. Walter was as happy as a sandboy. Although his sister, wishing us *bon voyage,* expressed sorrow at her brother's sudden change of plans. The journey took us through Stuttgart, Augsburg, and along the shores of the Rhine, where the first heavy damages of the air raids became visible. Walter and I avoided discussing the evidence before our very eyes as one never knew who was listening. As the journey continued we became tired and hoped that some of the passengers would get off so that we could stretch our legs. At Augsburg, several people did get off and we were the only two left for a little while. Soon Walter fell fast asleep. Although tired myself I was too keyed up to sleep, and looked through the windows to see how far we had got. I was worried about the outcome of it all.

The train kept travelling through the night, but I kept fully awake. Suddenly, a heavy-booted German patrol entered the compartment, and asked for Lieutenant Borg's papers. Walter was still asleep. Rather nervously I handed him mine instead, and the Corporal made some rude remark, saying: "He's tired already, what will you do when you get him home?" At once, Walter Borg jumped to his feet, putting on his jacket. Startled the Corporal saluted and left without checking any documents. "Lucky for him he is not from my Regiment, otherwise I would report him for neglect of duty," Walter said, so he could not have overheard what the Corporal had said to me. I refrained from commenting, so as not to invite discussion. However, I gathered another piece of mosaic which fitted in Walter's character. He was obviously still devoted to his country and the oath he had taken, so the greatest care on my part was necessary.

A wonderful morning dawned. The air was clear and still.

We looked through the open window to view the Cathedral of Strasbourg as it came into sight, closer and closer until the train stopped. It was so peaceful and secure – an omen that all would be well. We agreed to have breakfast, as many French people do, in a café beside the street in the open air, for I did not want to miss one moment of this lovely summer morning. It seemed that the town was still sleepy, but I was happy and confident. After a relatively good breakfast, Walter enquired about two rooms to rent. The waiter was most helpful and telephoned some friends of his. He told us that the people owned a large butcher's shop and there was still plenty to eat in the house. Stimulated by our good luck, we began to laugh and joke, remembering Baby left behind with his sister. The waiter, a Frenchman, gave Walter the address, with a small sketch of how to get there. We thanked him very much for his help and paid our bills. In a few minutes we found the house and were received with great courtesy. Promptly, we were shown our rooms. Walter excused himself to have a shave, whilst I went to freshen myself up. The lady of the house came and knocked on my door, asking me if I needed anything, but I declined. Opening the door, she said: "I sincerely hope you will like it here, we will take care of all your troubles." How grotesque, my troubles were only just beginning, and for a few moments, I regretted having not come alone. I thanked her kindly and she went away. Walter came in looking refreshed and elegant in his uniform. Before I was able to stop him, he opened my suitcase and took out my dress to put in the wardrobe. Suddenly he paused, holding up my fair wig exclaiming: "What are you doing with this, disguising yourself?" His eyes narrowed and he pushed me aside to further examine my case but found nothing else to help him with his already aroused suspicion. My legs felt wobbly as he reached for the handbag lying near by. I managed to wrestle it from his hand and he just stared at me. He began shutting the windows and then proceeded to lock the door. Unable to move, I just stood there. He came towards me, demanding an explanation, saying: "I will give you five minutes to tell me the truth." "And what will you do then Walter?" I asked. "Kill me like the Gestapo in cold blood, without a trial?" Borg was frantic and cried: "You destroy yourself and everyone who tries to help you." All my emotions surfaced and I began to explain. "I am trying to prevent you and many more soldiers from being killed — condemn me, but hear me first. The Allied armies are rapidly advancing in North Africa, two exhausting winter campaigns in Russia, millions of dead on both sides, slave camps all over Europe and the Gestapo more ruthless than ever, horrifying mankind." I had to pause to get my breath back and went on . . . "Is destruction the only way to prove that we love each other?" Borg looked at me crossly and said: "You are working for the enemy." "If you wish to put it that way Walter, but who is your enemy?" I answered. Although it was very hot I was shivering and Borg held my arm. "It is Hitler and his gang, who decide the fate of millions of Germans." "But Burgi," put in Walter, "what about the great sacrifices our people have already made, the killed and the maimed. If we capitulate we shall never be certain that we could not have won this war." "Walter, please sit down and listen to me," I said and he obeyed. I continued . . . "If we prolong this war, which was sheer madness to start in the first place, the Nazis will recruit the children and make them fight, until there are no more homes left to defend. The bravery of the soldiers is not mine to judge, nor to diminish, what will be on trial are the atrocities of the Gestapo and the Nazis sitting at home, shouting to you chaps not to retreat, calling you cowards. The inevitable will come and you and I will have to answer for the many crimes committed in the name of the Fuehrer. Let's change it now, before it is too late, Walter."

There was a long silence. Neither of us moved. Then Lieutenant Borg looked at me, uncomprehending, and said with great emphasis: "I never examined the Nazi propaganda before, but I must admit that you have managed to convince me of one thing, the senselessness of continuing this slaughter on all fronts. I am equally convinced that, with Hitler alive, there will never be peace." "Dear Walter," I said, "at least you are logical and can prepare yourself for your own survival, even if you don't wish to join the few who are actively fighting Hitler and his henchmen, thus risking a terrible fate if caught." Walter put his arm around me as he had done on the night of the raid, and I felt safe again. His calmness was wonderful and no other questions were asked about my movements at Strasbourg.

An hour later, I left for my appointment with Valentine. The café was as described to me by Schindler, well frequented by German soldiers and doing well. Behind the bar a pretty girl served. She asked for my wishes. "The Chef please," I said quietly. She showed me the side door which led to the kitchen and opened it. In there a man in his late thirties was making ice-cream. He was very swarthy looking and gave me little confidence. However, in my best French and complying with my orders, I asked him for his identity card. His reply was a nasty sharp knife right under my throat. "You are a *Bosche,*" he snarled, "I don't like to be questioned like this." How I remained calm, I don't know, but the mention of my other contact, Jack de la Traille, brought forth his card and I had a look at it before it was snatched from under my eyes. The important thing I had to know I saw, and told him his birthday . . . February 14, 1908. A rather savage laugh from him told me that I was safe at last, and I was certain this was Valentine. He embraced me, unleashing a flood of French whilst thanking me over and over again for coming to see him. Hastily, I handed him my secret papers. He glanced first at them and then at me, shaking his head and finally nodding approval, pushing them well under his shirt. Banging his chest, emotionally he said: "Please excuse my temper, but all I deal with now are *pigs*. You are very brave to come here. I hope no one has followed you."

He told me of eleven arrests in this area in the past twenty-four hours. He went on to mention names already in the hands of the Gestapo and begged me to be more than alert. He explained how his young cousin, Andre Valle of Mortagne, became a victim of the Gestapo and how on his way to their dungeons he swallowed some of the documents that might incriminate those not yet caught. Emotionally Valentine pleaded with me not to tell him my name so that, if he should get arrested, the Gestapo could never find out – not even under torture. For minutes I began to cry, overcome with what I had been told by this ordinary Frenchman with the heart of a lion. I implored him to make use of my papers and get them to England via the French Resistance, "It is our only chance to beat them," I kept repeating. He nodded understandingly and, to my utter surprise, crossed my forehead. He opened the back door carefully and ushered me out gently. We both gave the V sign and I departed, full of revulsion against the oppressors.

I expected to find Walter gone, although I was certain that he would not report me to the Gestapo for two good reasons: (a) I could feel he loved me and (b) his own implication by aiding me. He had seen Nazi 'justice' in action and the unhappiness of his only sister, whom he loved dearly. I was wrong with my first assumption, for Walter was still at the butcher's waiting for me. He never enquired where I had been and told me to rest as I looked tired. I wondered, how can one assess the nobility of a man's character? Was I a challenge to him and his nation, despite its humiliating implications, or did he only follow the passions of his heart? Early the following morning, we left Strasbourg, but I decided to travel on, avoiding Munich and his sister. We said good-bye on the train. As he held me close once more I wondered how I had sparked off this love, and how I had deserved it? The few minutes we had left, I wanted him to smile, to remember the 'Baby,' the air-raid shelter, and how we laughed the hours away. However, Walter for all his twenty-three years, was so dead serious and said: "Love is the greatest mystery, a divine truth partially revealed, but only too few recognize it when they find it. Our being together was so short, so tragically affected by the events of war, yet I was entrusted with something precious, if only for a brief time." I looked at my watch and we had only one more minute left. I felt guilty and unhappy, and thought if ever I was caught and executed by a firing squad, they had better not aim at my heart for how could I possibly have one? Walter left the train and remained on the platform adjusting his cap, whilst glancing at the open window and me. Rather firmly he stepped back and saluted as the train set off, parting us. "Good-bye Walter," I shouted . . . "good-bye and thank you." There I remained by the open window, waving, until Walter Borg was no more than a little dot in the distance.

One more mission behind me . . . one more illusion destroyed. I had certainly come a long way since 1938 and the

Nazi invasion. At first revenge was sweet, now it became a necessity to put a pistol at people's heads or be shot myself. The thin line between values in human encounters became blurred, the cloak and dagger business more demanding and ruthless, yet there could be only one decision for me, to remain loyal to my cause until Hitler and his henchmen were defeated.

My first visit was to Dr M —'s place. I felt awful and told him so. He poured me a glass of wine and ordered me to cheer up. However, nothing could sway me and I pointed out my fears of some impending peril. His reaction was fierce: "There are too many decaying corpses now to give in, the moral debasement of the Gestapo has reached its lowest level and no man can escape blame from the crimes now taking place if he does not protest." "But I am a woman," I snapped at him, "I've done my share." "None of us has, my girl," he shouted back, as if I was on trial. Bewildered I looked at him and left without saying good-bye. It was the first time I had ever left him like this — but my head was in a turmoil, rejecting all reasoning. The only sanctuary was my mother, although in her gentleness she could never comprehend the life I was leading. She advised me to trust in the Lord and be a warrior in the battle for salvation. In my opinion I complied with her ideals the only way I knew, by saving from destruction the people who wanted to be saved, and the innocent souls, the children condemned to death by bombing and starvation in camps. Never before in history was the question 'to be . . . or not to be' so relevant, unless we were prepared to sink into a world of darkness and despair. The ultimate goal had to be Victory and thus Salvation.

CHAPTER 8

THE SECRET WEAPON

The autumn of 1943 started with a bang and disaster. A hundred and fifty yards from our stables a British Lancaster came down in pieces. Dressed in trousers and wind-jacket, with my hair tucked under my cap and a scarf partly covering my face, I raced to the scene of the accident. Visibility was bad, but I was trying to beat the still wailing sirens and the German police.

As I approached the wreck, I realized that not many of the crew could be alive. The silence was deathly. Suspended between two trees hung the cockpit and from it the blood-covered face of the pilot glared at me. I shuddered, although I had seen and been subjected to plenty of violence and horror since the Nazi takeover in 1938. Carefully I looked around and the suspense was awful. Suddenly I slipped and fell over something. It felt round and muddy and, for a moment, I thought it was part of a human body. With trembling fingers I began to scrape off the dirt, deeper and deeper, fearing the worst, when suddenly I realized that I was trapped by the large wheel of the aeroplane. At last I managed to free myself. As far as my eyes could see through the fog lay wreckage, twisted metal, and in it, I suspected, the mangled bodies of the crew. I was right . . . the next thing I saw was the severed leg of a man, still stuck in his flying boot. It dangled ghost-like from another part of the tree, blood dripping down. I steadied myself by leaning on the tree, when the leg fell right in front of my feet. I gasped aloud, closed my eyes and walked past it, ready to run from this morgue on the hill. Then, from the debris, came murmurs of pain. The November fog was setting in as I strained my eyes to see. The sound grew louder and, on turning around, I saw a man, obviously one of the crew, sitting on the ground, pointing a pistol directly at me. "Stay where you are boy," he said, with his finger on the trigger. Somehow I could not help but smile, but there was no time for any introductions and I kept walking towards him regardless of his menacing gesture. Rather oddly, all fear had left me and all I could think of was the petrol left in the plane, and the few bombs which could go up at any second and reduce us both to ashes. Desperately I got hold of the airman, telling him that I came to help, and dragged him along as far as possible. He moaned in agony and I saw that his legs were injured, perhaps broken, but I kept going until I thought he was safe. I propped him against a tree, placing my woollen scarf at the back of his head for comfort. By now, with all the moving about, my shoulder-length hair had fallen from under my cap and he could see that I was a girl. He smiled and pushed his revolver into his pocket. Shaking his head in surprise he asked for my name and I said: "Notburga, but my parents call me Burgi," to which he replied in haste: "I may not be able to say it, but I won't forget it in a hurry." I sensed he was in great pain and told him not to speak. Cold pearls of perspiration stood on his forehead and, as I wiped them off, he insisted on telling me why he had covered me with his gun. "I saw two of my comrades shot at whilst bailing out about two miles from here and I was taking no chances with the Nazis." He drawled the word Nazi just as Churchill did. I told him that I was in the Resistance and listened to the BBC. Once more he shook his head, holding his leg in agony. I could see he wanted to speak again and I held my hand against his lips. Emotionally he held it and said: "We are friends . . . and we both have so little time . . ." He never finished the sentence. I felt his pulse and listened to his heart beat and I knew that he was alive. Gently I laid him on the ground, saying my own "good-bye" and left, for I could already hear the oncoming police and their barking dogs. Once more I turned around, saluted and made farther uphill to avoid the Germans.

I waited until complete darkness before heading for home. When I got back I discovered that I had lost my gold watch and remembered my scarf, wondering what would happen if the police discovered its owner?

The crash was hardly mentioned in the village, except that a British airman was taken prisoner. My own careful enquiries through my trusted friend, the local Doctor Ehrlich, led to the information that in fact, this P.O.W. was being attended to in hospital. A stone fell from my heart upon hearing this good news and new hope that all would be well inspired me. In a way I felt proud to have proof that British planes did venture far from their bases, penetrating deep into Germany and revenging the terror raids against England, but most of all making fools of Goering's invincible *Luftwaffe*.

At this time our Resistance Group was lying low and most of the population still believed in Hitler's victory, his military genius and, of course, his new and third *Wunderwaffe* – Wonder weapon. Baron Schindler kept needling me about my 'inactivity' for I was always expected to have news. My work regarding the British plane crash was taken for granted and orders to keep my eyes open doubled. Soon, the unknown British airman was forgotten, for outside my office of the *Bahnmeisterei* other important things began to take shape. Extra SS soldiers patrolled the periphery of St. Michael and parts of the rail junction were declared prohibited areas. Although I kept my eyes wide open, the elusive transports, heavily guarded, were shunted out of sight and disappeared like magic. An old friend of mine, the shunting-yard master, Herr F. Winkler, kept his eyes open and found out that the consignments were transported to Knittelfeld in great secrecy, yet no one knew why. I reported my observations to Dr M –. However, he was one step ahead of me and, according to his good friend, Frau Vogel, was in the possession of further vital facts, namely the increase of fighter planes at Zeltweg, near Knittelfeld. He had an idea and if he had one I usually found myself in the midst of it. "Frau Vogel," he said, "will provide the jumping-off board for us and you, my dear, our hearing aid."

Dr M – had obviously done his homework on Frau Vogel and gave me the details. Thirty-five years old, natural blonde, very attractive and mother of three young children. Ever since her husband, the Kraubart Schoolmaster, left to fight at the Russian Front, Frau Vogel believed in 'live and let live' all the way, and became the darling and party-hostess of the *Luftwaffen* boys stationed at Zeltweg. Dr M –'s dark eyes were twinkling as he explained: "Via Frau Koerting I've got you an invitation to attend one of Frau Vogel's parties next week," adding "by golly, I imagine you having some fun there." "I don't suppose they will neglect me, Dr M –." I flared back at him and his challenging smile vanished. However, realizing the importance of stumbling across some vital evidence useful to shorten the war, I accepted and promised to do my best. Teasing him not to lose his sense of humour I departed.

Saturday November 30, 1943. Dressed flamboyantly in an ice-blue taffeta silk dress with tiny silver straps crossed over my back, matching shoes and handbag, my hair hanging down around my shoulders, I set off by train for Kraubarth and the school-house where Frau Vogel lived. Many thoughts churned in my head: (a) how could I get vital information and (b) how tough was I really in the end? It was so easy to tell people how to be brave from a distance, and after all I was only human and a slip of a girl.

The party was in full swing. Dancers passed me in the lounge, which was cosy and warm. Frau Vogel dashed over, introduced me to 'her boys', and skipped off. One was the Flying Instructor, a Lieutenant Werner Fink, and he was without an escort. There was a pause, then he suddenly said: "What is a girl like you doing amongst the trollops?" I answered, my voice rising: "The same question applies to you, Herr Lieutenant, it's the case of the kettle calling the pot black." "Please forgive me," he countered, "and let's dance." He rather crushed me in his arms and we both laughed. His eyes were as green as the deepest sea and my militant thoughts vanished.

The later the hour the more boisterous the gathering and Lieutenant Fink complained about the excessive noise. At one time he reminded his boys to calm down and save their energy for flying. I watched his behaviour like a hawk, thus forming my views on how 'tough' he could be. But somehow, he was like a chameleon, changing his moods from hard to soft, from gay to sad. Champagne was bubbling in long stemmed glasses and, for one crazy moment, I was thinking about the British airman in a P.O.W. camp, lonely and hungry. What a topsy-turvy world to live in? We ate, we drank, we danced, we laughed and made love, and we were dead, but who cared . . . certainly not Hitler and his crew. Fink noticed my silence and asked what was wrong, but I smiled at him as I had done before to other men. "You know," he suddenly stated, "you must have plagued the thoughts of every man who saw you and put them in a spin." It was evident that his heart was somersaulting, yet my mission was only in its infant stages! He told me that he came from Burgstadt in Germany, was twenty-five years old and the only son in a family of two children. He was scheduled to stay at Zeltweg for at least three months, largely depending on the completion of a special assignment. Like thunder at dawn, the last two words registered and I knew that my contact was the right one and possibly dynamite. As expected, Werner drove me home in a borrowed car and we arranged a meeting for the next day, which was a Sunday. "I am looking forward to tomorrow," he said, kissing my hand. He saluted and left.

Rather bashfully I told my mother of Lieutenant Fink's visit, expecting her vetoes, but to my amazement she had no objections, hoping it would take my mind off Schlager, whom she disliked intensely. However, unexpectedly, before Werner Fink's arrival, Baron Schindler called on me, to assess the situation so far. He could not resist a tiny jab – had I found Aladdin's cave at Frau Vogel's. His glance was brooding and told me more than he cared to admit, but we were professionals in every sense.

Soon after Schindler left, Lieutenant Fink arrived. Tossing his cap aside he took me in his arms and kissed me. "I've waited thirteen hours for this," he whispered as he released me. Astonished at his behaviour, I asked him if he was always that eager with girls. "No," he said, "I haven't been able to stop thinking about you since I left you. My kind of love is not a cheap sensation, but the kind that men dream about and only a few lucky ones experience to the full." However honest his intentions, to me he had to remain a game. Only one thing mattered, information, or that is what my head told me. I could never forget that I was living on borrowed time and how easily one dropped into a state of confusion and desire. Werner's eyes were cross-examining me and, slightly amused, he asked: "There is no one else, *Liebling*, except me? I've decided to go on seeing a lot more of you, if it's all right with you." Werner pulled me towards him on the couch, explaining that all 'installations' would soon be finished and his hours of duty brought back to normal. An uneasy feeling of stolen happiness swept over me as he unfolded the details of what I wanted to know – the secret of Knittelfeld.

Like an ugly cloud it hung over me, ready to burst at any moment. Was there really any necessity for what I was doing? My country was raped and defenceless, occupied by the 'Master Race', yet their Fuehrer was in fact an Austrian. The more I reasoned, the less it made sense, and the only thing real was Werner next to me. His kisses were warm and relaxing, though my mind could never stop being inquisitive and the more he desired me, the firmer I retreated into an impregnable shell. Suddenly he said: "You are as elusive as Hitler's new secret weapon, the *Panzerfaust.*"

Had I heard right? I gulped. Glancing at my watch I pretended I had not heard, and casually mentioned how fast one hour had gone. Werner pressed my head against his shoulder, explaining that he should not have let the information slip out. "Please don't say any more," I pleaded, for suddenly I knew I loved this unlikely young man and the past – including all other men – ceased to exist. The swirling mist had lifted from my eyes as I stroked his face and in a way dreaded this moment of truth. With shaky hands he turned off the lamp, but the moon shone through my window bright and clear. Werner removed his jacket and bent over me. His shoulders were broad and square. He whispered: "There is nothing lovelier than a satin-smooth skin and yours is glowing pearl-like at me tempting me to forget that we had met only twenty-four hours ago. Let me drown in your kisses," he added desperately. Love and passion struggled with each other to break my willpower, but I had been swimming so long against the stream that, however alluring the prospect, turning round was impossible. I sat up, switched on the light and walked to the window. Werner, at a loss to understand me, apologized and left without saying good-bye. I thought that was that and the end of our friendship. I was wrong, for when I came home from my work at the Railway H.Q. a large bouquet of dark red roses greeted me and an enclosed card read: "I cannot stop loving you. Werner." However, I decided to keep detached and have a frank word with Dr. M –, if anyone could put me straight, he was the man.

The following day I told him that Lieutenant Fink spoke of a secret weapon being built at Knittelfeld, and the build-up of fighter planes near by in Zeltweg. I also mentioned our amorous affair. Dr M – looked very serious and was stunned by my honesty. He said: "Although I can understand your rebellious nature, your first duty lies with us. At the same time the information from this man is of paramount importance, it could save thousands of lives and even shorten the war." Laughingly, I replied: "Hitler is thinking on the same lines, my friend, except that if he managed to win this war, he would take revenge on millions everywhere." Dr M – shook me by my shoulders vigorously and answered firmly: "We must see that this never happens, the end justifies our means, this is not a war, but plain murder." Pleadingly, he went on: "Take advantage of Lieutenant Fink's emotion and remember that he is one of Goering's men – this fact alone should sober you down." The flare-up was over and I was determined to conquer my feelings as I thought of a plan.

To endorse the views of Dr M –, Baron Schindler called unexpectedly. It was just four days since I had first met Werner Fink. To take my mind off things, as Schindler called it, he instructed me how best to take photographs, in particular at short distances, of objects like the numbers of the waggons which were shunted on the doorstep of my office in St Michael. After a few jokes and wishing me luck, he left. Once more it was up to me to execute this dangerous job which most of all needed precision timing as SS guards policed the area . . . only at lunch time did they relax a little . . . my plans were set for 12.30 the next day.

As usual, I ate my meagre meal at the Bahnhof Restaurant by the station, but left a few minutes earlier and headed towards the bridge underneath which the cargo stood. I was hidden between three waggons and, having made sure of that, I focused my camera, for who should come near but a six foot SS guard with his Alsation dog. The animal snarled fiercely and, for a moment, I thought he was going to attack me. My heart was in my mouth, and trembling I tried to take a picture of the scene – it was my only chance. At last, the guard grinned, holding back the now barking animal. "Go ahead," he shouted, "the view from here is good, especially with me on it as well." Whether he was bluffing or not I had no choice and my camera clicked for the third time, but this time not only the waggon with the number but also the guard was on it. To be convincing I needed another shot. *"Oberscharfuehrer!"* I called. He was only an *Unterscharfuehrer* but a bit of flattery always pays. "Move to the left, please!" He obliged, undressing me with his eyes. Faintly, I remembered I had seen him before, after all I had worked here for the past nine months. "I've seen you as well," he exclaimed "with an old cow, going to the Restaurant." This remark brought me out in gay laughter, for the insolent man meant of course Wulser's assistant, Frau Schwaiger, a woman in her early forties. "Brrr," I said, girls would not last long with you at that rate." He tied up his dog by a waggon and came closer. Putting his arm around my waist he said: "Either you are so small, or I am too tall, but I've never heard of a mouse which was squashed under a hay-waggon." What enlightened poetry, but coming from an SS man it did not surprise me, for most of them were crude and sadistic. Nevertheless, my fantastic luck, my velvet touch with men outweighed all dangers and challenged the death dealt out so readily by so many at this period. My bluff deserved my best smile and it pleased this man, who surely must have been an ignoramus. Of course I promised to see him the following evening.

During the afternoon all I could think about was getting home. The crafty grey blue eyes of the SS guard haunted me, but tomorrow was twenty-four hours away and so much could happen before then. Optimism was one of my strong points and I willed my luck to hold firm. That night I took a long time at the mirror, brushing my hair and thinking, desperately blinking away my tears. Werner was my only safe bet and I decided to telephone him at once. He answered and his voice was warm and tender. I begged him to come for I needed to talk to him urgently. *"Liebling,"* his voice embraced me, "I'll be with you in an hour." The crisis was on with Werner racing to my assistance and it was the only thing I was really certain of. He came on a motorcycle, windswept but determined. We looked at each other and we both knew how much we loved each other but the acid test lay before him, as I searched for words to describe the incident of the afternoon. Oddly enough Werner never asked me why I was taking photographs at all, his only concern was to disentangle me from this situation. "There is only one solution," he said, "you have to tell him if he pesters you that you are engaged to me and if he has any sense he will keep his hands off you." "But if he has not any sense, Werner," I asked, knowing the sort of man I was dealing with. "Then he will get the boot from me, make no mistake," he replied. Werner remembered my camera and asked me to hand it to him. As this was impossible, I stalled for time and told him that I had left it at my office in St Michael. Although he believed me, I kept on saying: "You've got to believe me, you've got to believe me." He held me trembling in his arms saying: "You are overwrought my darling, yet I do love you so very much." Clasped tightly in his embrace, I tried to forget the nightmare of it all and his amazing calmness gave me hope.

Werner was not just a fluke of passion but an anchor to hold on to. He insisted that I rested on the couch with him holding my hand. His brown wavy hair was still wet and tousled by the wind and taking out the comb from his side pocket, I straightened it, whilst Werner switched on the radio standing beside us. From it came soft romantic music – we needed no words, no dialogue, just us. Zarah Leander was singing: *Kann Liebe Sünde sein?* Can love be sin? finishing off with the words . . . *lieber will ich sündigen einmal denn ohne Liebe sein* . . . (but rather I shall be a sinner, than live without love). Was she right? The moon was up and hung like a heavy golden fruit in the sky and my heart raced. Love is the greatest mystery of all.

The following day was, as I anticipated, a tense one. On arrival at my office, the Bahnmeister asked to see me at once. He informed me that an SS *Unterscharfuehrer Holzmeister* came to see him demanding information on me, the sort of girl I was and so on, but he refused to tell him anything until he had spoken to me. My boss ended the interview by saying: "He wishes to see the photographs as soon as they are ready." I half swayed, and talked myself out of the affair by turning it into a lark on my part and finally stated that I was engaged to a Lieutenant Fink who was now stationed at Zeltweg. In the hope of closing the case I said that my fiancé had confiscated the camera and film. The *Bahnmeister* was satisfied with what I had told him but advised me strongly to stop 'flirting' with the SS guards. I thanked him with a hidden smile and left his room. However, if I thought that this was the end of it, I was gravely mistaken. My SS 'friend' waylaid me on my journey home, demanding his 'rights'. I was furious to say the least, threatening to telephone my fiancé at once if he did not go. "We shall see who has the last word in this story," he fumed and walked off.

I decided to get rid of the camera at once and left by train for Leoben, telephoning my mother that I would be late home. Dr M – was in his flat. I felt relieved and hopeful that all would be well. When I mentioned the way I had obtained the pictures, and the SS man, Dr M – laughed heartily, congratulating me on my daring. Infected by his humour I joined in, suddenly forgetting the double trouble I was in. At 8 p.m. I was back home in St Stefan reporting to my mother that all was well with Aunty Berta, whom I was supposed to have visited. She then told me that Werner rang and was anxious to see me. Belittling the fuss she made over the telephone call, I could hardly calm myself, but assured her that I was in no trouble at all. Thankful for her departure from my room, I composed myself by arranging my hair. Looking in the mirror I saw my harassed face and wondered how long one could keep up this kind of pressure. I kept opening the door, but all I could see was rain and slosh until at last I heard a motorcycle. It was Werner. He rushed indoors and threw off his drenched flying jacket. Holding me close, he said: "The Gestapo is checking up on you, why I simply cannot understand." "I have done nothing wrong, Werner," I stammered and he agreed wiping off the wet transferred to me by his face. His only clue was the stupid SS guard, but I knew all along what was behind it, only this secret would have to stay with me forever, if necessary. "Those people have got a nerve," Werner thundered and I've told them so." Expressing my fears that he may have upset the Gestapo, thus making things worse for him and myself, he dismissed it by declaring that he would write personally to Goering, filing a complaint at being pestered by them. Although it may not have been wise, I told Werner that I lied to my boss and informed him that he had my camera. "Why, for goodness sake did you say that?" he demanded shaking me by the shoulders. "Because I've lost it with all this confusion around me," I gulped desperately. "Luckily they did not ask me outright for it," he said, but now I have an idea why they searched my possessions."

My only concern now was for Fink, so innocently involved, and suddenly I was afraid of the truth – of losing him. I was not prepared to let my new-found happiness be destroyed, I wanted to be loved like every other woman. Werner became all important and I clung to him like a drowning person. I dropped every veil of defence, crying my heart out and all efforts to calm me failed. He picked me up like a child and laid me on the couch, using his handkerchief to dry the flood of tears running down my neck, whispering in a voice trembling with emotion, "*Mein Liebling,* all I wish to hear from you is that you love me." My tear-stained face accepted his kisses. I felt his arm tightly around my shoulder and, as every movement of his body transferred to mine, I vibrated like a leaf in the wind. An irresistible force with scorching powers melted one man and one woman into Paradise. Faintly, I heard my mother's knocking on the door reminding us that it was twenty-three hours and time for Werner to leave, but I dreaded the thought of it. All other men before him were forgotten, none existed and I was confident that the time would come when I could tell Werner of the double life forced upon me by conviction and circumstances.

The next two nights Werner was night flying and I had time to reflect on so many things. However my involvement with the Resistance was so strong that to pull out was impossible. By now I had also heard that the photographs had turned out well and I hoped my Group would leave me alone, for a while anyway. Although Werner was not with me, I could feel his breath and the softness of his lips on my skin. It was as if I had only just discovered that I was attractive to men and owned a body which was desirable and a new feeling was taking away my senses. My reluctance to remain cool came more as a shock to me than the volcanic love Werner had to offer. Still I fought the tormenting lust which flooded through me like a wild and tempestuous river.

Frau Vogel's unexpected telephone call brought me back to reality. Werner was under arrest. Lieutenant K.H. Blohm, his friend whom I had met at the party, also confirmed it. I was dumbfounded, but prepared to see him at once if possible, though I could not utter one word. Frau Vogel shouted into the receiver: "Are you all right, Burgi?" whispering to Blohm, "she seems to have fainted." "Yes, I'm all right," I said, asking for details of the arrest. As expected the Gestapo was looking for this vital camera, now in the hands of Dr M –, though it was my property. I urged Lieutenant Blohm to tell Werner that I had found it and would bring it within the next three to four hours and to hang up, not to waste another minute talking. Only action could save Werner and I decided what I had to do.

At once, I set off for Leoben by bus, heading direct to the Labour Exchange where Dr M – was working, asking, demanding to see him. "Are you mad," he said, "to come here in broad daylight?" I had no time to waste or choose and I told him so. Angrily he told me to go to his flat and wait until he came. Like a cat on hot bricks, I walked up and down the street, eager to settle the matter about the camera. At last Dr M – arrived and we went inside – he bolted the door behind us. Without explanation, I asked for my camera, and film. "What's the hurry?" Dr M – demanded. "Someone innocent, outside the Resistance, is in Gestapo hands and will not be free unless I can produce the camera." As if all Hell was let loose, Dr M – got hold of me by my neck and threatened to cut it from one end to the other if my further explanation was as stupid as my request. We were quite alone and Dr M – was much stronger than I and he was certainly not bluffing. Neither was I. Obviously he thought he was dealing with the seventeen-year-old girl of two years past, but he soon changed his mind, when he felt the Luger, which I had hidden in my handbag, right at his chest, and he removed his hands from my throat. As he complimented me on my toughness, I reminded him that I was the product of his training, a brain child of his but with a free mind to decide, begging the question – or was I just a tool to remove one dictatorship only to replace it with another? Dr M – went to fetch my property with me covering him all the way. I checked the film and found two pictures cut off, but agreed that I had to chance it, as long as the SS man was on it somewhere. "My word I've trained you well, my girl," Dr M – said. Still blazing away, I refused to give an account of what I intended to do, much to the disappointment of Dr M – and it was the first time that he realized I was a force to be reckoned with.

By now we had both calmed down, but in the process I discovered a weakness in our relationship, lack of faith which to me was all important. Our loyalty had suffered its first showdown and the hurt went much deeper than I cared to admit. Dr M – stared at me in silence for a while, then said: "Whoever you are doing this for is a very lucky person." Upon leaving Dr M –'s house, I replied in all seriousness: "You're mistaken, this time it is I who am the lucky one."

Rather shaken, I went straight to the Leoben Station and took the next train to Zeltweg. My head was aching for I had not eaten for hours, but all I could think about was Werner and his plight. Half an hour later I was there. Making my way to the Base I asked to see Lieutenant Fink. The guard showed me into the visitors' room and told me to wait.

They brought Werner and he smiled at me. I wanted to say something, but I was silent, afraid that he would disappear. It was as if I had recovered consciousness after a severe blow. Despite the guard, he took me in his arms, his eyes searching my face, his lips coming closer, whispering: "Please don't say anything, just kiss me, so that I know that I'm alive."

Incomprehensibly the secret of love lay in higher regions, boundless, turning guilt into innocence and innocence into passion.

Suddenly he spotted the camera. Grabbing it eagerly he waved it under the nose of the policeman. "That's the damn thing they are looking for," he shouted so loud that other guards came to investigate. Triumphantly, he introduced me, as if to say: "We have won all the way." But had we?

Werner Fink was free again. We celebrated our reunion at my home that very evening with my mother making a splendid dinner which we ate by candlelight. Afterwards, we played the gramophone and danced to *Heute Nacht oder nie, sollst Du mir sagen ob Du Deine Liebe mir gibst . . .* (Tonight or never you must tell me that you are mine) . . . a forbidden record sung by the great Jewish tenor, Josef Schmidt, in keeping with the forbidden love of ours, and because of it we thrilled to the rhythm of our hearts – all that mattered was one man and one woman.

"Will you ever regret what happened between us?" Werner asked. "Never," I replied and he pulled me a shade closer and I began to sing with Schmidt: *"Ich hüll Dich in Liebe ein, Du wirst mein Alles, mein Schicksal sein."* (I engulf you in my love). I kept on singing and our dancing became more of a love-making, until, like a siren, the telephone rang. Werner touched his forehead, as if to collect his thoughts and answered it. "The Base," he said, "I have to return at once, it's an emergency." Brief, to the point of cruelty, a military order and the man who had just melted under my kisses was off.

After his departure I pondered over our relationship. His words of love still rang in my ears – there was nothing hypocritical about him. However, the Gestapo had ways and means to get even with us and I, for one, should know better. The only way to defeat them was to fight them and, by recognizing this fact, I was back at square one . . . the Resistance. My schooldays flashed past and, with them,my pet subject, history. What did Admiral Nelson say at the height of the battle? "England expects that every man will do his duty". Was I on the verge of deserting my ship, my cause? However much I tried to find the answer, in my mental state I failed to do so. All I felt were pangs of regret, and half a woman without Werner. *Ich hüll Dich in Liebe ein . . .* I engulf you in my love . . . my brain hammered and I counted the hours for my lover to come again. Indeed, the following evening as usual he came bringing with him flowers and two grey leather boxes. I opened them and found two gold rings, with large initials *'W'* and *'B'*. The one with *'W'* was mine and the other with *'B'* was Werner's. Inside the rings was written . . . *'For ever'*. "Now it's all legal," he said, "now you can travel with me to Burgstadt and meet my mother and sister." Taking me in his arms, he whispered: "And for your dessert, I'll take you with me to Prague . . . where I am scheduled to train with new aeroplanes. As I needed time to collect my thoughts, I asked him to explain the situation slowly. Werner did so, more explicitly than I could ever have hoped for. The plant and equipment to make the new weapon called *Panzerfaust* was now safely at the Email Factory in Knittelfeld. Casually I enquired what a *Panzerfaust* was and he told me – a one-man Bazooka which could be carried on one's shoulders but was powerful enough to destroy the heaviest of tanks. It was simple to operate, thus saving valuable time in training the infantry, and should be in action before the end of 1944. I listened with astonishment and interest. A marriage proposal and details of utmost military importance were handed me on a plate at the same time and I felt as though I was sitting on the edge of madness. Werner excused himself to go and have a word with my mother who lived next door to me, obviously asking her permission for me to travel with him. Whatever the reason was, I could hardly wait to be alone, to digest the vital information. My positive thinking added up to one fact; for the first time since becoming a courier and taking orders I was holding my own trump card – Hitler's Third Secret Weapon, which was now being made right under our noses at Knittelfeld. How ingenious – a little insignificant town between mountains, difficult to attack from the air, but most of all where no one would suspect. Then I remembered what happened to the man who tried to transmit the position of the dreaded battleship, *Bismarck,* in Norway and shuddered. Riddled with bullets they found him in a shed, his icy fingers still holding on to the morse apparatus. My ideas of being heroic diminished, but only for the time being.

Mother and Werner came back into my room full of ideas regarding our journey, with me adding my own brand of humour referring to my grandfather who was born in Prague and to my Bohemian shaped nose, rather resembling an upturned ski jump. We had a good laugh, but underneath it all I trembled at the magnitude of visiting occupied Czechoslovakia and seeing my relatives. During the following days I deliberated what to do, but decided against informing Dr M –. The secret of Knittelfeld was all mine until I was good and ready to disclose it, least of all to a man I had to beware of. Too many people in the Resistance got killed by being too eager, overestimating their friends and underestimating the Gestapo. I did neither! The only friends I had were men and most of them only wanted my body, some also my soul and, as they could get neither, they contented themselves by picking my brain and sending me across Europe, hoping for results. Up till now I had never failed, if I had, they would have never heard of me again. This knowledge made me hard, but efficient and dangerous to my enemies. Now much bigger things presented themselves, the possible destruction of the *Panzerfaust* Factory in its infant stages. The very thought of it set me aglow and I was certain that thousands of lives could be saved. A total war demanded total action and I thought of the men in the Allied tanks trying to liberate us from the Nazis being blown to bits and maimed for life by one single young Nazi firing this weapon. Somehow, I had to stop it however silly it sounded. I had to stop it!

My contacts with France were limited, three to be exact, but I had to try every possibility to get there, come hell or high water, and if Lieutenant Fink was to be a stepping-stone, so much the better, for I had no illusions as to what would happen to me if I failed.

January 18, 1944. My travel papers were signed once more and I embarked on my new journey with Werner to visit his mother in Burgstadt. Neatly my own plan was falling into shape, thus combining business with a little pleasure.

Unfortunately the latter did not last very long – at a dinner given to us by Werner's mother, his sister's fiancé, Walter, caused an uproar by declaring that Austria was now part of the "Thousand Year Reich", and that the flying bombs would level off every town in England, thus saving the crews for other targets. Werner tried to restrain Walter from his outbursts, but to no avail so I got up and walked out, packed my things in my room and was about to leave the house but Werner prevented me. His mother pointed out the dangers of being against the Fuehrer, agreeing with her future son-in-law that Germany had no option but to fight to the last man if necessary. I told her that I only hoped it would not be her son but Walter – she ordered me from her home. I gladly left, followed immediately by Werner. However, this unfortunate incident only brought us closer together and we celebrated January 21, my twenty-first birthday, at a hotel belonging to his best friend. Despite the war, the food was wonderful with delicious salads, game and chicken, plus the best French wine. A lonely candle flickered on the table as we danced and basked in the warmth of love and the enchantment of the hour. Werner the incurable romantic and optimist could switch off reality, wreathing around us a symphony of beauty and defying man's efforts to destroy it. "Tell me no other woman is loved as much as you," he demanded to know as we were dancing. I dreaded to think who gave me such powers to multiply such feelings, to subjugate men, to find me so fascinating.

The days of wine and roses went past, with sightseeing and photographing, one of Werner's great hobbies. One evening a Lieutenant Bruell, a school friend of Werners, telephoned asking us to come and visit him in Burgstadt. At first I was not very keen, but when I heard that he was stationed in Paris I changed my mind.

Bruell lived with his widowed mother and was delighted to see his old friend again. They talked about the *Luftwaffe* and the various types of planes they were flying, and I talked about Paris and all its magic. Before the evening was over, I gathered valuable information. It was obvious the fight between Goering and Himmler was on, for each tried to outdo the other by giving their men powers far beyond their wildest expectations. As France was always associated with *l'amour* and girls, the two played a vital part in keeping the troops happy, if only for one glorious night. Bruell made no secret of the fact that brothels were set up close to every *Luftwaffen* base and sometimes girls were forced to attend regularly. "What a sinister set up," I exclaimed to the surprise of both men. "It may be so to you, Fräulein Burgi," Bruell said sharply, "but to a pilot with a plane and no fuel it's a way to escape reality."

Soon after this statement, Werner and I left, rather subdued. On our way back to the hotel, I brought up the subject of us visiting Paris, if only for one day, and Werner was astounded, but promised to find out if this were possible from Will Bruell. "After all his uncle, Colonel von Beck, is an administrator in Paris," he added. Dampening down my enthusiasm he asked me not to put the cart before the horse. However, I had the feeling my contact, Marcel Auboyer, was within my reach. In remarkable order things developed, with Werner asking his friend for a weekend pass, and finding him most adaptable. Bruell was not only successful but also offered us his lodgings in Paris for our stay. In an almost offhand fashion he produced the documents, flamboyantly clowning about, setting me in a daze and clogging my senses, but not for long. Logic, and my studies in psychology had paid off, thus bringing me one step closer to my objective.

January 31, 1944. Werner and I left for Paris and, as expected, Bruell was at the station to collect us, driving us direct to his quarters. Stage one of my fifth mission was accomplished. Looking out of the window, Paris stretched before me, romantic and sad, with my mind focusing on the centre and the Hotel St James de Albany. In the afternoon we went for a drive through the city and I could not help but wonder for how much longer it would be under German rule. Badly washed-off 'V' signs appeared on houses and I knew that the message of General de Gaulle had come through, loud and clear. We drove under the Arc de Triomph and I felt a lump in my throat on seeing the Swastikas blowing in the wind, the final humiliation of the French Nation, when my *Luftwaffen* friends pointed at them with pride. At moments like these, I was very angry with myself for listening to the young lions' roar and my thoughts became a loaded weapon against me. Further 'V' signs came in sight and, as a sort of retaliation, I asked Werner to look. With a rebuke in his voice he said: "People who write these signs are fools and wind up in the cages of the Gestapo." A sudden silence fell and we decided to return home.

The villa in which Lieutenant Bruell was lodging had belonged to a French business man and was confiscated by the Germans in 1940. It was mostly used by *Luftwaffen* personnel as a Club, with an odd visitor now and then.

I was certainly in a most precarious situation, with a highly dangerous objective, yet I could not retreat. Perhaps the excitement of pulling off a feat of this calibre spurred me on and boosted my ego. Luckily for me, Werner's mind operated in another direction, thus giving me time to adjust both wavelengths. He excused himself to have a drink with the boys and I was glad to be left alone. In Werner's pocket book was a little map of Paris and I began to study the route to the Rue Saint Honore, where the Hotel St James was situated. My big worry – was Auboyer still working there? However, this was a chance I had to take and take it quickly with or without Werner. Whatever my deliberations, I had to tell Werner some sort of watertight story to enable me to go there . . . and to retreat if necessary. As I nervously paced the floor, dismissing ideas, Werner came back to ask me to join him at the Club. I changed my dress. Werner watched, then, as he did up the zip, his hands trembled as he outlined my shape and he said that the garment felt like a mountain stream running down, lazily cooling the curves. I laughed, silkily asking him for a favour. Suddenly, the telephone rang and Werner was called away by another officer. Subconsciously, I placed my hand to my bra as if to memorize the coded message secreted there, hoping Auboyer would decipher my system of an abridgment . . . S.W.S.W. KNFLD. A. my brain repeated until Werner came back, assured me that all was well, and urged me to hurry up. "By the way," he reminded me, "what is the great favour you want me to do, show you Paris in my Me 110?" adding anxiously, "Let's have it, Burgi, what is bothering you, ever since we came here you have been restless. If I could, I'd get you the blue out of the sky." "My request is much nearer to earth, Werner," I said, taking a deep breath, and I told him of the two French prisoners who were working for my step-father. "They are nice boys," I continued, "although I should not say so, but they have not heard from home lately, particularly Gavin who is worried about his little son." I watched Werner's reaction closely and suddenly he said: "I understand, you would like a message sent to their families?" "Not a letter," I replied, "but a small present for the boy, St James de Albany in Paris." Stressing this act of kindness to a child separated by war from his father worked wonders. Werner agreed to help me and endorsed his desire to come with me and deliver the gift. "What gift *Liebling*" he asked suddenly. I suggested the little trumpet we bought at the Burgstadt Fair would do, plus a note that his father was well. Watching every gesture and pondering each word I had said like a pharmacist his drugs, Werner considered how best to get to the Hotel without causing a stir. He was well aware that even doing this harmless favour could be misinterpreted and have severe consequences. Nothing was to impede this mission as far as I was concerned and I willed Werner to take the risk. Somehow I became another person pursuing my objective with precision, cancelling all other feelings. If that seems wicked and heartless in the eyes of some, remember I was taught by 'Masters' without any mercy for mankind.

In the morning Werner went to organize a car. I used this time to remove the note from my bra, dismantle the mouthpiece of the trumpet, push the note deep inside and reassemble the toy. However I waited for Werner to wrap it and print a message that Gavin was well. All was set. We arrived at the Hotel by approximately ten o'clock. The porter, who bowed too low and spoke German too well, enquired our wishes. Rather stunned, I answered in French and told him to fetch Monsieur Auboyer. Screwing his eyes together he paused and for seconds I felt as though I were in a trap, but he departed and fetched Marcel Auboyer. "May I see your work permit," Werner intervened, and I was glad for I knew he made this request to cross-examine the name. Looking at me and nodding, I continued my conversation in

French, telling him of his brother-in-law working for my father and that it was he who told me of this address. I also mentioned the full name "Gavin Souchal" and waited for his reply. However, Monsieur Auboyer stared at me in amazement and for a further dreadful moment I thought he might disclaim knowing him. Werner's restless behaviour told me to go, but I just stood there holding the parcel in my hand, challenging the Frenchman to take it. At last he took it and I emphasized that it was for Gavin's son; he smiled and I understood. Carefully he opened the parcel and showed the toy to his friend. He then examined the workmanship, turning it around and upside down – my nerves were in a state of turmoil. Suddenly Auboyer put the trumpet to his mouth to blow it. For seconds my heart stood still and I felt all blood leaving my head, anticipating the distorted noise through the note inside. The short duration of anguish must have shown in my face and Auboyer grinned, removing the toy and making a blowing noise himself. It was obvious that, in this gesture, he revealed the thinking of a wise man. Unpretentiously he took his leave and disappeared up the stairs, slightly waving the little trumpet. Werner asked me to go and opened the door with his back to the now retreating Frenchman who fleetingly gave me the 'V' sign. I nodded and was certain Monsieur Auboyer was the right man for the job I had in mind and that we were the giant dwarfs who would break Hitler's back, thus saving civilization. It was with great relief that I departed from 211, Rue Saint Honore. As we drove off the sun was up and it seemed as if it set fire to every branch, twig by twig, and that the destruction of the *Panzerfaust* Factory was only a matter of time.

Our last night in Paris closed in and Bruell staged an ostentatious party with savoury dishes. The officers present toasted us and the glorious *Luftwaffe* of Herman Goering, while my mind contemplated much more realistic things – Prague. The raucous gathering increased with the advancing hours and it proved how careless they were in entrusting themselves to a female. In point of fact, I could have blown up the lot, stolen vital documents and vanished into the French Resistance without a trace. I should also like to state here that if one had the right connections and opportunities everything was possible. Underhandedness and deception had reached their zenith and high-placed mistresses were a common feature of life. Nearly all the Top Brass indulged in clandestine affairs and to snatch a little happiness before going to the much dreaded Russian Front outweighed the risks. For the first time in my young life I became truly aware of the devastating power sex has and, instead of promoting it, Hitler would have been wiser to have banned it.

February 2, 1944. PRAGUE, the birthplace of my grandparents was within my reach. Driven on by an unseen force and sanctioned by the Nazi laws, I managed to add further mileage to my already startling war record of travelling, thus making the authorities a laughing stock if nothing else. With restrictions and obstacles galore, I bamboozled my way through all ranks, stretching my luck to the maximum, transforming wolves into gentlemen-in-waiting, with the bird flown in other directions. Puzzled by this fact, I was wondering if possibly I did have the devil in me . . . or was destiny trying to have the final say? Was I to bear witness at a later stage on its behalf and those who fell by the wayside? There are moments in one's life when one doubts the very existence of sanity and I felt that I was coming dangerously close to qualify. However, whatever explanation was the right one, there was no doubt at all that I was here in Czechoslovakia, safe and sound.

Werner and I were taken in a truck to HRADCANY – or Hradschiner Platz Square, and to my lodgings at the Old Town of Prague. Glancing through the. handmade lace curtains at the window, I noticed the place deserted, with only SS patrols now and then visible. As Werner had to leave at once for his Base Prague Russin, we agreed to meet at six that evening, and I started unpacking. The convent-like silence was frightening, so I decided to go downstairs and so get to know my landlady, Frau Havranek. Hearing the clutter of dishes, I knocked and was promptly invited in. Her beady eyes struck me like lightning and I sensed that she resented me. However, I stretched out my hand, which she declined, making me feel rather small and it was the first time in my life that I was stuck for words. I told her who I was and that I should be staying here for at least one week, to which she replied in broken German: "I don't mind *gnädige* Frau, sooner or later all the Germans will have to leave." Seeing how miserable she was, I told her that my mother and her parents were Czechs and that I came from Austria. Suddenly her face drooped and she began to cry, as she came towards me. Still afraid of offending her, I put my arm around her shoulders and she did not resist. "How old do you think I am?" "Fifty-five," I answered. "I'm not thirty," she said, sobbing away, adding: "I was two years in a German concentration camp." How lucky I was so far I thought, thereupon excusing myself to return to my room and still thinking of the old-young woman in the faded wool jumper, with no warmth left in her.

Although I had not eaten for quite a while, I did not seem hungry, for I was far too busy combing the past, knocking my head against a brick wall. What did have priority, I asked myself . . . always the present, with the future in the hands of the Gestapo. Nevertheless, I had to see my uncle, Professor Zdenko Peithner who lived in Prag VII Vewerkastrasse 6, as I had last heard of him in March 1943. My thoughts were like an avalanche, hurtling down at me, overflowing, not even Werner made sense and I was relieved when he telephoned to tell me that he was night-flying. Soon after Frau Havranek asked me to have something to eat and I accepted with thanks. We talked very little, knowing the danger of saying too much, but I guessed that the Germans were a thorn in her side and that she prayed for for their defeat. Our wishing was mutual, yet paradoxically I was in love with a German.

The following day I decided to visit my uncle and I took with me a few precious cigarettes, knowing that he was a heavy smoker. As I approached the house I noticed an absence of life. All the curtains were drawn, only the neighbours moved slightly as if someone was keeping an eye on me. Uneasily, I rang the door bell. After a while a woman peeped through a small window asking me what I wanted. I told her who I was and she let me in, leading me to the dining-room which was blacked out. As I had difficulty in understanding her, I begged her to speak up, but she indicated that people were listening. "Where?" I said, and she pointed to the walls. Her odd behaviour was frightening and, for a moment, I wished that I had never come at all. However, I demanded to know where my uncle was and told her to pull herself together. She did and explained amid tears what had happened the previous Monday. A truck load of SS men came, searched the entire house and found British weapons which had been smuggled into Czechoslovakia by British planes. Obviously my uncle had hidden them and was betrayed. Frau Kubelka, who by now had introduced herself, told me that both the Professor and his seventeen year old son, Bernd, were taken away and were at the Gestapo H.Q. at Prag VII Bredauer Gasse 20. I was shocked at the news, but I knew my uncle was a determined man and loathed the Nazis. The fact that I was so helpless and could do nothing to aid him grieved me. Frau Kubelka offered me some coffee which which I gladly accepted, for I was shaken to the core. The more I thought of Zdenko, the prouder I became, for it took nerve to harbour British arms under the noses of the Germans and, when this war was over, he would be one of the Few of whom Winston Churchill had spoken. Suddenly Frau Kubelka burst into tears and told me the rest of her story, of how Professor Peithner's wife obtained a permit to visit her husband, only to find him in a shocking state. His face was badly swollen from punches and his right arm wrenched from the shoulder. When she fainted she was tossed out on the road by the Gestapo, but somehow managed to get home where she committed suicide. A note hidden in a saucepan documented the happenings and Frau Kubelka gave it to me. Immediately I realised this note had value and asked the old woman if I might keep it, to which she agreed. While she cleared away the dishes I studied the note which said: "I cannot go on any longer, but the man who betrayed us was known as 'Spider' and telephoned Prag 097 Extension 143." "This man will be brought to heel one day," I said confidently to the still sobbing woman as she showed me out, after cross checking that all the curtains were drawn.

Walking over the uneven path, the earth smelt of blood and tears. I wondered if there still was anything left that men could not kill, that made life worth while? Dachau and

Ravensbruck came to my mind and the awful realization of what lay behind those places. All my aggressiveness rose, as with my fur collar tucked against my face, I hurried home, searching the deserted roads for people, but all I noticed were a few SS officers prowling like wolves, and a man on crutches hopping across the street. Against this vicious background I could no longer remain the loving woman, refusing to see the facts before me, and I decided to tell Werner the truth, shame the devil and hang the consequences.

As expected he came at six to take me to their Mess, but I refused, telling him bluntly that I had been working for the Resistance since 1941. Shocked, he drew the curtains and locked the door. "Making sure I don't escape?" I asked sarcastically and added, "this seems the fashion now in Czechoslovakia, since you lot came here." "Oh," was his sharp reply, "I have not noticed yet, but if I am to understand you rightly, you are in very grave danger." "So are millions more under Hitler, my friend. I have just returned from a visit to my uncle, but only found a terrified old woman who told me how the Gestapo dealt with him, his son and wife." I told Werner of the tortures and suicide. He begged me to stop talking, expressing his personal disgust for the methods of the Gestapo. "They all say that when told by a woman," I cried, "but no one is prepared to stop this lunatic, Hitler." Werner took me in his arms and said in a grim voice: "If I believed that there was no other way out for you than to wind up in a Gestapo prison, I would kill you myself, I would fire every bullet of my revolver into your heart to make certain that you were dead." "I believe you would, Werner," I answered, stroking his hair and suddenly he pressed me against him as if to reassure me. His eyes were burning into mine, expressing a sad but beautiful love, above and beyond Hitler's barbaric war and I said: "You and I should be thinking of living not dying, the more grievous the world, the more we need the luminous beauty at the centre of life . . . Love . . . and we have yet to fathom it all." "You should have been a poet, not a woman haggling with death," Werner countered, adding, "How did the great Nietzsche put it? *Mut, der angreift; der schlaegt noch den Tod tot, denn er spricht; War das das Leben? Wohlan. Nocheinmal* . . . Courage, which attacks will kill death dead, then say: Was that life? Very well, let's live it again." Suddenly we felt relaxed, reclining on the couch, thinking and searching for solutions to our dilemma. No awards were being given for being in love, only for killing and I was frightened and startled by the unquenchable desire for both. Our enemy, that implacable foe – the hands of the clock – showed nearly twenty-three hours and Werner had to leave, yet his heart was burdened with the added weight of my cruel secret from which it was impossible to escape. Only his love was unshaken and I knew it.

The crucial points were over and we settled down to a few more days under the golden roofs of Prague. The blazing hell of war encompassed many things, most being violent, but also the dream of a sad, beautiful love. What lay before me no one knew and, as if someone had turned off a celestial tap, my stay had ended and Werner and I said good-bye.

Back home again in Austria life was far from being stable. City people moved their possessions into the country as the German armies retreated towards the crumbling Reich, heedless of destruction, still churning up turbulence and fear. Our house was like a storage barn, filled with two grand pianos, various paintings and fur coats, some of them had seen the 'merry-go-rounds' of the Austria-Hungary Empire and the senseless horror of war. In addition to all the hardships, the 'Hamsterers' (beggars) became an hourly nuisance, offering and exchanging everything for a little food. It was particularly heartbreaking to send away small children, who begged one slice of bread. However, our own stock was exhausted, with only Frau Lucy Koerting having a claim on mother's reserve. As we were outsiders, but knew that she was Jewish, this singles her out in my story.

One afternoon, I attended the five o'clock dance at the Post Hotel at Knittelfeld, owned by Lucy's mother-in-law, as a cover-up for getting some food. Unfortunately I met Werner's old friend Lieutenant Karl Heinz Blohm, for whom I had no admiration. He was ruthless, arrogant and ditched more girls than I care to remember. As he asked me to dance I had little option but to accept. The music was low and seductive and one did not need a crystal ball to see that he had designs on me. Looking down with a critical eye he said: "There are two things I look for in a woman – eyes and mouth; the first have to be tender and sensual, the latter wide lipped, registering emotions." "Oh, indeed," I answered cooly, hoping the music would stop. With his eyes like a firework he kept whispering sweet nothings in my ears, until I asked to sit down. Angrily he asked: "Is it true that your friend is Jewish?" I thought he meant Werner and ridiculed his question, but raising his voice for all to hear, he referred to poor Lucy. Disgusted and worried I told him not to believe any rumours for they were only 'red herrings' to distract from the real issue. Quietened, he told me that Lucy's mother-in-law was spreading the news and that he had every reason to believe it, until now. Luckily for me a striking girl sat herself next to our table, thus Blohm's racial interest soon vanished, as he concentrated his charms on her, and my own departure was appreciated.

One week later Werner returned to Zeltweg for a six weeks' training period on a new system of night fighter interception. Although I had written to him asking to terminate our affair, his reply was simple: "For you I have given up my family, my home; I am still prepared to go all the way, to accept hard labour and, if necessary, the gallows." How could I end a relationship like ours? Time alone would tell and I hoped and prayed for victory and forgiveness. At the same time, how could I allow him to love me, with other missions in the pipe-line? Exasperated, I waited for the last blow to fall. However, Werner's brain was engaged with other plans, far more startling than any of my past adventures.

It was the middle of May 1944 and his first weekend leave, which he spent with me and my parents. His chief interest was exploring the large horse run, measuring the distances between the fencing and then staring at the opposite mountains standing there like goal-posts. Puzzled I asked him for his sudden interest in the scenery. Calmly and decisively he said: "If I could land unobtrusively at the back of your stables, you and I could be in Switzerland in no time," adding, "Hess did it and made Scotland safely." I laughed and I cried until Werner slapped my face. "Don't play-act with me, Burgi," he shouted, "it's torture to be with you and hell to be without you." "That's why it has to stop now," I demanded, "this nonsense that you cannot live without me. Men have said it before you. I have had to play-act ever since Hitler came and at that time I did not even know what made a baby grow in a woman's womb." Werner sat down and listened, covering his face with his hands. I told him of my years in the Resistance, my struggles with myself and how I learned to hold at bay the men I needed to assist me by raising my eyes a little above their level and by breaking every rule as far as promises were concerned. Werner came to life once more, insisting that this was now over and done with, as long as I had faith in him and his daring plan to escape.

On the Sunday night before Werner left to return to his Base at Zeltweg, we walked the circumference of our horse run. We never spoke, the place had become an aerodrome. With a tense air of expectancy I could feel a tremor running through my body and raindrops falling from the brim of my hat. Werner took me in his arms, pulled my face towards him, and kissed me fiercely. A vision of a better world lay before us. Werner Fink certainly had pluck and rose above the limitations of a uniform.

During the next few days my mind went over the past and the picture before my eyes could tell me the truth, but it was too real so I shut them tightly. I came to realize that things depended on how you looked at them and I suddenly wanted to be the master of my own fate. Etched on my mind was the clear picture of Werner's face as he tried to do the seemingly impossible, but inside me I wanted to believe in him. At night I became tense and listened to the sound of engines in the sky. As the *Luftwaffe* was always circling around this area, people took no notice, only I lay awake chalking off the hours in my mind.

May 30, 1944. After a restless night I woke early and opened my window, staring at the sun in the sky. Suddenly the telephone rang like a sharp stab of pain. Fearful, I picked up the receiver and heard Blohm's voice . . . unlike him, he sounded shocked. "Werner crashed into the mountain . . . he is dead," he said, and I sank to my knees, bringing down the telephone with me. I don't know what I answered, but

Blohm urged me to see him soon to collect a note Werner had left for me.

Mother found me, stunned and face down on my bed sobbing bitterly. Nothing made sense any more and I believed that there was no justice at all in this world. My vigil was over and I had come down to earth with a bang. As the day progressed the full force of the tragedy dawned and I was unable to attend to my work. In the back of my mind I blamed the Nazis for all that had happened, including Werner's death. They were the villains wretchedly responsible for hunting down defenceless people and churning out hatred. All I could think about was revenge, not vindictiveness but absolute satisfaction through the destruction of the Knittelfeld factory. Nothing less would do and, with that objective in view, the sunless sky became bright again.

A few days later a second telephone call from Lieutenant Blohm reminded me to come and see him urgently as a military enquiry into Werner's crash was ordered. A jolt went through my body . . . how much did Blohm know? To satisfy my curiosity I agreed to meet him that same evening. Dead on six I arrived at the Base and asked to see Lieutenant Blohm. A few minutes later he walked through the gate. Pushing his arm under mine he rushed me off to walk the small path along the river Mur. Spring was evident and Blohm fondled the tender green leaves. "I am truly sorry about Werner's death," he said in a hushed voice, pulling out his cigarettes and offering me one. I declined as I did not smoke and he countered laughingly, after having first taken a puff at his cigarette: "You've got other vices, yes?" He stopped, placing himself in front of me and I noticed how much taller than Werner he was. His gloved hand pulled me closer as he said: "Although Werner has never mentioned a successor, I could fill his place admirably." I slapped his face so hard that his cap fell off.

Blohm became transformed into a snarling animal. Getting hold of my wrist he turned it until I fell to my knees, as he shouted insults: "I don't give a damn what the others think, or you for that matter, life is fleeting and one has to grasp every chance and you have got what I want. I like women with fire, but impertinence I will not have, especially from a traitor." I had underestimated Blohm, thinking that his only follies were sex and drink, and I decided to calm down for he was far too dangerous a man to trifle with. Quietly I asked him why he had wanted to see me so urgently? "To give you a chance, my pigeon, for I am much more reasonable and understanding than a Court Martial," he said, pushing a small note into my hand which was in Werner's handwriting and read: "Beloved, be ready tonight. I love you and I shall free you." Summoning all my strength I retorted flippantly: "Don't be silly you are not seriously suggesting that this little note would be taken earnestly by any Court, to start off with, it's addressed to no one in particular." "But I do know who it was meant for," he snapped back, "and I could give evidence." "Only your interpretation my friend," I said, making an all-out attempt to stop his argument. He gave in and I saw in his face the disappointment of a loser. Blohm's blackmail had not come off, not yet anyway.

I tore up the note, scattering the pieces amongst the leaves; a slight breeze caught them and blew them finally into the water. Slowly but deliberately I walked back to the town, with Blohm close on my heels. In a state of grief, I was play-acting, killing the minutes until my train arrived. This man was dangerous and there was no time to relax, so I hinted at seeing him again. At once he took advantage of this 'invitation' and tried to kiss me. I pushed him from me thus arousing renewed anger. "You unpredictable bitch," he shouted, "why do you want to promote heaven, when hell is much more profitable?" "That's the privilege of a lady, Herr Lieutenant," I answered, turning my back on him. Feeling sick and exhausted I boarded my train in mental distress. It was almost dark and the blacked-out lights soothed my eyes, though inside me was a restlessness, the shadows of a game that had now ended and I was afraid of the truth. In the next compartment, someone played a mouth organ . . . *Der Wind hat mir ein Lied erzaehlt . . . von einem Glueck unsagbar schoen* . . . The wind has told me a song . . . of happiness indescribably beautiful . . . It sounded so wonderful, but happiness was only a dream, reality was life and death, an eternal battle between peace and war. I removed my hat and laid it on my lap, stroking the brim and I could feel the hot tears running down the felt. Only the destruction of the Secret Weapon* could atone for our sacrifices, uplift our crushed spirits and repay our services on behalf of the Allied Cause.

*On February 23, 1945, allied Bomber Squadrons coming from the South of Italy, attacked Knittelfeld and totally destroyed the Factory where this dangerous weapon was made.

CHAPTER 9

THE STORM CLOUDS ARE GATHERING

August 1944. The heat was unbearable and somehow I sensed impending trouble. My sixth sense told me that something was going to happen, but my mother, a devout Catholic, refused to listen and suggested a change of scenery, a visit to my relatives in Vienna. However, time was running out on me and I was arrested by the Gestapo at 10 a.m. on August 6th in the presence of my mother. They refused to let us embrace, and pushed me into the back of their car. Flanked by two SS officers I reached the Gestapo H.Q. at Leoben in about twenty minutes. Without being charged I was locked in an empty room, but as none of my jewellery was taken from me I had hopes of release. However, after eight hours had elapsed my hopes dwindled and I resigned myself to the inevitable. Nagging hunger forced me to look at my watch and, as it was ten o'clock at night, I decided to lie on the floor, using my jacket as a pillow. Racking my brain as to what had gone wrong I thought of Socrates, the Greek Philosopher who taught the principles of clear thinking, realizing that this might be the only weapon to help me survive.

Tired and hungry, I dozed off until dawn. Someone opened my door, pushed through black coffee and a dry piece of bread, then closed it hastily. Minutes later a Wardress took me to the toilet, emphasizing that I had only a short while before my interrogation by the Chief. As anticipated, she came back to collect me and took me to his office which was situated on the same floor.

Sitting by an ornate desk and playing with a long whip he X-rayed me with his eyes from head to toe, once or twice hitting the chair beside me. I was aware of their methods and did not flinch, using my mental retaliation until he got the message. "Sit down, it will take quite a while," he said with a grin and I obeyed. Pointing at the file before him he spoke again: "Your file, as you can see, we kept up-to-date with your various journeys and with your boy-friends." His hate-filled bulging eyes beneath his short forehead stared at me as he reached across the desk to grab hold of my neck – he pressed it until I nearly fainted. Someone said: "Let her talk first," and I felt his grip loosening. Dazed, I noticed a much younger man standing there and I suddenly remembered where I had seen him before. At the tive o'clock Tea Dance at the Café Bauer; then he had worn a civilian suit, but he was now in SS uniform. Not that it did much for his sloppy shoulders, I thought, and caught myself smiling at him. Obviously he also knew who I was and returned my smile with a frivolous glance, before following his boss into the adjoining room and leaving the door open deliberately. Clearly I could hear the C.O. saying: "I've got your number, Willi, you've got your eyes on her, but to possess her, you may have to kill her," and, after some general laughter, added: "This is not a bad solution at all, my boy." Shivering with fear and disgust, I listened to their further conversation which developed into an attestation of proof as to my guilt, I heard them mention the mystery crash of Werner Fink. It was very evident the Gestapo wanted a conviction one way or the other. "She shed her men as a snake sheds its skins and thought nothing of it," the boss shouted, "but we've got her now, with Schlager's letter as conclusive evidence."

The men returned to the room. Since I had heard the word 'Schlager' my mind was in a whirl. The Chief produced a letter. It was in Schlager's handwriting and on the usual yellow paper. He held it right under my nose, saying: "Do you recognise this letter?" "Yes it is Franz Schlager's," I said and added, "but how did you get it?" "What an impertinence to ask. We have every right to censor the mail, to catch the traitors," he raved at me. "I shall only read part of it to prove that you are a traitor," and he read:

My dearest Burgi,

Strasbourg
4.8.1944.

When I tried to adopt your attitude towards the Fuehrer and Germany, the reaction proved that I was more than ever their loyal servant. Though I must hurt you I can no longer pretend and must tell you the truth. I could live with Germany and a wife who would share this feeling with me, but to live with a wife alone, although I loved her as much as I loved you, but without my beloved Fuehrer, that I could never do, that would go beyond myself. For a long time I tried to please you but I must honestly tell you that I am deeply ashamed of this. You can curse me, you can blame me, I tried to understand your views on humanity and I knew that in your own heart you believed that you were right. Again, I must repeat, here I stand and here is my fight and that I will never alter my views to the very end, that my loyalty belongs to the Reich and my Fuehrer and that I believe in his great victory.

The Gestapo officer paused and looked at me angrily, then he began to rave and shout: "You are guilty in the first degree of *Zersetzung der Deutschen Wehrmacht* and for this crime stands the gallows." He meant, of course, that I was guilty of undermining the morale of the German Forces and that death was the due punishment for it. In my view, I only undermined the morale of the Nazis (if they had any) and secondly Franz Schlager was an Austrian and was engaged, like myself, against his will by the Germans. I knew that I was lost and that no one could help me. Both men began to shout at me to defend myself, but what could I say? Provoked by my silence, the Chief hit me across the face with the back of his hand and his SS signet ring cut my cheek open. Blood and tears mingled as they fell, but he continued screaming at me: "You will be sent to a Concentration Camp to rot like a bad apple, hanging is too good for you." The other man got hold of my shoulders as I began to sway off the chair and pressed me towards his chest. Could that gesture have had any meaning to him? For me it was revolting and I closed my eyes in disgust. Finally, he half dragged me back to my room and handed me to a woman wardress who shut me in.

Hamburg den 4.8.1944.

Meine liebe Burgi!

Bevor ich Dir in einigen Zeilen ein bischen mein Herz ausschütte, will ich gleich zu Beginn meines Schreibens meines alten Hoffens gedenken und vor allem wünschen daß Dich diese Zeilen bei bester Gesundheit antreffen mögen. Auch will ich nicht vergessen Dich auch auf das Herzlichste zu grüßen … Ich hoffe, daß diesen Brief … Du gerade Zeit hast und vor allem fühlst Dich mit den Gedanken eines so unscheinbaren Mannes, wie ich es bin, zu befassen. Damit Du Dir auch nicht vielleicht die geringsten Sorgen um mich machst, kann ich Dir Gott sei Dank mitteilen, daß ich immer wohlauf und gesund bin.

[illegible] … schon … nicht … lich … bel … liche … schen … einen … nen … eintrage … mit … Zweifel … der … mich … mich …

oder … ver … ge … und … solche … nicht … ich … Tat … endi … und … aber … auch … en.

gemüt … selligen … Immer … Kraft … erlügen … ver … mgelt … Gramel

Schlager's Letter

"Please God, don't forsake me now." I kept saying it over and over again. Despair gripped my heart and it was the first time in my life that I had given up hope of ever seeing my mother again.

The following day I was transported to their H.Q. at Graz, which was in fact close to my godmother's manor, at Parkring No.4. Her residence was at No.3 and my mind back to my happy childhood at this place and its surroundings. Within a stone's throw was the skating rink and the beautiful park where I used to feed the squirrels, while my father talked to his best friend, Sauruck. I smiled . . . for I could do with him now – he was the biggest and toughest man I had ever seen. His strength was feared by all, including the law, and the newspapers were full of episodes describing Erhard Sauruck as the hero of the day. Once he got in a row over smoking his pipe in a prohibited place and was tackled by a young policeman, who soon found out that he was no match for the old warrior (a hundred per cent invalid) and wound up in the river, minus his revolver. It took six policemen to arrest him but not before he had actually bitten off one man's finger. Nearly twenty-one years of my life were spent in this environment and now the stone walls of this building held me prisoner.

August 8, 1944. My first interrogation here was similar to the one at Leoben, except that one of the Gestapo officers used another tactic to begin with, persuasion. "Your record shows that you are of Aryan descent so why do you help the Jews who are responsible for this war?" As I shook my head he got into a rage, shaking me by the hair and forcing me to look him straight in the eyes. Luckily for me he could not know what I was thinking, or he would have killed me there and then. The demagogues witch-hunting defenceless people, even killing unborn babies in their mothers' bodies, yet trying to prove that history had selected them to sort out the rest of the world and if need be, to exterminate millions! Nervously walking up and down and picking his fingers, he stared at me just standing there, saying nothing. Somehow I was far too unruffled for him and he produced a paper from his pocket. Holding it before me, he asked me to sign it, but my eyes picked out the gist of the wording: "I hereby declare of my own free will that Herr F. Mueller aided my escape, rendering valuable assistance." In whispers he explained that this document was to be used if he should fall into Allied hands. To his amazement I refused to sign it and said: "If you dine with the devil, you need a long spoon, but I prefer to take my last supper with the other prisoners and chance the outcome." Furious, he replied: "Don't underestimate my position, but if you should wish to be reasonable, I'll be around." Walking past me to the door, he knocked on my forehead saying: "To make you see sense, I may have to penetrate this thick skull."

All I wanted was to be left alone. My battles of wits and wills with men were past and I accepted defeat, but only in a restrictive sense. Fortunately the human heart always waits for a miracle and mine was no exception. Strenuously I kept thinking . . . if only we could inject love like a serum and outlaw hatred to create an ideal standard for everyone. What intolerable thoughts to have whilst waiting to join the procession of doomed people?

August 9, 1944. After a frugal breakfast, a man came to see me who said that he was the resident doctor and I had no reason to disbelieve him. Only when he forcefully took me to another room where it was almost dark did I become very suspicious of the set-up. These suspicions were confirmed by the arrival of two SS men who strapped me to my seat and I had a good idea of what could follow – one of their interrogations, as they called it. Suddenly the Gestapo officer, whose paper I refused to sign, came in and said: "Show me your hands," which I did, trembling. Turning to the man in the white overall he remarked: "Her fingernails could do with a manicure." "No, no". I screamed, so loudly that the men were startled. Perspiration stood on my forehead as I wrestled with the leather straps holding me down. I had heard of Gestapo tortures. The men came close to me, nearly all of them asking at the same time; "What information did Schlager give you and why was he deeply ashamed of it?" "Give us one of your humanitarian answers," Mueller said with a sinister grin. When I did not reply, the latter hit me over the head with a stick and I felt pain and blood trickling down my forehead . . . then the 'doctor' was cutting my nails . . . shorter and shorter until I lost consciousness.

Back in my room I returned slowly to reality, lying on the floor, bleeding from my fingers. I could not bear to examine them, they were so painful, but I felt some were still there. I managed to put my handkerchief around my hands, holding them upwards to ease the pain and bleeding. As though to add to the torture the wardress arrived with a fairly good meal, placing it on my chair. I told her that I could not eat with my hands. "Then you must eat like an animal, or I shall have to report you for disobedience, and you know what that means." As she gloated over me I managed to eat somehow, mostly using my mouth only, I was so ravenously hungry and staying alive was foremost in my mind. Agonising as it was I finished my 'dinner'; kicking the plate towards her with my foot I shouted: "Remember this day, you bitch, for Hell has no fury compared to mine when I'm free again."

She spat in my face and departed.

"They will never break my spirit," I kept saying aloud, as if to reassure myself of the fact. My next visitor was Herr Mueller and he ordered me to get ready to join my friends, the Jews, at their 'Holiday Camp' at Dachau. To me this was good news, for getting away from this place was all I wanted. Although only eight hours had elapsed since my ordeal, I felt very much better and knew that half my fingernails were still on and that, for some reason, they overlooked my watch and ring.

I was ordered to line up with four other women and taken away to the waiting van. As we passed an SS guard he suddenly came forward, extinguished his cigarette on the right side of my face, and wished me a pleasant journey. The pain of the burn seemed small to the inferno inside me, for I had still enough fire left to burn down Hitler and his Reichschancellery.

At last the van drove off and in it five women huddled together, destitute, desperate, and destination – Dachau. A few minutes later we arrived at the Graz Rail station and were placed in a wagon filled with straw, and smelling ghastly. However, we did have room enough to stretch our legs and to lie down. Slowly the train moved on, the wheels rattling away below us monotonously until we halted. I had no idea where it was, but I could hear some shouting going on and looked through the slits of the wood. Faintly, in the darkness I could see soldiers and heard them saying: "This war will be over by Christmas, most of Germany, and in particular the Ruhrgebiet (Essen area) is destroyed." Incredible, I thought, a conversation like this was unthinkable six months ago. We started moving again, but not for very long, for the sound of the sirens announced: "Air raid imminent" and I listened to the running footsteps. "They are leaving us alone," I exclaimed to the others, but had little response. As I could hardly see them I kept walking about, shaking them by their shoulders and telling them never to miss a chance of an escape. Soon realizing that, save one, they were at least twenty years older than I and perhaps beyond caring, I gave up, and retreated to my corner. Above us were the sounds of heavy bombers flying over . . . like old coffee mills they sounded, grinding their engines and I knew that their load was still undisposed of. I closed my eyes and thought, how one direct hit could end our suffering at Dachau, or, at its best, blast open a way to escape – which was always on my mind. Somehow I refused to believe that going to Dachau was inevitable, although the Polish woman, with whom I was able to speak a little, disagreed. Yet I kept on talking to her to keep up her will to stay alive, but gradually I realized that the poor demented woman only understood part of what I said. By now I considered myself a prisoner of war whose duty it was to try and escape however remote the chances. Thinking on those lines I felt in co-operation with the Allied Forces . . . I was one of them fighting on the beaches, the landing grounds, in the fields, in the streets and on the hills . . . never to surrender.

The flak had begun to burst in all directions and explosions could be heard around us, but to escape from a locked waggon was impossible. Nevertheless, I kept on the look-out and saw the guard approaching. I banged the door and asked for bread, pleading hunger. My aim was really to see what he looked like, for most of them doing this job, although specially selected for their known cruelty, were at the same time utter simpletons. I counted to a large degree on the latter. To my surprise, he opened the waggon and gave me half a loaf of bread, ogling me whilst telling me to keep my mouth shut. Still, I had had a good look at him and knew he was in his fifties, had a slight limp, and had been wounded. Sharing my 'gift' with the other women, we began to eat as if it was some succulent meat, but if I thought that this would arouse them to see the state we were in I was very much mistaken, for they turned over and went back to sleep. Frustrated, I got up examining by feeling the inside of our waggon. Suddenly I heard the voice of a man I had known for many years and it came closer. Holding my breath and touching my pulse I glanced through my peep-hole. "No," I said aloud, crossing myself and fearing that I was going out of my mind, "it cannot be true." The man I saw was Sepp Schneider, my mother's godson and one of the most ardent boyfriends I have had.

Cold perspiration stood on my forehead as I fell on to the straw like a sack, telling myself to be reasonable, all this was impossible. Between doubts and reality lay such a small margin so I pressed my ears against the wooden planks in the hope of hearing this voice again, and I did. Sepp's steps came right past me and if it had not been for the wall between us, I could have touched him, "I shall be damn glad to hand over these women at Vienna, my place is with my comrades in Russia," he exclaimed. My thoughts went back to Spring 1940, when I first met him again, after a five year's absence. Devilishly good looking, his clear cut face a sculptor's dream, enhanced by a perfect figure with a narrow waist and broad shoulders. His grey blue eyes with deep black thick eyelashes mirrored passion, plus a roguish twinkle and, when he smiled, his evenly-shaped mouth told you to beware or surrender.

Sepp was very fond of my mother, who helped him after his own mother's death and he delighted in visiting her. However, by 1940 I was fast growing up and his memories of me in gay little dresses were blotted out by seeing a half grown woman. Immediately, Sepp began courting me and made no effort to conceal his feelings, until my mother put a halt to his desires. Her ideas lay in other directions, by marrying him off to the richest girl in the village. Her name was Hedy and she was, in my opinion, rather pretty, but Sepp thought differently. Smilingly, I kept digging up the past. The poor rich girl throwing herself at this hunk of a man, with him pulling out the best way he could without openly offending her. Although Mother pushed me into the background, to give Hedy a chance, it was of no use. Sepp only had eyes for me, using every opportunity to make this clear. I told him how I felt about the Nazis and the SS of which he was a member, but to no avail. "All I want is you," he confessed. One day I teased him about the off-on wedding with Hedy and he replied sharply: "If that was the only way to being rich and to gaining you, I would do it, but Hedy would soon find herself at the bottom of their well." Sepp Schneider frightened me, for I knew he meant it.

Still hearing his firm footsteps outside the waggon, I went on dreaming and wondering, if *now* he had enough power to fulfil all his wishes. I also thought of our stolen kisses behind my mother's back, followed by rapturous declarations of eternal love and his complete surrender to all my whims. Now it was my turn to try, however slender my chances. Like lightning, a plan came to my head.

It was eleven-thirty at night and we were still stationary. Suddenly I heard footsteps again and someone opening our door. A torch shone into my face and I recognized the guard, a Corporal about twice my own age. He told me to step down and I obeyed, only to find him giving me a sandwich. Thankfully I reached for it when he held it high and said: "This must be worth a little loving, Fräulein." Full of revulsion but startled I realized that fate had come once more to my aid, so I asked him first for a favour before considering his request. "What is it?" he grunted and I told him to take my own identity-card to Sturmfuehrer Schneider. Open-mouthed, obviously wondering how I could possibly know his boss, he nodded, examining the card offered to him. Reading his mind, I ventured a guess, namely that he believed that I was a spy sent along with the others to get information. Scratching his head, he read the back of my card which stated: "Special qualifications – speaks four languages." I knew my line of thinking was right, for he cleared off nearly forgetting to put me back with the other prisoners. My outlook suddenly changed and I concentrated all my willpower on a man I had rejected four years ago – Sepp Schneider! The waiting seemed eternal – did he, I wondered, remember me? Ten minutes later my question was answered, for Sepp remembered me and I was collected by the same guard.

As he led me to the darkened train I trembled with fear and excitement. Soon we were there and once inside this waggon, the smell of drink greeted me and I was handed through a door into a compartment upholstered in crimson velvet. There, stretched out on the seat, was the man I had not seen for four years; he did not bother to get up, just dismissed the guard. Seconds later he jumped to his feet, embraced me, and said: "What have they done to you Burgi, I'll bet you wished that you had married me," adding, "damn it all I'm not such a bad fellow." "Perhaps you're right Sepp," I said, "I might as well have done so," and told him of my ten day marriage to Schaile. Releasing his hold on me slightly, he shook his head, examined my injuries and exclaimed angrily; "And that is how they treat a war widow, so what would they do to the enemy?" Still blazing with fury he began caressing me as if to make sure that I was real. With me in his arms at last, he murmured: "God, have they no mercy on a girl . . . men, I can understand getting the full treatment, but women . . . no," adding very strongly: "They would have to shoot me first for disobeying orders." I knew that Sepp was speaking the truth as his face showed shock and indignation. Reaching for a tin he said; "You must forgive me, for the only thing I can think of is giving you food."

He produced ham and butter with a choice of wine. Still in a daze, I did not quite know what to do so he began feeding me like a baby, now and then stroking my hair. Suddenly I thought about Rudolf and how close we came to loving each other. How odd, how incalculable are one's feelings? Sepp urged me to eat, while asking me how much I was involved with the Resistance. I told him the truth. He seemed not very disturbed. "You and I are made of the same material," he said. "We should have teamed up . . . but on my side of the fence." "I am not so certain," I countered, "the position of the Allied Forces is getting better every day." Sepp's smile disappeared suddenly and he reminded me that I was still a prisoner on this side of the border and I bowed to his better judgment. After having eaten I felt much better and got up to have a look in the mirror. Deliberately Sepp jumped up, blocking my view with his back. I understood and said: "Only a woman would wish to see how she looked in my state."

All his outward control was gone and he took me in his arms, kissing the burn on my temple, which was swollen, telling me that he loved me more than ever. I noticed his ring and to cool him down asked him if he was married. "Of course," he said sneeringly," and with the Fuehrer's blessing." Challenging me: "Don't you know the Reich needs children to replace their fathers killed in action?" Feeling sorry for him was no use, so I asked him to tell me all if he felt like it. "My wife is wonderfully balanced, ugly and rich," he said cynically, adding "so I kept her all to myself, but shared her money amongst the Top Brass, buying favours now and then." His mood suddenly changed and he asked me why I had come to see him, adding: "Surely not to find out if I was married or not." "No," I said boldly, but firstly to see if I had not gone out of my mind when hearing your voice and secondly to ask you to help me escape." Placing his hand over my mouth, he countered breathlessly: "You are mad, if you think I could aid you, thus putting a rope around my own neck." However, to give up now would be unthinkable, so I kept holding on to him in desperation reminding him of Spring 1940 and how much he desired me then, willing Sepp to see me as I was then and how I could be again, given a chance. The more I pleaded, the closer he held me, so I blazed away dismissing his doubts to atoms until they had all gone and Sepp Schneider, the man, interrupted, shouting: "You know damn well that I could not make love to you in the state you are in, I am not that sort of a pig, yet the temptation of making up for lost time is scintillating and tantalizing." Somehow I could feel his torment, wrestling with the obvious, his virility as a man cornered by an impossible situation, yet he was weakening under the bombardment of my persuasion. To underline my plea, I referred to the thousands of deserters on the run and the present chaos caused by the heavy bombing raids, adding my personal observation at the 'offer' from his Corporal. Sepp was at a loss to get a word in, but his holding became a passionate embrace, he searched my face, his lips were mine and I knew that I had won my battle. Between kisses he said: "When I think how much I could have loved you in these past years, I go beserk. You could have shared with me all the SS had to offer and never known the torments you went through, by simply saying 'Yes' in 1941."

Although Sepp's passion loomed before me, all I could think of was my freedom, my revenge against the Nazis, and to escape the living hell of Dachau. In a strange way, Sepp's confessions of how he was cheated by the Fuehrer and his High Command, went in one ear and out the other, but he went on: "Perhaps you had to come back into my life to give me another chance of happiness, before the Russians get me and I am damn well going to take it." Sepp checked his watch and fifteen minutes had gone, but he indicated that there was nothing to worry about, explaining how through a wife of an SS Officer having had a baby he was put in charge of this transport. "Lucky Siever," he added, "is now on special leave, while I have to do his dirty work." By now he saw my reappearance as a hint from destiny and I was certain if anyone at this moment were to enter, to take me away, it would have been a fight to the death for all concerned.

Sepp asked me to listen carefully: "I shall destroy your record, hand over four instead of five women and, if necessary, say that I had to kill you as you were trying to escape," adding, "however, should the H.Q. at Graz have time for enquiries, which I doubt, with the cases they have to deal with, they will be looking for a needle in a haystack." Finally he emphasized that many a prisoner of the SS never reached their Camps, as they were killed, sometimes beaten to death by drunken guards. I shuddered, although it made sense and diminished my doubts of failure. Sepp's final instructions were: "Next time the train stops for more than ten minutes, we are there and I shall give you a tapping signal and unlock the padlock. Jump, run to the right over the lines and hide wherever you can . . . I may have to fire a few shots." Once more he pulled me close and I was in a trance, not because Sepp kissed me, but knowing the doors of Dachau would never close behind me. The world, I felt, was full of miracles, if only we would believe in them. Sepp called the guard, telling him to take good care of me, thus planting the seeds of suspicion deeper in his mind. Walking back to the truck was like floating on clouds, ignoring the chatter of the Corporal and reading into his apologies my wishful thinking. Freedom was within my grasp.

The first hour of August 11, 1944, had begun and the train had halted. As I could not read my watch, I counted one thousand and knew we were there. All I possessed was me, shivering cold with fear and worry in case Sepp had changed his mind . . . or something had not worked to plan. There was no sound, the others were fast asleep. While holding my breath the signal came, but my legs gave way and I sank to the floor. "I have to make it or perish," my brain hammered, giving me the strength to act. I pushed the door back wide enough to get out and jumped. The wind blew around me slightly, making noises and I listened in suspense. Hiding by the wheel of the second waggon I noticed someone hurriedly putting the padlock back in its former place. My heart was pulsating like mad with my brain working out my next move, when suddenly, I felt a gloved hand over my mouth and nearly collapsed. It was Sepp, who ordered me to run with him towards some outbuildings. I obeyed, but my feet seemed numb and he half dragged me along. Before I realized, he locked me into an out-door toilet, taking the key with him. Amazed at the speed of his action (approximately one minute) I settled down, weighing up my position, but decided to trust Sepp. As he did not come back for a while, I got worried. Obviously the handover took longer than anticipated. I dared not even think of the alternative to failure, although it was in the back of my mind, slowly driving me crazy with anxiety.

Someone was coming – the door opened, and Sepp was standing there grinning, exclaiming: "Even the Tommy (meaning the RAF) was aiding us last night; they are still clearing up the mess from the raid and I had a job to find the prison train to hand over my little lot." "Oh, Sepp," I cried and fell into his arms, "you don't know what it means to be free again." Holding me firmly, he said: "I do – I have just seen some two thousand men, women and children locked up like wild animals *en route* for Dachau."

Sepp took off his long leather coat and placed it over my shivering shoulders, and as he guided me towards the nearby road he still rambled on about the prisoners. "Poor devils," he said, "most of them won't last till Dachau." He began to laugh, but this was the other Sepp, the professional killer, the man with a chest full of medals – he found it amusing to note that they certainly wouldn't miss me.

It was still dark and we walked on until we saw what seemed to be a farm and Sepp went ahead. Soon he returned to tell me that the farmer was willing to take us in for the night. "By the way," he said "I've told the old boy that you were in the bombing raid and a bit of a mess." Now we both laughed and the last hours of horrors melted away in prospects of an incredibly new life.

The farmer made us welcome, heating us milk and giving us food, and enquiring what had happened to me. Rather startled by his questions, Sepp answered for me, pointing out that his 'wife' was very tired and needed rest, so I was shown to our bedroom. Sepp and I were alone and I knew the meaning of this. To begin with he made a bold statement; "You have only one chance, that is to come with me to Poland. My Unit is stationed at Lodz and luckily for you there are many SS wives and pretenders staying with them, they are well cared for and no one asks questions. We are a sort of suicide battalion, the last outpost of Himmler." Sitting on the edge of the bed, I listened in amazement as he said: "I can see no reason why you should not come with me and enjoy what there is left of our lives." "I suppose not," I said, looking past him. Suddenly he got hold of me fully dressed and bundled me into the bed, telling me off for being so childish and afraid. He was right. I was a big girl now and my game of playing Russian roulette was over. My game of chance had reached the dotted line and Sepp had every reason as winner to collect his prize.

I've waited four years to see you again so a little longer will make no difference to my love for you," he said putting on his heavy leather coat and bending over me he whispered: "This time you will be mine, all mine, a voluntary submission, promise?" Sepp left, without my answer, thus giving me time to think. Soon I was asleep, relieved from the problems of tomorrow.

Four hours later I awoke. Someone was approaching. Thank God it was Sepp, looking refreshed and full of ideas. Fidgetting with my identity card he said: "There are two ways to get to Poland, by brute-force or with a travel-pass." I guessed what Sepp had in mind and was going to add my own ideas, when he continued: "Now let me think, – who do I know in the latter business." Suddenly, he changed the subject and asked: "Guess what I've brought you?" placing a parcel on my bed. I opened and found a new green coat. My common sense told me how he 'bought' it, but I accepted it without question.

Sepp urged me to get ready for breakfast, as he had to leave as soon as possible, to "explore the lay-out" as he said, adding: "If I don't come back before dawn, get going and head for Vienna and your aunt's place. Sepp pulled me close, kissed me and left. After his departure, I tried on the coat and found it much too big, thus I decided to do a little tailoring, soothing my nerves whilst waiting. It all seemed so unreal – last night en-route to Dachau, today in this farmhouse sharing my fate with a man I had rejected four years ago, utterly depending on his help. Hundreds of thoughts went through my mind, with now and then the farmer coming in to see how I was, amusing me with old tales of weather forecasts. I even declined food offered to me, for I was tingling with anxiety and suspense. Night was falling and I got more and more worried, until at last I heard Sepp's footsteps. Out of breath he ushered me to our room, ordering me to close my eyes until he told me to look. Apprehensively, I waited. "Now you may look," he exclaimed . . . . . and I gazed at a document: "Frau Notburga Schaile has permission to travel to Freistadt and back to visit her husband." This duly stamped travel pass lay before me, yet I was afraid to pick it up in case it vanished, so Sepp kept holding it, reassuring me of its validity until I burst into tears. Taking it from me, he said: "We can't have it wet, *Liebling,* the ink on

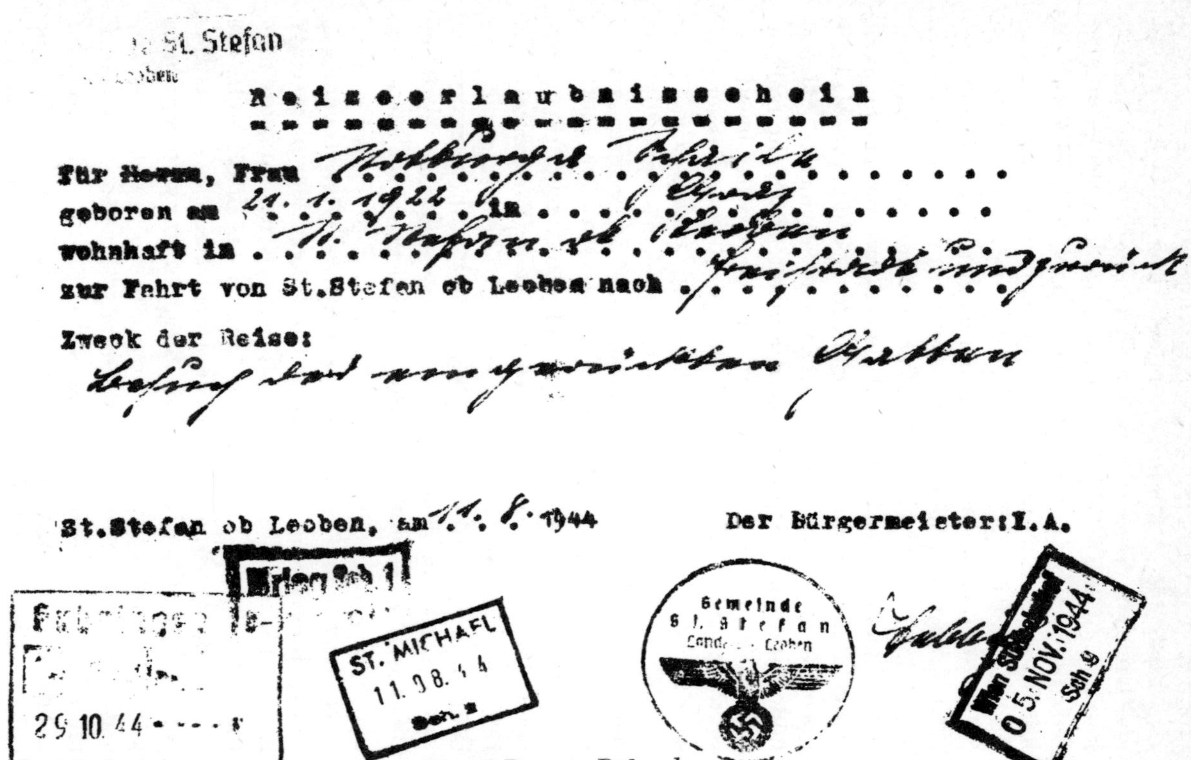

St. Stefan

Reiseerlaubnisschein

Für Herrn, Frau [illegible] . . . .

geboren am 21. 1. 1922 in Graz . . . .

wohnhaft in . . St. Stefan ob Leoben . . . . . .

zur Fahrt von St. Stefan ob Leoben nach Generalgouvernement . . . .

Zweck der Reise:

Besuch des verwundeten Gatten

St. Stefan ob Leoben, am 11. 8. 1944

Der Bürgermeister: I. A.

Travel Pass to Poland

it is hardly dry." Composing myself, I enquired into the ifs and buts, but Sepp maintained that no one could possibly know that I was a widow, that I was not his wife, or that the only thing relevant, the name on the pass, coincided with my identity card. "In any case," Sepp explained, once we are in Lodz I'll take over." I demanded to know how and he said: "If at the present I could collect a mark for each person with a false identity, I should be a very rich man and the women living in Poland with SS officers is nobody's business." Sepp's audacity fascinated and bewildered me, yet he made sense. Rather jokingly, I exclaimed: "The new Madame Pompadour on her way to the Eastern Provinces." "That is how I like you," Sepp answered jubilant, that's the real you again." In a way I shuddered to think to what lengths he might go for his face was aglow with ideas as I listened in astonishment. "You will be staying with friends of mine, the Adams on the outskirts of Lodz. By the way, they are important Nazis and have everything." It seemed as if he was trying to punish them in advance for the suffering inflicted on me by the Gestapo. "I could never do to any woman what they did to you, Burgi," he kept repeating until I kissed him gently on the cheek. For one moment I believed Sepp would take full advantage of the situation but he only held me close to him. "No one will harm you while I am around; they would have to take me apart first," he said resolutely.

We looked out of the window; some fires were still burning in the distance and Sepp said: "The face of War is very ugly and we go on killing for killing's sake. My wife once told me that I frightened her at times, but she was proud to be the mother of my children." He went on: "She named the boy, Adolf, after Hitler, and the girl, Sieglinde, for victory, what a joke." I tried to change his mood, but he felt like confessing and I knew how comforting it can be. "Did you ever think of me, Burgi?" he asked rather sadly. "Now and then," I answered truthfully, but added: "Mother often spoke of you very kindly." "Yes, she would, she is a very good woman," he said, "but it was you who was on my mind so many times, particularly when I first got married. I was glad to be called to the Front. Real happiness could only be with you," he finished. It was the first time since I had taken the path to fight the Nazis that I thought of myself first and believed I had earned this privilege. Sepp held the key to my freedom and if I played my cards right all would be well. New-found confidence inspired my plans.

The following day we left for Lodz, or Freistadt, as the Germans named it, and arrived at approximately two in the morning. It was August 13, and I wondered if that was a bad omen. Sepp, as promised, took me to stay with a family called Adam. Somehow they did not mind my early arrival and waking up the entire household, in fact Frau Adam was delighted to meet me, or shall I say to see Sepp again. Sleepy eyed I was shown to my room, helped to bed by Frau Adam and wished a "very good rest". After her departure, Sepp informed me that he had to report at the Barracks and to register the arrival of his 'wife'. Too tired to care, I asked no questions and Sepp left. The agonies of the past week were over and all I remembered was Dr. M-'s words . . . "You will get past any obstacle, particularly if it is a man." Flattery or truth, a sunny morning dawned and here I was with more than a thousand kilometers between me and the living hell of Dachau. I tried to find a cool scientific reason for my escape but ended up in a labyrinth of fantastic circumstances. However I was going to live and cheat the Nazis of their desire to see me rot like a bad apple, as the Gestapo officer in Leoben had predicted. My thoughts were interrupted by a pretty girl bringing my breakfast on a tray. She introduced herself as Helga Adam, the only daughter of the house. Whilst I was eating, she told me about herself and her life in Poland and we established that she was two years younger than I. I noticed a beautiful ring on her finger and enquired who the lucky man was, to which she replied: "SS Sturmfuehrer Krause and we hope to be married next Saturday," adding, "but one never knows, so much could happen in a week." "Yes, how right you are Helga," I countered, "one never knows." I examined her face, it was sweet and childlike and I felt sorry that she should be marrying an SS Officer. After explaining the details of the house, she left gracefully like a butterfly, obviously unaware of the state the world was in.

An hour later, when I was dressed, I looked out of the

window, and to my amazement everything was peaceful. What did I expect – riots? Obviously the SS saw to it that no Pole lifted his head without their permission, yet the strange calm was rather frightening. A car came up the drive and I recognised Sepp. He laughed and waved, so I knew all was well – up till now. He came into the room loaded with goods which he placed before me. "All for you, *mein Liebling,*" he shouted . . . and I began to unpack. A grey two-piece suit, a gorgeous blue silk dress and a flame red dressing-gown with pyjamas to match. I could hardly believe my eyes, as I held the garments against me, fooling about, and Sepp looked at a new woman, for the moment living in her ivory tower. Being a female, I decided to try on my clothes at once and Sepp agreed, sitting himself in the armchair, waiting for the 'Fashion Show' to begin. Nearly everything fitted except for the length and I asked Sepp how he managed to get hold of such treasures, but all he said was: "The SS has connections everywhere, *Liebling*, and that is all I am going to say in this matter." In a way he was right, I thought, justifying the 'purchase', why should the Nazis not compensate me, and smilingly put on the last ensemble, making my entrance from behind two open wardrobe doors. This time Sepp stared at me. "With this colour you're as beautiful as sin and I like it", and he pulled me towards him.

Unexpectedly, Frau Adam entered the room. She was as big as she was tactless and began to talk like a waterfall. I could not rid myself of the feeling that she wanted to flirt with Sepp. "I am very angry with you for not letting me know that your wife was coming. After all we have been the best of friends for over one year. Now that she is here, let me have a good look at her in the daylight." She stared me up and down as if I was for sale. Being looked at made me nervous and uneasy, but most of all I kept hiding my fingers in case she noticed the shortness of my nails. Her withdrawal was greatly appreciated and we both ushered her to the door. Sepp made sure that she had gone, then bolted the door. "Brrr," he said, "what a relief, but in view of this wedding you cannot stop here, one never knows who may turn up." Sepp paused to add: "Willi Fegerle, this pig for instance, he's the only one who has ever seen my wife." Sepp whispered the last word, as if she did not exist and I enquired why he called Fegerle a pig. His eyes narrowed to a mere slit and he replied: "Willi was an *Oberscharfuehrer* in my Unit and when we took Warsaw most Polish people fled in panic and lots of shooting was going on. Suddenly I noticed Fegerle drunken with victory and power screaming and firing at fleeing women, one of whom was pregnant." Schneider turned away from me emphasizing that he could never forget this sight as long as he lived. Disgusted by what he'd told me, I expressed my opinion that Fegerle should be put on trial by a court-martial, but Sepp laughed and answered: "Might is right and the rules are made by Himmler, but they can be broken and the one who's smart enough to live can tell the tale." Although I had known it for years, the reality seemed so much more shocking – I lived amongst cold-blooded killers, and I pretended to be the wife of one of them. Forty-eight hours after my safe arrival in Poland, I was back at square one – I must defend myself the best way I could. However, there was one consolation . . . Sepp's loyalty towards me was unshaken and I accepted that he had jeopardized his life for me.

On my third day at Lodz, Sepp informed me that all resident wives of the SS had to undergo a training in firearms at the nearby shooting range outside the town. We arranged to go the same afternoon, and Sepp brought the horses to the house. It was a lovely day and we rode along an alley flanked by trees with a brilliant blue sky above us and we hardly spoke at all. Some twenty-five minutes later we arrived, but the place was deserted apart from a few SS officers. Sepp explained that most of the others were down by the warm lake enjoying a swim. We dismounted, Sepp put the horses away and fetching the weapons from a nearby depot, whilst I examined the distance of the targets, some of which were dangling 'men' filled with straw.

Sepp and I took up our positions; he explained the latest machine gun and showed me how to take it apart and put it together again. As the magazine got stuck I kept fiddling about. "If you take that long, you will be dead before firing a shot." Of course I tried until he was satisfied, but got a little angry over his shouting. He then put a Luger 38 into my hand, teasing me to have a go. For one moment I thought of bluffing him by pretending ignorance, then my professional pride took over and I showed him how to shoot, hitting the bull's eye with every shot. Sepp exclaimed: "I'm glad I am not at the other end." Whilst Sepp went to move the targets farther away, I turned on my back remembering who first gave me a Luger so that I would not feel so naked, and smiled. Suddenly Sepp stood above me, asking what was so funny. How could I tell him the truth in the first place? I had to be on guard twenty-four hours a day, knowing full well that my quickest way of committing suicide was to mention another man. I pretended that his remark was the reason for my smile and he accepted my explanation, taking the Luger from me.

Sepp went on practising on the new target and I watched him, when suddenly I began to concentrate my mind on him. There he lay, all of his six feet two inches in the black Panzer uniform. His slim waist enhanced by the belt and his already broad chest widened by the large lapels of his battle jacket. As if guessing my thoughts he turned over, slightly lifting his body off the ground, playfully twisting his deadly weapon. We just stared at each other as if caught out, Sepp put his revolver to his lips, blowing at it as if to cool it down. I watched him smilingly, unable to utter one word, knowing that the next move was his. Putting the Luger away, he flashed those white, white teeth into a broad smile, his mouth beckoning me to come closer and I obeyed. His 'on-target-eyes' with a reddish glint told me: "Surrender, you fool" and Sepp kissed me into oblivion. For a brief while reality ceased to exist in a world of cruelty where guns presided over life and death. However, my will to live was too strong, it was too intoxicating to give up, for all that I had endured since 1938 came alive, repeating itself in my head. Struggling to free myself, I reminded Sepp that we were not alone and succeeded. He asked me: "Can the future redeem the past, *mein Liebling?*" "Yes, why not," I said casually, trying to calm him down and begging him to move from here.

Sepp got up, adjusted his uniform, secured his revolver, and warned me not to toy with him. In a way I wished I did not have to, for Sepp was the epitome of manhood to any red-blooded woman, yet I dreaded any sexual contact with him. Perhaps in the back of my mind I knew that we were two of a kind which would obviously lead to disastrous consequences one way or the other. The natural or logical result in those days was having a baby, for the German soldiers were neither equipped nor asked to restrain themselves from breeding a 'Master race'. With that in mind, and the fact of being a fugitive from the dreaded Gestapo, I had enough to occupy my brain, without giving in to the normal pleasures of life.

Sepp fetched the horses and we rode home in silence. Although it was still as beautiful as before, the unmistakable shadow of an impending crisis was evident, judging by the face of the man riding next to me. Lodz came within sight of us and with it the Adams' house which stood rather imposingly, dwarfing the others at the entrance to the town. Sepp helped me to dismount, lead the horses to the stables at the rear, and I went into the house and washed my hands. Soon Sepp joined me, but his face still looked solemn, if not worse, and I was relieved to hear him speak: "How much longer are you going to torment me . . . or is this part of your training in the Resistance?" It was the first time that he had mentioned the latter in this house and I knew what he meant, but kept silent, conscious of the grave implication and hoping to cool the situation. However, Sepp looked wild, like a wounded animal and I made for the door. Unfortunately, it was too late and he got hold of me, twisted my right arm, flinging me on to the bed stating angrily: "In 1938 you were too young at fifteen, a year later you let me kiss you to install yourself into my system only to reject me in 1940. Despite this humiliation I went on writing to you, making a fool of myself." Stretching my arms as if to crucify me and smouldering with internal fire he went on talking: "By then I was an Officer of the SS and had my pick of women, marrying a less stubborn girl, plus plenty of money." Wickedly laughing he continued, whilst pressing his body against mine, causing me pain and knowing it, but Sepp was in a state of complete abandon, unreservedly exclaiming: "I lay awake at nights craving for your sexual arrogance, your excessive beauty, visualizing you in my arms, taking leave of my senses." Finally, he released his grip on my right arm and I placed my hand over his mouth to stop this mental torture for I feared that Sepp would go out of his mind. At last he calmed down, and with his lips on my neck, whispered: "A few days ago all my desires, however wicked, came true and there you stood before me, helpless, begging for mercy, reminding me of our love."

What could I say to this man, half crazed with passion? Only that it was biologically impossible to make love to me and Sepp understood. Rather desperately, I borrowed five more days in the fight for my survival. Sepp's attitude suddenly changed, he sat up, mild as a kitten, holding my hand, saying relieved: "How could I possibly think that all you wanted of me was the key to your freedom and to escape Dachau?" To avoid answering him, I offered to make some coffee, leaving for the kitchen pondering what remains ineradicable in the heart of a female. How long could I go on using excuses? The answers lay in the wind and however much I tormented my brain, it could not yield a solution. Perhaps fate was catching up with me, for I had toyed with too many men.

The aroma of the coffee worked wonders, putting a breath of victory up my nostrils – smiling to myself I acknowledged the fact that certain drinks can change one's mood. When I re-entered the room Sepp looked relaxed and apologized for his behaviour, which I happily accepted. After coffee he left for the barracks to collect his mail, always fearing a letter from his wife. However, we were extremely lucky for she believed him to be in the front line, thus holding back her letters until he informed her to the contrary. The following night the Russian guns were blasting away, but I lay awake reassuring myself that all would end well, however inexplicable my position. Of course Sepp was fully aware of our predicament and willed our fate to hold firm, using his dare-devil approach to life, backed by his gun, to safeguard us or, at the worst, to end it all. With this knowledge, to be happy one had to be a fool and desperately in love, yet I was neither. Survival was my paramount desire, to destroy the Nazi regime.

After breakfast Sepp collected me for a drive to the next village to fetch some ammunition. He was in charge of the transport preceding the convoy of three lorries. It was just nine o'clock. Cool breezes heralding the autumn blew around me as I sat next to Sepp in the open car, which was chauffeur driven. We made small talk and I noticed the ground became obscured by fog. Suddenly a flash of lightning cut through the passing wood. Sepp pulled me to the floor of the car, giving orders for the driver to fire the already mounted machine gun. Was this my end, I thought, an ambush by Polish partisans? Oh how crazy life can be.

Sepp crawled out of the car, firing his Luger to the right from which direction the shots were coming. A stick of dynamite exploded near the car and I felt my end was near when I saw the driver hit, and slump over the seat. Being fairly small, I managed to get in front to man the gun. This was no longer adventure but life and death challenging each other. Never had I dreamed for one moment that an occasion could arise when I would fight the people I wanted to liberate. My fingers were numb and cold sweat stood on my forehead as I faced a decision worse than that of my encounter with Sepp. Fierce shooting was going on everywhere. The road became impassable with dead bodies, but Sepp was still alive and in complete authority, slowly pushing his men forward with the partisans pulling back into the darkness of the wood. Suddenly, open mouthed, a woman partisan, a rifle still in her hands, faced me squarely saying something in Polish. She looked utterly exhausted and I told her to give me her weapon. She did so. Sepp hurried over, telling his men to take her prisoner. Her hostile eyes met his and I knew exactly how she felt but there was nothing I could do.

After an hour or so we left the battle scene, heading back to Lodz where Sepp was to make his report of the incident. His own casualties were two wounded, the SS killed eight partisans and injured several others, but most of them escaped into the wood. Sepp dropped me off at the Adam's house, telling me to forget the ambush and to keep quiet, but how could I? In point of fact my mind kept analysing where the partisans went wrong, coming to the conclusion that too many attacked at the same point, thus risking defeat with unnecessary losses.

At five thirty Sepp returned from the barracks, looking serious, but made no reference to what had happened, nor the outcome, so I asked him about the fate of the woman prisoner. As he was noticably quiet, I repeated my question. "She is dead," he stated, "they shot her without a trial." Suddenly her death reminded me that I was far from being safe, and I buried my face in Sepp's uniform, banging his chest with my fist. "It's no use feeling sorry, Burgi, you must accept our terms by now," Sepp demanded, but I threw myself on to the bed sobbing. Being relatively free in Poland had lost its attraction for me and the frustration of being useless, subjected to the orders of a man who was technically my enemy, added a humiliating note. In the irony of my position I longed for action, to help the oppressed to free themselves, thus fulfilling the oath I had taken when joining the Resistance. The harder I thought, the tougher the decision. There was no let up in suspense as far as my life was concerned. The horoscope forecast, at which I had laughed at one time, had come true. Born under Aquarius, with Saturn and Uranius as my reigning stars, the latter, known as the 'casue of suddenness', had never failed me yet.

It was on a Sunday, six days after my arrival in Poland, that I took my leave of the Adams family. Luckily for me Frau Adam was so busy with her daughter's wedding that she forgot to ask for my new address, so we got away with relative ease. Sepp drove me to our new lodgings. The house belonged to an eighty-years-old Polish Officer's widow and was ideal as a hide-out, quiet and rambling, with heavy lace curtains covering the windows. However, Madam Muschinsky was a very sunny and lovable person and I knew instinctively that we could be friends. She showed us the place with Sepp picking up the doilies until I told him not to be so silly. "Our first public tiff," I thought and smiled at him as he excused himself to fetch the food rations from the barracks. With the old lady's assistance, I unpacked my clothing. Somehow, I did not feel so well and kept excusing myself to go to the toilet which, most inconveniently, was at the end of the garden. My excessive bowel movement increased to the point of great abdominal pains and Madam Muschinsky put me to bed, taking my temperature which was nearly one hundred and three. Sepp returned at five-thirty and was amazed to find me ill in bed. At once, although I begged him not to, he went to fetch the SS Doctor who, after a thorough examination, diagnosed diarrhoea of a serious nature, as he called it. Prescribing weak tea and boiled milk after every bowel movement to replace the fluids, he left. Upon the doctor's leaving, I heard him say to Sepp that I seemed fatigued and it was evident by my short fingernails that I was living on my nerves. Hearing the latter, I gulped, shaking with fear, but Sepp insisted that nothing would go wrong as long as he was about.

The events leading to living twenty-four hours on a knife's edge, maximum tensions, plus irregular food had finally caught up with me, proving my theory that I was young and fit was an error of judgment. Sepp's fine example of standing by me, manifesting his love, was an act of heaven but, when I told him so, he smilingly said: "Heaven is where you are – you know I don't believe in God." When ill one's mind wanders to more serene thinking and I wanted Sepp to believe in a higher Being, yet he avoided all conversation leading to it. I waited for him to return from the barracks to talk to me, but all he could think of was willing me to get better. Sepp moved my bed to the window, thus getting more sunshine and the view of the lovely garden, whilst seeing him come and go with his beautiful horse, Rio. My face pressed against the window glass, I watched, and dreamed away the days and weeks, praying for a full recovery. I also reconstructed my life, imagining how it might have been with Sepp as my real husband . . . two hot tempers in eternal combat with each other, fighting and loving it out, with missiles crossing the air.

October 4, 1944. I felt well enough to get up. As I entered the sitting-room I saw it was filled with gladiolli and golden dahlias and, to my surprise, Sepp standing by the sofa stretching out his arms to me. "You look fit enough to go to the Opera Ball," he cried, hugging me and I agreed to please him, pointing out his 'W' hairline, standing for will power, and we both laughed as if we had not a care in the world. Suddenly, he was still and exclaimed to my utter amazement: "Thou shalt not . . . yet my longing for you never ceased, despite the fact that I managed to read a Bible whilst you were ill." Incapable of a reply, with tears in my eyes I thanked him for all his help and love during my illness and wondered what had gone on in his mind during those critical weeks. Suddenly he said: "Your illness gave me time to examine myself and recognize the fact that one does not have to be in bed with a woman to love her as much as I love you. I've never been educated like you, Burgi, all I was taught was to use brute force." Holding me very close he continued: "You have no idea, the power I held in my hands at times, I could give orders to burn down a village and all that was in it and get a medal for it."

With closed eyes, my head on his chest, I listened with horror, but let him talk, for who was I to judge him in the first place? He saved me from the terror he knew only too well, risking his life every moment of the day and for this alone I owed him something. Humbly, he went on: "There is so much I have to be thankful for, a damn good life, whilst it lasted and, most of all you, bewitching and tormenting me as I kept coming back, asking for more."

Sepp told me that he was leaving in the morning for the Front line, which was now near Warsaw as the Jewish Ghetto was in uproar. We discussed at great length the consequences of his leaving but, as far as the food rations were concerned, I was safe. However, he urged me to get out of Poland as soon as possible and I agreed. Although he never mentioned the name Fegerle, I knew it was on his mind and he handed me his Luger to protect myself. "Shoot to kill, if anyone tackles you," he begged, "don't let them get you." Anxiously his eyes surveyed my face, expressing hope, determination and a love I could or would not accept. There was really no definition of what I felt for Sepp, too many aches of different kinds had pierced my heart, rendering it to a state of numbness, with only the normal physical attraction between man and woman still alive.

Madam Muschinsky made us some coffee and Sepp relaxed for a while, putting up his feet on the sofa. Somehow I dared not touch him for fear of awakening a desire and our 'good-bye' became an ordeal without any concession on my part. Grim looking and dejected he got to his feet, bracing himself for the last few minutes of being together. It was all over and I sensed a feeling of relief in both of us, but I was glad that Sepp's toughness dominated the situation to the very end. His kiss exuded the explosiveness and stored away passions of a man who demanded of life the ultimate, with me the loser, and I had to concede to his last sentence: "You still were mine, although you've fought me and your kisses will linger to the end of my days." Without turning around, he left the house, straightening his cap and adjusting his revolver. Our physical tests between love and war were over, although our fight for survival was still on but entering its last climax.

With Sepp gone I had to reshuffle my position and decided on a change of address until I was fit to travel home. People by the English sounding name of Fitzroy sprang to my mind, and I set out to visit them. To the best of my knowledge they were not Nazis, although they mixed with the Adam's family, like someone trying to keep close to the enemy. I ran into Frau Adam and she insisted on my going with her for a chat. To get away from her was like wrestling with an octopus so I went to her home. After an 'inquiry' as to Sepp's absence she told me all about her daughter's marriage, and the illustrious Nazis who attended. I listened for one single name – Fergele – and I was relieved to note its omission. As I was still feeling weak from the reaction of my illness, Frau Adams' loud and boisterous voice, and the endless gossip worked like hammer-blows on my poor head. She enquired into my plans, thus giving me little choice but to tell her of my intention to stay with the Fitzroys, adding my hope that they would have me. "Of course they will," she cried, "they are lonely elderly people and could do with livening up," and with a glint in her round eyes she added; "Now that you are alone, Frau Schneider, you can have some fun like me, husbands tend to get in one's way sometimes." I had to hand it to her – Frau Adam was still game to flirt despite fifty years and her fifteen stone figure.

We walked into the lavishly furnished sitting-room and I

thought of the old Polish widow just down the road. What a contrast! Frau Adam excused herself to telephone the Fitzroys with a view to preparing the ground for me. "How kind of you," I said, swallowing the words "to interfere". Relaxed I sat on the deep cushioned couch, whilst opposite me Hitler's life-size portrait stared down and I began to study it more closely. Pompous, with madness in his eyes, he looked down on me and it was the first time that I had ever laughed loudly at a picture. As Frau Adam entered the room she asked me what was so funny, I said, rather truthfully: "Everything, come to think of it my being here at all."

After hearing some more tittle-tattle, I left for the Fitzroys' home knowing by Frau Adam's telephone conversation that they were pleased to have me as a lodger. Madam Muschinsky was sad to see me leave, but agreed that it was best for both of us with Sepp gone. Had she guessed my grim secret?

The same evening I moved to the Fitzroys who received me very kindly. Nevertheless, I could not help but notice the luxury in furnishings and food – where did it come from?

Before going to bed I was invited to a cup of coffee which I accepted. Avoiding talk about Sepp, I told them of Austria, only to be reminded it was called 'Ostmark'. However, the evening was soon over and we retired to our rooms. I thought about Mr. Churchill and the headaches he gave Hitler and decided to listen to the BBC again on my radio given me by Sepp and made in Czechoslovakia, and called *Blaupunkt*. Unfortunately ever since I fell ill I had not been able to use it, now was my chance. Switching on I waited for the familiar tapping signal of Beethoven's Fifth Symphony. After some whistling it came through, loud and clear, transplanting me into another world – to me a dream world where human lives have value and dignity. The news from London was good and there was a message from Mr. Churchill saying: "My friends in occupied countries, the end of the Nazis is near, but keep on fighting and don't yield an inch . . . ours will be the glory." I loved his drawling of the word 'Nazis' – he summed up my own feelings and I knew that oppression had had its day. Lying on the rug, covered with the eiderdown, radio underneath the bed and my room in darkness, my heart was like a shining flame as I hoped with all my being that the words of this man would become reality.

Suddenly I heard footsteps – someone put a head through the door. It was Frau Fitzroy but I was too late to get back into my bed and she walked in. I managed to hide the set but she realized what I had been doing. "You appreciate if they catch you listening to the BBC, the penalty is death?" She switched on the lamp by my bedside table. "I know, Frau Fitzroy," I said bitterly. "Death is everywhere, on the fronts, in the homes and the open streets so one more will make little difference." "Good God child," she answered, "don't talk like this, I would never betray you. All I want you to be is sensible and wait for the War to finish," and she added, "you are so young, the whole world lies before you." There were too many people waiting for this war to end, especially the Nazi fellow-travellers; what was wanted was action. Too many had perished already and if one single life could be saved it would be worth-while.

Next day I sorted out my wardrobe, as it was getting very cold. Through many gifts from various people, I was in possession of really good clothing. A Polish doctor's wife gave me a real Astrakhan jacket, which once belonged to her mother. From Frau Fitzroy I received a soft brown fur, intended for trimming the Astrakhan jacket, to give it the younger look. Fitting my newly acquired fur to the collar, I went to look in the mirror in the corridor, turning from side to side. For one moment I gasped for behind me stood the SS Commandant of Lodz. He was rather a short man for an SS officer, but very efficient, according to Sepp. I recognized him at once, but he said: "Now where have we met before Madame," adding with a sigh, "yes, of course, you are Schneider's wife," and I nodded. Rather forcefully he grabbed my arm, marching me into the living-room to the amazement of Frau Fitzroy. Without much ado he came to the point of his visit and told me that he needed an entertainer for his SS Club. For one awful second I thought he had come to challenge my identity! There were so many questions I wanted to ask him, and how he found out that I could sing, but time was short and I could not afford to arouse any suspicion, so I said: "You flatter me, but it is a long time since I made a public appearance. However, I am best at doing impersonations of film stars like Zarah Leander and Marikka Röck." Arranging his tie vainly he replied: "I shall be the judge of what you can do, Madam, and what you will be singing in my club."

He insisted that I got my coat at once, and we left in his elegant Mercedes for the SS Club. It was in the main street, called the 'Herman Goering Strasse'. The poorly lit place was half full of officers, some of them unsteady on their feet. As the Commandant and I walked past, junior officers kept jumping to attention, saluting. The pianist was Polish and, as I commented on his beautiful playing, the Colonel retorted: "Don't forget he is a Pole and we are only using him because our pianist is needed at the Front." After a few songs the Colonel seemed pleased, indicating "enough for now". He had me driven back to the Fitzroys, reminding me to turn up for rehearsals at the same time the following day. The concert was within a week. What a hoax! I, their most vehement opponent, was chosen to entertain the SS for their farewell dinner. If the fact of my being in Poland was fantastic, this latest development was sheer madness, an extravaganza I could do without, yet I found it fascinating.

The last touches to improve my act went smoothly – impersonating the voice of Dr. Goebbel's much praised Leander suited me. Although she was a woman of forty, nearly twice my age, her appeal was highly tempestuous and sultry, turning her disadvantages, big feet and rather shapeless legs, into a mystery. She put emphasis on her face and immaculate décolleté. The notes she could not reach, she sang low, giving her songs a new meaning. To sum up Zahrah Leander, she conveyed more with a look or flicker of her eyelashes than most of her compatriots could do by taking their clothes off. I had certainly set myself a big task.

The choice of the dress was left to me and, with the help of Frau Fitzroy, I redesigned her old evening gown of red and multicoloured taffeta. She practically pinned me to it, taking out the sleeves and splitting half the back, folding it to a large 'V'. How apt, I thought, my silent protest for all to see. She gave me a large black-laced picture hat, trimming it with a huge red rose. When I saw the finished product in the mirror I could hardly believe it was me – the pathetic little girl who rose from the depth of despair, near to death, to the now dazzling woman. Near to tears, I took everything off, explaining that I wanted to be alone, while Frau Fitzroy wondered what was the matter.

"Three more days and nights," I kept saying to myself, I never imagined in my wildest dreams that one day I should have a First Night at an SS Club. With my nerves fading by the hour, Frau Fitzroy took over, reminding me that I owed her some gratitude as well, and must do justice to my husband's reputation, a hero in the front line. It was all far too complicated even to reason things out and I accepted the inevitable to go on stage and show them what material I was made of, perhaps in more than one sense.

November 3, 1944. The Club was filled with some two hundred and fifty officers and a few wives. I arrived fully dressed, trembling like a leaf behind the curtains, awaiting my signal. The stage was in darkness, the music began to play and I began to sing: *Allein, bin ich in der Nacht, meine Seele wacht und lauscht* . . . (Alone, am I in the night, my soul awake and listening . . .) The spotlight fell on me and I could hear gasps from hungry men, most of whom had not seen a woman for over one year and there I was flouting temptation like throwing sweets to an audience of children and I sensed that I was safe in a jungle of passions rewarding me with undulated vibrations of confidence. Those men down there willed me to interpret my song their way and, to my own astonishment, I expressed my hidden longing, the torments of my soul and my true self, to the point of exposing my heart. The song had a lovely lyric and I made the best of it, especially with the refrain: *"Der Wind hat mir ein Lied erzaehlt, von einem Glueck unsagbar schoen . . . er weiss was meinem Herzen fehlt, fuer wen es schlaegt und glünt, er weis fuer wen . . . Komm . . . Komm."* (The wind has told me of a song and happiness beyond all dreams, he knows what my heart is missing and to whom it belongs and for whom it beats . . . come . . . come).

There was terrific applause and shouts for more. At this

moment I was only an artiste knowing that I had done well. The thought that the crowd down there were my enemies added to the exhilaration. Now I was sure of myself and started my next act with ease. I changed from the rather unhappy to the frivolous woman as I sang: *Eine Frau wird erst schoen durch die Liebe, ganz, allein nur durch die Liebe, ach wenn es nur ewig so bliebe, nur die Liebe macht erst schoen.* The gist of this song was: "A woman is only beautiful when she is in love, only through love (sighing) Oh if it only could be so for ever, because love alone makes beautiful". Even before I finished, the entire audience rose to its feet applauding and cheering me for about three minutes. The Commandant looked straight at me, nodded and smiled. I held his glance for some time, turned to my pianist, and tossed him my standby music score. It was Lehars "Girls were made to love and kiss". "Play it slowly," I said commandingly. He obeyed, rather awed as I began to move forward into the audience. Standing by the table of the Commandant and his all male party, I started to sing Lehar's melody, using my own wording which I had made up the previous night at the Fitzroys. In a way, it was my answer to the Commandant's speech which I had heard after last night's rehearsal, namely that his men should be proud to die for the Fuehrer. Looking over his shoulder, I sang loud and clear: *Männer sind zum lieben da . . . Und jeder Mann der sagt zur Liebe ja . . . Ist kein Held . . . Nur ein Mann der liebt . . . Und eine Frau ist seine ganze Welt . . ."* After these first few lines of telling them that men were made to love, not to be heroes, they began to cheer me, stamping their feet shouting: "Bravo, bravo! More!" I had little option but to carry on and sang: "*Ja glaub mir* . . . believe me . . ." when, turning round I saw a revolver lying on a table facing me but continued to sing directly at the officer in question; "*Nie nahm ich die Liebe schwer . . . ich kuesste heiss, gab mir mehr und mehr,*" thus declaring, amongst roars of laughter: "Love was just a game to me, but oh so nice and full of ecstasy."

If I thought I had reached the zenith of my performance and that they were going to stop me, I was mistaken, for they stood up cheering me, daring me to go on and I did, with the Commandant's eyes burning a hole into my body. Through an archway of outstretched hands I reached the stage, finishing off my song: "I have known love that was bitter sweet, I have known passion, I've known retreat, I have explored all the channels of bliss, And I have tasted, never wasted one kiss." It was a hilarious feeling, with Frau Fitzroy protecting me from officers offering to take me home, with me saying over and over again: *"Aber meine Herren beruhigen Sie sich doch, ich bin ja eine Ehefrau* – (But Gentlemen, calm down, I am a married woman).

We drove home in a horse-drawn carriage, with Herr Fitzroy laying out the red carpet by producing champagne. Although it was past 2 a.m. I could not possibly go to sleep, I was too full of fun, if only for one glorious night. However my friends saw to it that I went to bed and I did, humming the melodies I had sung and thinking of Sepp and strangely wishing him near me. The glamorous night was over and, to my surprise, was followed by an unexpected visitor, the Commandant. Brazen-faced he walked into my bedroom. Startled, I pulled up my eiderdown. Grinning all over his face he said: "Don't worry, you are not the only woman I have seen like this." Realizing that I could not afford to affront him, I asked the reason for his visit. Adjusting his jacket before my dressing-table he answered: "To see if you look as good in daylight," and, prancing around my bed, he added, "I must confess you have not deteriorated since last night." I could have hit him for his rudeness, but what damage would it do to the poor Fitzroys and myself. So I smiled and asked him to hand me my dressing-gown which he did teasingly. Flinging it over me, I got up and tried to leave the room, but the Commandant barred the door. "First a kiss, *mein Schatz* (Darling)". Holding me very close he whispered ardently: "You've tempted me beyond endurance with your poetry and I have come to the same conclusion as you, namely that men were made to love and kiss." I felt his wet lips on my mouth and they seemed like a snake's bite, horribly sickening. All the world turned around me and, full of repulsion against this man, I struck him in the middle of his face, hard and deliberate. He got hold of me furiously, shouting: "You little nobody, you Austrian idiot, every woman in Lodz would give her right arm to be mine, do you understand?" He fumbled with his revolver, but I knew he was far too excited to fire it so I flung myself at him and his mercy, imploring him to use his common sense. Eventually he put the weapon away and I tried to reason with him by quoting some of his Master's rules and regulations, such as: "You know the Fuehrer's penalty for having an affair with the wife of an Officer fighting at the front." If I thought it would frighten him I was mistaken, he became more angry and shouted: "Hitler is in Berlin and I am right here in Poland and here *I* decide who shall live and die." The Commandant got hold of me again, crazy with lust, and we wrestled on the floor, when Herr Fitzroy entered and pulled him off me. "You will regret this deeply, I promise you," he snarled at Fitzroy, who himself was shaking like a leaf.

At last he left. Herr Fitzroy and his wife comforted me like a child but my deepest fear was now for them in case this man unleashed his fury on my protectors. If all the anguish of this morning was not enough, more was to come in the next few hours. Frau Fitzroy asked me to take a parcel to the Post Office which was in the centre of the town. When I arrived a long queue of poorly dressed people were standing in the mud, whilst a much smaller one stood on the pavement. There were two large notices: "Germans to be served first" and "Poles". I simply felt I had to stand with the second-class citizens. All the humiliations of the past years came to my mind and hatred was the only thing left, keeping me alive.

Suddenly a woman pinched me on my back, saying: "Hello there." It was Frau Spitz from Hamburg, whom I had previously met at the Adam's house. She looked well and fat and her boy of four was expensively dressed. Rather pathetically, next to him stood a little Polish child without shoes, its feet wrapped in rags. God have mercy, I suddenly thought and was on the verge of giving the child one mark, when Frau Spitz said: "You are in the wrong queue, Frau Schneider," thus leaving me no alternative but to join her. For a while I listened to the latest news concerning Frau Adam, but suddenly she waved to some people not far from us, explaining to me: "There is Fegerle and his wife." "Who?" I asked in a state of shock and she replied: "*Oberscharfuehrer* Fegerle, don't you remember, he was amongst the first SS Troops to enter Warsaw," adding, "your Sepp knew him fairly well." I hoped the earth would open up and swallow me, but I regained my composure and nodded. Like a rabbit fascinated by a cobra, I stared at him, for I wanted to remember his face after this war was over and the War Criminals would be dealt with, according to the broadcast of Mr. Churchill.

At last our queue moved forward and I found myself inside the Post Office getting rid of my parcel and rid of Frau Spitz, watching her leave through the exit. My heart was lighter, for I feared that she might join the Fegerles and talk to them, obviously stating who I was, thus setting off a time-bomb for me. As quickly as possible I left the building and made for home. My chances of Fegerle not asking who I was seemed remote and if so, I had had it. There was a man at the end of his reign of terror, who had already killed defenceless women and children, confronted with a situation too intoxicating not to make use of, plus his opportunity of getting even with Schneider who was a thorn in his side. The suspense was terrible, a state of uncertainty with adequate suspicion and only one way out . . . to leave Lodz immediately.

Back home at the Fitzroys, I went straight to my room and checked my Luger. Somehow, holding the cold steel in my hands gave me hope, although my commonsense told me that I did not stand a dog's chance. There were no stop-gap solutions to my dilemma, only stark reality staring in my face. Now I had two men after my blood. The Commandant enraged by my refusal, and Fegerle, the pathological killer . . . once he found out that I was not Schneider's wife, he would probe deeper into my background and perhaps find the answer. These thoughts increased my speed in packing and I informed Frau Fitzroy that I had to depart at once. Relieved at her thinking it was due to the fracas with the Commandant, which was partly true, I thanked her for everything, and was ready to leave. However, she insisted that I took the address of their Polish shoemaker, Mr Dabrovska, who lived in a dingy sidestreet close to the rail station, thus giving me a further chance to hide if need be. Somehow, I dreaded another contact, but accepted it as a standby, a port in a storm, refraining to disclose my own plans, thus saving us both admissions, particularly if the Fitzroys were questioned by the Gestapo.

Loaded with two large suitcases, I set off, having said 'good-bye' to the people who had sheltered me for several weeks. It was very dark and frosty, with my footsteps echoing down the cobbled roads and making me jump at every human sound, until at last I arrived at the cobbler's house. Mr Dabrovska's window was blacked-out, yet the curtains moved slightly and I sensed that someone was behind them, watching me. By now my nerves had reached breaking point and I was afraid of lulling myself into a false sense of security, so I pulled out my Luger and knocked on the window. I could hear the shuffling of feet and someone opening the door, asking me to come in, but rather oddly the voice did not sound very Polish and I requested Mr Dabrovska to come out, which he did. Having seen him once at the Fitzroys I followed the Pole into the house. To his amazement I locked the door, keeping the key until I felt certain that we were alone. Eventually, he smiled at my strange behaviour, but the look in his eyes told me that he understood only too well. With a sigh of relief, we shook hands and he informed me that he had to learn German in order to survive, adding: "Four years of being taught German is a long time for an old man who lost his only son at the beginning of the war." I suddenly felt very sorry for him and nervously checked my watch. Like a cat on hot bricks passing up and down, he assured me all would be well if I was lucky enough to get on the train – but I told him I could not afford any ifs. Mr Dabrovska had noticed my shoes – shabby and nearly worn through. Smiling as though he had some secret surprise, he told me to take them off. Then, placing a large box wrapped in layers of newspaper before me, he began to unpack and out of it came the most beautiful black leather boots. "Try them on," he urged me, "they are your size, four and a half." They fitted like gloves and were soft as a kitten. Nostalgically he told me how he made them for a lady who was killed during the first bombing raids on Warsaw and I was sure she was his wife. Caught in a web of the past, we reminisced, forgetting that I was waiting for a train to save my life, until the hands of the clock indicated that it was time to go.

Mr Dabrovska got out a handcart, placed my cases in it, and off we set for the little wooden station of Lodz. Taking no chances, I walked beside him, my revolver at the ready, for I feared that by now Fegerle knew my secret and was on the look out. If he came gunning for me he'd better make sure that I was dead before he was or he would have the surprise of his life. The station was filled with a ramshackle mob. Sitting on my cases, we waited, perceptively surveying every man in uniform and suspicious of everyone that looked at me. Ten minutes later the train arrived and an indescribable rush from all sides set in. If ever I needed assurance, now was the time. I was determined that nothing should stand in my way – it was a case of the survival of the fittest. Mr Dabrovska's gaunt frame pushed me into the open door, using my heavy suitcases like torpedoes and, to my relief, I made it. Standing upright, squeezed between the human cargo, I waved my good friend, never knowing if he saw me, with more people still climbing through the smashed windows. The much overloaded train moved out of Lodz, puffing westwards towards my home.

Brieg came in sight which meant changing trains and I got ready for the battle to get on the other train. People were trampling down the old and ill and little abandoned children cried for their mothers . . . this was Hitler's hideous, merciless war at its last stages.

Although I managed to have my travel pass stamped, I was unable to get a train back to Vienna. Life was tough, with hundreds of thousands of refugees from the East and those Nazis who, in the first place, made use of Hitler's conquered *Lebensraum,* or land on which to expand, were fleeing from the fast advancing Russians. They congested the roads and created an unimaginable chaos in the already panic-stricken areas. The food position was hopeless, with babies dying in the arms of their mothers for lack of milk and from exposure. The situation worsened and I was prepared to abandon my precious suitcases to lighten my load, when suddenly I spotted a Red Cross van. Taking a deep breath, I approached the stationary vehicle and asked the driver, a woman, for a lift. She looked as startled as if she was being ambushed, for I caught her counting money, lots of money. Obviously we understood each other from the onset. We were both in a 'jam', heading for Austria and possible safety. She told me to get into the van . . . she pretended to the others that she was out of fuel, doubtless having good reason to do so. However, my aim was mobility one way or the other and I complied with all she said. As she was waiting for her 'doctor' we talked of our experiences, with her envying my 'career' as a troop entertainer; "Ever since I was old enough, all I could think about were men, loads of handsome men to have my pick from." "Oh, really," I answered bemused, "so did I, only in my case it became a necessity." Soon afterwards we were joined by her friend and set off at last, with people screaming and swearing at us, as we started digging our way through the desperate crowds. Half an hour later we halted; the doctor placed a Red Cross band on my arm, in case of a check up. Smilingly I hoped that no one would be depending on my 'skill' as a nurse, and lay myself in the back of the van. Once we reached the country roads it was better and my friends increased speed, only to stop now and then for further consultations.

Luck that had played such a big part in my past seemed still with me, although I guessed I was in the hands of two deserters and, judging by their wealth, utter rogues. However, with every kilometer I came closer to Austria and that was really all that mattered to me. Up till now I had had little time to think or take a good look at myself, as men did it for me in rapid succession, yet it was nice to know that my formula to fight and beat the Nazis had worked . . . through women's strongest weapon – sex – if used the right way. Physical beauty in the eyes of the beholder can play havoc and I had had a head start. Men showered me with adulations, attended to my wishes and pulled me through all sorts of troubles – all for a kiss, an embrace, an aura of make believe. Combined with circumstances, I managed to escape the fate of so many – to breed for the Fuehrer. I certainly had no desire for the latter, but whenever I tried to become a one-man woman, my fight for the freedom of mankind loomed before me, love had to be sacrificed regardless of the hurt. Bruised in exchanges, but still in one piece, I focused my goal on a freedom for which women have fought in the past, realizing that my world and I were part of each other. Fate allowed me to glimpse the dizzy heights of passion against the most vicious background possible, with moments of pain, horror and great exultation, ending in humility and gratitude.

November 15, 1944. I reached Vienna after this incredible journey, crowded with obstacles, and went under cover at my aunt's manor as a stop-gap solution. Part five of my life was over and, although I was only twenty-one, I felt that I had lived a hundred years, with the willingness to believe that Peace was within my grasp.

CHAPTER 10

THE WEARY WEHRWOLFS

November 1944. Lying low at my aunt's house in Vienna was not at all my cup of tea, for one cannot live a life of action such as I had experienced and be cut off like oxygen from a breathing bottle. Since I had seen my relatives, Vienna had changed indeed. The cosmopolitan crowd, among them many great Nobles, were huddled in old clothing, exchanging their most valuable possessions for food to survive. For instance, my cousin, Baroness Urbanek-Haan, a relative of the once incredibly rich Habsburgs, exchanged a solid gold watch, worth about fifty-five pounds, for one loaf of bread, two pounds of lard and two pounds of flour.

She was nearly in serious trouble through her dog, an Irish Setter called Tommy. A few weeks before my return from Poland, the dog had run away during an air-raid and was caught by the police. Its name and address were written on an elaborate silver-plated collar. Suddenly my cousin found herself under arrest and, to her utter amazement, was told that she could not call her dog 'Tommy' as this was primarily an English name and affectionately used by the British people for their soldiers. Cornelia Urbanek-Haan, dumbfounded for seconds, flew into a temper and told the Gestapo officer if the name of her dog was to blame for the military setbacks in the past years, then it was high time he went to serve in the front line and give up his post to a much older man. Fearing my cousin's intervention through some high ranking people to implement her suggestion, he dismissed her as an old decrepit aristocrat and 'let sleeping dogs lie'. Baroness Urbanek-Haan insisted that never was there a quotation more aptly applied, and I agreed.

At the beginning of December 1944, I ventured a letter to my mother in the country. To my surprise I received an answer within days, asking me to come at once. It obviously meant that I was safe, otherwise she would have worded her letter differently. On December 9, using my official escape pass, I left Vienna. The only trouble was to board the train as it was filled to capacity hours ahead. However, crawling through a window, I succeeded, but had to stand the entire one hundred and fifty kilometres, guarding my cases like a hawk.

Six hours later I was home and my mother could hardly believe it. She cried to the point of making the neighbours suspicious, until I reminded her that the war was not over yet, and the hatred of the Nazis was in its last and most cruel stage. To counter my anxiety, Mother had good news, although this was not due to my presence but to the magic of her cooking and the ability to stretch one chicken to last one week and to feed three people. "Who is the number three in our family now?" I asked and Mother advised me to wait and see, for the mystery guest was due at six. Punctually he arrived, introducing himself as Major Hans Schoepf, Commandant of the anti-aircraft-defence *Fliegerabwehr* stationed at St Stefan. He seemed delighted to meet me, but my first impression of him was that of a fox taking cover after having devoured its prey. The Major explained to me his work at the Unit, and the fact that he was a Doctor at Law in civil life and a German Officer minus decorations. The purpose of his visiting my parents was his hobby – playing cards. Clicking his heels and bowing slightly to me, he followed my mother into the kitchen, extracting from under his long coat a parcel, then shutting the door in my face. In a way I had to laugh, despite my mother's advance instructions "to conduct myself in a ladylike manner." Home again, after four months on the run, criss-crossing Europe and witnessing the awful spectacle of Hitler's war, the cruelties perpetrated against millions of Jews and citizens and the senseless slaughter on the fronts, I had at last an opportunity to play cards and "be ladylike". What a crazy world to live in!

As anticipated, after a good dinner out came the cards and the play began. My step-father partnered my mother and I had the expert and skilful knowledge of Major Schoepf to go on with. At times only the ticking of our big clock was evident and the briskly spoken rules if one had enough points. However, during the shuffling of the cards our guest made polite conversation and I found him rather suave and intelligent, until he suddenly exclaimed that in the event of a German frontal collapse he would fight on as a *Wehrwolf.* With Mother expecting at any moment my humorous reaction and fearing the consequences, I diluted her anxiety by excusing myself to fetch a glass of milk, thus avoiding what might have been a tricky situation. To prove my will power, I endured the company of this *Wehrwolf* for a further two hours, but, needless to state, his departure was a great relief to us all. However, I should like to stress that, if ever awards were due for the 'Best Actress of the Year' I deserved it for my impeccable performance. By now I had met them all, the young Lions, the Patriots and the Cowards, but this one was so tragically funny that I knew with certainty that Victory was within reach.

Christmas 1944, and most of Mother's food-stock was exhausted. Only our *Wehrwolf's* supply of purloined goods kept us going, ensuring one simple meal per day. Although we knew he took it from his men, we accepted it eagerly. Hunger is perhaps the most demoralizing force of all and to stay alive we needed food. The agonizing wait for the end of the war had reached the final stages. It was at this time that I began to write down some of my escapades, excluding names, although the fate of my comrades was always on my mind, wondering if they were still alive and well. My life was very quiet now, fulfilling the daily round of work, mostly helping my step-father with his one hundred and twenty horses. Apart from this my mother kept me on a close range and, with Major Schoepf's gastronomical and moral support, I had little opportunity but to be good.

It was January 1945 but the calendar of horrors was still slowly unfolding. Mass arrests and air-raids in our area and, in particular, Donawitz, the great Iron and Steel Works, fifteen kilometres from my home. Now and then Major Schoepf's anti-aircraft guns were to be heard, but it was a rather pathetic noise and the fighter planes of the R.A.F. flew so low over the guns that their crews could see the pilots' faces. Schoepf felt humiliated by the 'sauciness' of the English.

Early in January 1945 I had to go to Donawitz and Major Schoepf gave me a lift. As we got there the sirens sounded and we both went into the Works' tunnel. Lots of other people were there already. It was a heavy air-raid and the blast knocked several people over. Major Schoepf held me tightly and, to my amazement, said: "If I look at you much longer, I shall kiss you in front of all these people." I looked at him startled and said: "As a former Judge, you surprise me indeed, I always thought you were infallible." Schoepf laughed and released his hold on me. After the 'all clear' we went to visit some friends of mine and continued to the Villa Oberhaus. The owners of this place were most charming people, highly educated, but owing to Nazi persecution, rather down and out. Frau Oberhauser was a very good friend of mine and in the Resistance. I could trust her completely. She informed me that she would be coming to St Stefan soon and hoped to get hold of a little food.

About a week later she came. My mother fixed her up with some potatoes, eggs and flour at my personal request, and Major Schoepf arranged a lift on a military lorry back to Leoben. I decided to accompany her. On our way back we were stopped by a rather flamboyant woman in a fur coat, waving her arms about, and the driver, a Corporal, helped her on to the vehicle for which she hardly thanked him. As she ignored us, Frau Oberhauser and I continued our conversation as quietly as possible, moving closer to the driver's cabin, turning our backs towards her. We discussed the conditions of the British prisoners of war stationed at Goess working at the Cement and Gravel Works just above the Oberhauser Villa. I mentioned my crazy plan to help them escape but she explained that, in her husband's view, they were safer where they were for once they were out they would have little chance of survival. We went on complaining about the starvation rations and I stated that Hitler was a madman and should be in an asylum. I had hardly finished the sentence when our fellow passenger knocked at the driver's window ordering him to stop the lorry at once. She declared that Frau Oberhauser and I were traitors and demanded that the Corporal reported to the nearest Military police, which he did. Our 'friend' disclosed that she was an ex-singer and the wife of the Director from the Opera at Graz, well-known as a faithful Nazi and witch hunter in sorting out the Jewish elements from his Theatre. Suddenly it dawned on us – the predicament we were in if this woman managed to make her charges stick. She made a full statement, repeating the conversation she overheard in the van until the driver insisted upon giving his version, namely that such conversation could never have taken place without attracting his attention. Bewildered, I looked at him, for one moment fearing to upset his line of thinking. Why did he wish to help us? First one had to consider his own implication if we were found guilty, thus boomeranging on him for not keeping his ears open as demanded by Goebbels, and secondly had he, perhaps, an axe to grind against the Nazis? Whatever his motive, it gave hope.

The Police took over, bundling us back into the van, reconstructing the events, whilst two officers sat in the front of the van, keeping the engine running. "Talk as loud as you can," they shouted at us and we obeyed. However, they understood only partly what we said, thus confirming the Corporal's views. Slamming the doors in anger, they told us to clear off but I shall never forget the venomous look the *Prima Donna* gave us, knowing that we were free to go. Frau Oberhauser was going to embrace the driver but I restrained her firmly, for we could not afford any trace of suspicion which might harm our true friend. By now I had learned to be so hard and to accept every facet of life.

Back home, I told mother of our narrow escape and her wagging finger told me to beware, to stop playing with fire all over again. Apart from this my home life was surprisingly happy, with Major Schoepf popping in and out, encouraging my step-father's chip-on-the-shoulder self pity, whilst hoping to increase his popularity with me.

February 1945 was here and all it brought was more violence on the so-called Home Front. The Brownshirt Nazis took over and, in co-operation with the Gestapo, set up a regime of terror unparalleled in history. No one was safe and on-the-spot trials became a very common feature, with corpses littering the sides of the road.

February 23, 1945. Towards midday we heard the familiar sounds of Bomber Squadrons flying over our village. We rushed outside to get a good view and there they were, glittering in the bright sunshine, hurrying along to their targets. We wondered what town was doomed. A few minutes later explosions went off and we went into the house for shelter. However, they increased and the earth began to tremble. Unfortunately we had visitors, the waiter, Otto Kowaschitz from the St Michael Restaurant and his bride. Frightened, they crawled under the table, with Otto having little difficulty being only four feet five inches tall, yet his wife, who was five feet seven inches in height banged her head, lamenting the disaster and the possibility of having to die. Although I knew it was in bad taste to giggle, I could not help myself – my mother told me off from under her bed. Suddenly our front door lifted from its hinges and the blast blew me on to the floor, bringing me up to date with the seriousness of the situation.

How long I remained in this undignified pose I don't know, but Herr Kemp, the Air-Raid Warden, appeared like an Indian smoke signal, shouting that Knittelfeld was destroyed. Hysterically, he insisted this raid was due to inside information because the Fuehrer's secret weapon, the *Panzerfaust* was made there. Adjusting the Swastika on his arm he added, with indignation: "By the way, your friend, the Jewess has flown from her hotel and I wonder who has warned her?" He meant, of course, Frau Lucy Körting, and it was no secret that we were good friends, despite several warnings to stay away from her. At last Kemp departed in anger.

The first reports on the destruction of Knittelfeld were coming in over the radio. I knew that my message to France had reached the right place after all.

"Good old Auboyer," I thought, tingling with excitement. There could be no other explanation of why at this late stage of the war large Bomber Squadrons should single out a little town of some twelve thousand people and devastate it. Perhaps to some people standing on the other side of the fence, telling us to be brave, it may sound cruel to feel as I did over the bombing of my neighbouring town, and the grief which inevitably came with it, yet there will always be people in different countries who are prepared to stand up for the rights of the individual and, by doing so, receive criticism and indignation as thanks. My choice was either to aid Hitler's war machine or help to destroy it, thus saving countless millions of lives. I knew by doing the latter I invited the bombing of military objectives and the death of some civilians. But what was the alternative?

At eight thirty in the morning on February 24 I was arrested and taken to the Gestapo H.Q. in Leoben. My mother was frantic. They accused me of being partly responsible for the raid on Knittelfeld and the *Panzerfaust* factory. I had nothing to say. Two men questioned me simultaneously and I realized that one was called Schneider and that he was an Austrian. Wondering if this was a good omen, I felt more confident. However, the questions put to me seemed silly: "Why did you cancel your appointment at your Knittelfeld hairdresser on February 23, and why were you playing the gramophone on this day, as reported by Herr Kemp?" As I had no replies to these ridiculous questions the Austrian Gestapo took over. The officer urging me to make a confession, and thus save my neck. In sheer desperation and, as a last and faint hope, I declared that I was married to an SS Officer killed in Russia and produced my escape travelling pass, clearly stating the purpose of my visit to Poland. As if a bomb had hit the room, both men stared at me and left the room, not bothering to close the door. History seemed to repeat itself in my life . . . a man named Schneider had once saved me from certain death by means of a door left ajar and it was on a train journey of no return. Perhaps at times like these one is very prone to wishful thinking. Nevertheless, what went on inside this other room made my hair stand on end and I listened most carefully; "We cannot delay our getaway," Schneider said, adding: "don't be a fool Karl, the Allies are only a stone's throw away. Remember, I kept my mouth shut when you killed Pavliceck and I disposed of the body, now it is your turn to help me, for my family lives at Leoben." "What has this got to do with this girl?" the German snarled. "Everything," said Schneider, "I've done my homework on her long before this arrest. She's clever, well-known and liked, but most of all, if the Russians should come first, I shall have an alibi, by referring to how I saved her from hanging." "But why and who is going to tell the Russians this crazy tale?" Karl asked in a tone of despair. "She, of course, Du Dumkopf, for the Resistance will be the heroes and we the villians," Schneider explained in a laughing voice. There they were carving me up between them, two murderers without pity, exploring a 'case' which suddenly proved to be a hindrance to their swift escape, and once more I heard Schneider's plea: "Let her free Karl, we don't want unnecessary paper work now at this stage, nor a corpse to dispose of." I closed my eyes and folded my hands . . . not praying, but willing God to help me. White-faced Schneider approached me, my fate on his mind and I trembled as he led me out of the room, along the stairs and escorted me to the bridge leading over the river Mur. There he spoke: "Clear out of Leoben, girl, and fast, this is your last chance. Remember me after this war is over." He held out his hand to me – I could not shake it but said 'thank you' loud and clear, gazing at a handsome face with clear blue eyes which had witnessed so much horror and got used to it.

Back home at Mother's she agreed that I should flee as soon as possible. To my surprise our friend, Major Schoepf, was of the same opinion and planned to accompany me. He, of course, believed that I was innocent and a victim of the Gestapo. I stood between the devil and the deep blue sea. By now I was determined that I would see the end of this war, come hell or high water. Luckily for me, Dr. Schoepf was a first-class organiser. A staff car, filled with petrol, and most important of all, food he very thoughtfully stole from his Unit before his departure, was put at our disposal.

February 25, 1945. With snow on the ground, we set off. There was a time when my mother would have strongly objected to my leaving travelling unaccompanied with a man to wherever he chose to take me. Now she prayed and kept her fingers crossed. After five years of war, hunger and the indescribable cruelties of the Nazis, one got so hard that nothing else mattered except survival.

We reached Bruck, twenty-five kilometres from my home, at night time. The sirens were howling but the chaos that reigned was so awful that we just sat in the car until the 'all clear' sounded. The roads were congested with all types of vehicles, an inferno in itself. As we continued our journey, now and then the headlamps would pick up the dramas played out on the open roads – ugly and pitiful sights, death and struggling everywhere. The bulging bodies of dead horses hindered our drive and we both had to get out and push them out of the way. At one place we came on a soldier, dead on his horse, with his icy fingers still holding a revolver. I insisted that we lay him in the ditch so that the oncoming lorry would not tear him apart. Dr. Schoepf was shocked to see how I handled the dead body and remarked: "I suppose you would do the same thing for me?" We travelled on for another fifteen kilometres until Gratwein came in sight and with it the first halt as far as I was concerned. Dr Schoepf bundled me into a villa which belonged to a good and loyal friend of his, an architect. Without asking any questions they took me in and gave us a meal.

Outside on the by-pass Hitler's debris kept moving past, columns of human cargo on the retreat and I was wondering how many would live to see the end of this war. Major Schoepf made himself at home in no time, getting out a bottle of wine and looking for glasses. Pouring a drink for me he exclaimed: "First, here's to our future," and he smiled magnanimously. A little amazed, I toasted his health and expressed my hope for peace. Sitting himself on the arm of my chair, he stroked my untidy hair. If ever there was a man in my life who meant less to me than Schoepf did, he would have known it instantly, but this man was blind and deaf at the same time. Bending over me he whispered, "You are the only female who has caused a furore in my heart." What could I possibly answer, I needed his help and this shelter, and when his lips came closer and closer, I shut my eyes. He spoke of the gracious living he had in mind for us, rather ironically forgetting the plight we both were in, but stressing the 'inevitable' fate which had brought us together. If he had not been so serious, I would have laughed, but in a way it amused me to see a mature man, some twenty years my senior express himself so romantically, and thus mocking his former resolve to fight on as a *Wehrwolf* to the bitter end. He excused himself to get some more wine from the cellar, whilst I explored what was to be my home for the next few days. Obviously, my benefactors must have been Nazis to live in such luxury, but to me being alive and staying alive was the important thing. Most of my worldly possessions had been destroyed, I had only memories of days gone by.

With my head resting on the velvet cushion I began to remember the men who had mattered in my young life:

1939. **Rudi Reinbacher** who used his father's power to exempt me from National Service, thus forming the basis of my strategy against the Nazis.

1939. **Armin Torggler**, the partly Jewish Surgeon who saved my life and wound up in prison.

1941-45. **Baron Schindler**, cynical, detached, the born avenger sacrificing everything for his cause.

1941. **Count Jarlsberg**, the fanatical Gestapo agent, who came so close to love, yet demanded a price incompatible with my ideals.

1942. **Rudolf**, the partisan, rugged unrelenting and honest, who disciplined his body and lost his heart.

1942. **Georg Schaile** and my December shot-gun wedding to save my family from the hands of the Gestapo.

1943. **Lieutenant Walter Borg**, the interlude, the decoy, the romancer who tried to plant a flower in a desert of war.

1943. **Pilot Officer Schlager**, responsible for my betrayal and consequent suffering at the hands of the Gestapo.

1943. **Lieutenant Werner Fink**, refusing to accept reality, thus giving his life for an unattainable target and burning to death in sheets of flames, with a love that was inextinguishable.

1944. **Sepp Schneider**, the SS Officer responsible for my escape on my way to Dachau. A man of courage and unbridled passions, gambling against all odds to enforce a past that had eluded him.

Major Schoepf's return reminded me of the present. Nonchalant, he combed his fingers through my hair alluding to the motives for falling in love, asking if sex was really the goal or only the by-product. Viewing me from all angles he stated: "I suppose in your case, it is all rolled into one by igniting an explosive, only to find out that it has got a timing device, controlled by you." "Cruel in peace-time," I answered laughingly, "but very necessary in years of war." A violent knock made us jump up and Schoepf reached for his revolver. He opened the door. Two Nazi Brownshirts demanded to check our identity cards. "I am on transfer to Linz *meine Herren*" said Schoepf coolly, adding "and this is . . ." when one of the Nazis pointed at me, touching me with his hand. "Your card, please," he demanded but Major Schoepf pushed him back. Herr Balzer, the architect, came in and produced a document which one of the Brownshirts studied – he gulped and made his exit in a hurry. After his departure my host explained that this paper was signed by the *Gauleiter* of Graz, one of the most powerful and dangerous men in this area. We all had a good laugh and I realized once more how the arm of my enemies protected me in a very strange way. Major Schoepf, who by now was of course a deserter from his unit, decided to get going and made for Linz. Our farewell was brief, to the point and in keeping with our 'love affair'. Holding me close, he suddenly exclaimed: "Remember Burgi, you are the last woman to have rested your head on my Fuehrer's uniform." Before he had said this, I felt gratitude for him, but now I was laughing inwardly and glad to see him depart, cross-checking the time of day in order to compose myself. It was 2.30 p.m. on the last day of February 1945.

The following day was to be a very special one for

Frau Balzer announced chicken for lunch. However the sirens never stopped and the blasts from various guns made additional noises, forcing us to stay in the cellar. Nevertheless all I could think of was the smell of chicken and I volunteered to go upstairs and prepare the feast. Frying the pieces and licking my lips, I defied all sirens, until the unmistakable noise of Spitfires came closer and closer, firing in all directions. There I stood with my half-fried chicken, holding it before me in the frying-pan, when a bomb went off behind the Villa and I found myself in the road, still holding the pan, running along to the next *Luftwaffen* shelter across the field. Swearing at the Royal Air Force and oblivious of the planes above me, I made the shelter. To my amazement others were there already reaching ravenously for pieces of my chicken and all I managed to eat was one half of a leg, and to think for that I nearly risked my life. The 'all clear' dispersed my 'friends' and I just sat there with my empty frying-pan, tears streaming down my face. Perhaps only when one has really experienced hunger as I had one can truly understand my feelings.

With the Balzer's place badly hit I decided to move on. There was no problem with luggage for all I possessed was the clothing I had on. I did take a small case with an automatic rifle which Schoepf left me, to defend myself, also some food my hostess kindly packed for me.

I was heading for Graz, some twenty kilometres away and hoped to make it in two days. The main roads were far too risky as they had SS patrols, who mostly shot to kill, so I waddled along the snowy path through the nearby woods. At a snail's pace, I advanced, deeper and deeper into the forest. At times I felt sick, seeing dead horses with blown-up bodies, and discarded weapons covering human corpses, their sometimes open eyes staring at me. I increased my speed, but every strange sound made me stop and hide and imagine danger. Suddenly I spotted a little wooden hut and made for it. I was exhausted and needed shelter for the night, so I decided to investigate. An abandoned horse came towards me and I got hold of its reins to examine its saddle. My heart was in my mouth for on it was stamped 'SS'. I was about to retreat when I heard men's voices in the hut. My decision was made as I had little choice to weigh up my chances. Cautiously, I opened my case and assembled my automatic rifle. Pushing my hair right under my cap I made for the door, kicked it open with my boot, and brandished my deadly weapon. But what a sight met my eyes! . . . There before me on the floor sat three men in uniform, squabbling over some pieces of dry bread. Oblivious to my menacing gesture, one of the men who by the sign on his collar I believed to be a doctor, said rather impatiently: "Put your *pushka* (gun) away boy and shut the door." The situation was pathetic, as I could see he meant it, so I walked in and did what the man asked me . . . shut the door. The doctor made the introductions, very informally, describing himself as "Dr Hans Held, a surgeon without a surgery and my name is misplaced from the start." I looked at him sadly, knowing what he meant, for 'Held' in German or Deutsch means hero. Then he spoke again: "I'm no hero at all, only a deserter who has buried his pride at Stalingrad." Somehow this broke the ice and I shook hands with the other two, a Hungarian captain, and an Austrian sailor wearing a 'borrowed' Major's jacket. I felt unhappy amongst these men . . . once they must have had pride and belonged to someone, now all there was left of them were empty burned out bodies with large eyes mirroring hunger and despair. Near to tears I left the hut to get some of my food, and offered it to them. I had never seen anything like it, although I had seen plenty since Hitler promised to make 'his Austria' into a flowering garden. Ravenously they ate up everything in minutes, including the small bones of the chops, and the apples complete with cores and pips. To save face I made a joke, telling them that they should go on stage with this 'vanishing trick'. After a good laugh we settled down – the doctor took off my wool cap. In sheer bewilderment the men stared at me and I reached for my gun, but they assured me that I had nothing to fear. Without a smile they accepted the fact that I was a girl and on the run like them, and their dirty bearded faces disclosed human beings behind a façade of astonishment. Suddenly they became more amicable and told me their stories.

The twenty-one year old sailor had escaped from a U boat

at Hamburg. He had reached Austria after weeks of travelling and with the help of numerous girl friends. His wish was to reach home, twenty-five kilometres away.

The Hungarian captain, a man of forty, was a professional soldier with twenty years' service. After his Regiment was wiped out by the Russians, he had deserted, counting on the kindness of the Austrians to give him shelter.

Finally, the doctor, a man of the same age, had served in many field-hospitals in Russia. He was sick to death with amputating frozen limbs, at times without any pain-killer, and revolted by the cruelties of the Nazis during the retreat from Stalingrad. Holding his head in his hands he kept saying: "I can never forget that three hundred and sixty thousand young men, the elite of Austria perished because this madman Hitler ordered NO retreat." With tears streaming down his face, he declared: "Only top Nazis were flown out from the encirclement of Stalingrad, by the order of Himmler, the others perished. I have seen men with their bare hands hanging on to the icy wings of planes, begging to be rescued . . . and men inside shooting them down like mad dogs." Petrified I listened; watching a grown man cry like this was frightening. The cold wind lashing against the thin wooden hut added to the fury this man expressed for the four people gathered together by fate.

Someone was shouting outside: "Come out with your hands up, one by one, or we will set fire to the place and burn you out like hornets." My lips were trembling as I looked at my party. The captain jumped through the only wood boarded window and began to shoot from his revolver. We lay flat on the floor, weapons at the ready. Several shots rang out, then silence, which was worse than the shooting, so the sailor went outside to investigate. A machine gun rattled and with a scream he fell to the ground. Through a small slit I could see that he was badly hurt and waved the doctor, but he ordered me to lie still. For a few seconds he opened the door to look and we saw in the distance some fifty yards away an SS man who shouted: "Come out or we kill you in there, you scum." No one gave me a mandate to answer, but I did: "Come and get us you pigs." The doctor nudged my arm as if to agree with what I had said and crawled towards the door, rolling over towards the injured sailor, but he signalled me that he was dead. Using the body as cover, he began to fire. Now I was alone in the hut, frightened, but equally determined to survive. I could see the captain rushing behind a tree and opening up fire from behind the SS men. One fell to the ground like a stone, face forward, with the captain screaming: "I've got him . . . I've got him, there is only one more left." I rushed outside, firing like mad, but the doctor pulled me down and took over my machine gun. We could hear movements and waited, then there was an explosion, obviously from a hand-grenade, but it went to our right and we glanced at each other. He noticed that my cheeks were cut but this was caused by pressing my face down for cover in the snow. Suddenly the second SS man came forward, his hands up high. My mouth was wide open when I saw how young he was and how wild he looked. The Hungarian took no chances. There was a little argument between him and the doctor and the SS man fell dead to the ground. "Now I've settled the score for the little boy over there who did not make it," he said firmly.

I packed my few things and we parted company, leaving three dead men scattered in the snow. Worst of all the two living showed no sign of compassion. With tears in my eyes I soldiered on asking myself the question: Why did God allow a monster like Hitler to create so much misery and suffering?

After a six hour solid walk, I reached my Aunt Betty's villa, and waited for the darkness to hide me before I rang the doorbell. My aunt was deeply shocked to see me in such a tired state, with filthy clothing covering me, but agreed to let me stay.

Frau Betty Kus was in her fifties, relatively wealthy and well known for her many charities, and as a devout Christian. I felt guilty but I had no option, for her villa was hidden away, but most of all she was, in the opinion of the neighbours, above suspicion so far as harbouring undesirable elements was concerned. Pointing this out to my aunt made her laugh, but she made it clear never even to think on those lines. To her the Nazis were repugnant and I a sort of 'Joan of Arc' driving them out. Our great problem was food. Betty made tea from *Herbs-Kamillen*, and Spinach from stinging nettles, so keeping us alive for the next twenty-four hours. Hope was what we really lived on, and wild rumours were sweeping the town of Graz. People were found hanging from trees, in particular in a wood called *Kaiserwald* (Emperor's wood) some three kilometres from Graz. Heavy air-raids forced us into the cellar day and night, and we became used to the darkness and dampness of the walls. Even the goldfish had had enough – they curled up and died and we fed them to the hungry cats of the neighbourhood. Despite this total war, I decided to visit my grandmother, Mina von Bolzano, who lived near the Schlossberg in the centre of the town. I had to know if she was still alive and the only way to find out was to get there.

My grandmother had been a widow since 1922 and was the eldest daughter of the Industrialist Baron von Ludwig and the sister of a retired Fieldmarshal. Evicted from the family Mansion at Rosenberg-guertel 28, in 1938, she was placed in a modest three-roomed flat, with a Nazi widow to take care of her. This truly could be interpreted in a sinister way, for my grandmother was spied upon and forced to allow the woman to eat with her. In return Frau Kruz would call my grandmother 'the old Jewess' because she was the former widow of a Jewish Surgeon, before marrying my grandfather. Still deep in thought, I arrived at the flat and, luckily for me, the 'Dragon', as my grandmother named Frau Kruz, was out. Although the old lady was delighted to see me, she came to the point, asking me if I was in any trouble and I told her part of my adventures. Leaning against her silver-knobbed stick, I noticed how thin and ill she looked and forgot my troubles, leaving the talking to her. Happily her spirit was still in one piece and she rose to her status, 'ordering' me to put on the crimson velvet tablecloth which was in Frau Kruz's room. I made tea, using the best Meissen China. With a glint in her eyes she said: "I do hope Frau Kruz comes now, for I am just in the right frame of mind to tell her where she belongs – in the kitchen."

During tea, Grandmother reminded me to keep up my singing, to improve myself, in order to have a chance of making good after this war was over. Holding my hand she exclaimed: "My child, you can be everything, if you want to be. You've got the capacity for perceiving the ludicrous elements in life, yet a sympathetic imagination for regarding things, but most of all you are a humanitarian who regards the interests of mankind as of supreme importance." We reminisced about the years before Hitler came and how the *enfant terrible* (me) grew up . . . from child to girl . . . from girl to woman.

I had been just one hour with my grandmother when the sirens sounded. Immediately we left for the shelter in the Schlossberg tunnel, some ten minutes away. People were coming from all sides, pushing and pulling prams, hoping to make it. Once in there, Grandmother sat down and we listened to the loud speaker's announcement that unidentified Bomber Squadrons had attacked the town and that further waves of aeroplanes were expected. We could hear the first explosions as the smell of dust and smoke filled the air, and people started to cough. Suddenly the light in the tunnel began to flicker and went out. Children cried in the darkness. At last, the emergency lamps lit up again and the loud speaker was giving out instructions.

Unexpectedly they dragged someone along the floor, right past our feet and I noticed by the uniform it was a British P.O.W. I heard people say that he had been killed by a falling rock and wondered what he was doing outside the tunnel. He was an awful sight, with his white teeth sticking all over his head and blood running down his arms. "Poor fellow," one man said, "he nearly made it," when I saw a Nazi Brownshirt charging this man, shouting: "Are you a traitor, the Englander will never win this war, do you understand!" A tumult broke out, with the Guard rolling the dead P.O.W. to one side by his boots, while the same Brownshirt, his eyes flashing, pulled the rifle from the soldier and fired at another P.O.W. He sank to the ground – people shouted like mad: "Kill all the prisoners, beat them to death, they are bombing our city and destroying our homes." Grandmother was trembling all over and I myself was not too steady, but there was nothing I could do save urge the few next to me not to be silly, for this was murder, not war. Some began to attack me by my hair, with my grandmother hitting back with her stick until we noticed other British P.O.W.s behind a single wooden fence, their fingers holding on to the planks. Expecting another upheaval, our attackers let go of us, turning their attention towards the P.O.Ws. Someone brought along chains and I held my breath, awaiting the outcome. The Brownshirt tied them together, stating at the top of his voice: "Everybody is judge in the holy fight for the Vaterland." The men were to be shot and were marched off.

To think clearly was impossible, killing defenceless P.O.Ws in cold blood was inconceivable and against the Geneva agreement, but who cared? After the all-clear, I escorted Grandmother home – we were unable to speak. Back at Aunt Betty's I had a good cry and told her what had happened and she exclaimed: "We must pray very earnestly." All I could think of was revenge and action to prevent further crimes like these.

The next morning brought more air-raids, but Aunt Betty and I refused to go into the cellar for fear of being buried alive. Rather oddly her brother-in-law, Colonel Getreu, called and brought a note from my step-father asking me to come home at once as Mother was very ill. There could be only one answer, whatever the risk, but how I was going to make the eighty-five kilometres home, I did not know. I was willing to try, and Betty gave me one half loaf of brown bread, two apples and her blessing. Two days later I was home. The most unlikely transports came my way proving the absurd and comical side of war. Somehow I was always on the move from somewhere, or to somewhere, and home was often just a word.

This time my home was deserted, my parents were up in the mountain-house usually reserved for the summer months, so I got out my horse, saddled it and rode off for Lobning. On the mountain road I was suddenly confronted by the local police chief. He certainly was no friend of mine and ordered me to dismount. "You are the last person on earth I expected to see," he said angrily, adding: "But your gallivanting days are over Fräulein Triller, or Frau Schaile, or whatever you call yourself now." Realizing how dangerous this man was I played it humble, calling him Herr Commandant, but with little success. He stressed how he had followed my activities in silence, overshadowed by the 'Mighty' who signed my documents and that now at last he had a chance to get even with me. "But you hang, whatever you do to me," I said, changing my tune to the only language the Nazis understood . . . fear. He reached for his revolver and I knew that I did not stand a chance, being unarmed for the first time in four years, so I kept at him, telling him the Russians were in Leoben and possibly in the woods behind us laughing their heads off at his pathetic attempt to kill me and for good measure reminding him that he had a daughter my own age, who might be taken as hostage to Siberia. Cold sweat stood on the little man's forehead as I raved on, desperately hoping to save my life. When he put his gun away I knew I had succeeded and he told me to clear out before he changed his mind. I swung myself back into the saddle and rode off as quickly as possible. Feeling safe, I halted to get back my breath, laying my head against the horse's neck and I thought of the quotation . . . "An eye for an eye . . ."

At last I made the Lobning and the Almhouse. My mother had passed the crisis of her illness, but she could hardly speak. She indicated that now she could die in peace, having seen me safe. A few days later she was much better, asking me to bring some food to the Oberhausers in Goess, and I agreed though knowing the renewed danger facing me on this nine kilometres journey. In a way, I wanted to see my friends again and a tingle of excitement came over me, with the knowledge that I was back in harness and with the Resistance.

April 1945. The Oberhauser Villa was still in one piece and we rejoiced at seeing each other. However, the fact that British P.O.Ws were hiding in their loft made my hair stand on end. We only talked in whispers, for the penalties of aiding them was death by hanging. Frau Oberhauser begged me to bring some more food and I nodded, knowing full well that roadblocks were set up and manned by the SS. Like the lion who had tasted blood and could not leave it alone, I set off, willing myself to make it or be damned, thinking of the latest official figures in the Resistance in Austria: thirty-five thousand one hundred and ninety executed – with most of the women guillotined. Thank God I made it, and swiftly returned with more food to Goess. I managed to get lifts by army trucks and staff cars loaded with deserters in all directions. Some, of course, still believed in the miracle victory and I had to change my tales to fit in with my masters. One lift I had from a *Ritterkreuztraeger*, the highest order given by Hitler, and who referred to me as a 'damsel in distress', gallantly ordering his driver to take me to the Oberhaus, then getting out and escorting me to the door. This surely was Socratic irony.

April 15, 1945. I was followed all the way back to the Lobning by two men of the Gestapo. Without much ado they questioned me regarding the whereabouts of the British prisoners. I shook my head and they got very angry indeed. "Don't lie, girl, we know the Englander are in this area," one shouted. "How should my daughter know where they are?" my mother intervened. This infuriated the men more and they began searching the entire house, flinging furniture out of the window and finally turning over my mother's linen. "You won't find any Englanders in there," she exclaimed and in return was struck across the face by one of the Gestapo. As her nose began to bleed I went to her aid, but the other man grabbed hold of me and shouted: "Where are the P.O.W.s . . . or we kill your mother." How can one describe a decision like this in plain words, it is the agony of a lifetime combined into one terrifying moment – the borderline between the animal and the human being, the ultimate judgment of right and wrong and the ability to assess . . . is it bluff or reality? For seconds I closed my eyes and thought hard for the answer. I was just twenty-two years old, but I had lived one hundred years and blasted the foxes out of their holes . . . to give in now would have been a betrayal of all, including my own mother, and that I knew she would have never expected from me. As if all life had left my body I said firmly: "I have no idea what you are talking about, I know nothing of P.O.Ws." The man holding my mother pushed her aside and they left grinning, promising to hang me next time.

After they had gone I went to my room, for I had to be alone. Love for my mother and loyalty to my cause had clashed head on, I had taken a great risk but my gamble had paid off.

Graz, am 21/12 1967

Meine liebe Burgi.

Verzeihe mir diese Aufschrift nachdem Du doch heute eine verheiratete Frau bist. aber ich habe Dich auch vor 30 Jahren nicht anders genannt. Ich bin ganz erstaunt, daß doch Du dich noch immer erinnern kannst. aber ich weiß es genau wie wenn es jetzt 1 Jahr wäre, wie man uns auf Tritt u. Schritt verfolgt hat, erst am meisten wie wir die Plakate aufgemacht haben, wozu ja Du treibende Kraft warst. Ich hatte auch hier in Graz als Gastwirt noch einen Aufstand z. B in dem Haus wo ich mein Geschäft hatte war im I. Stock ein großer Saal, dort hatten die Nazis eine Versammlung, einen Tag vorher holte man mich zur Versammlung durch den Hausmeister. ich sagte ihm, er soll den Ortsgruppenleiter sagen, ich habe ein Geschäft nicht so wie er von der Versammlung und ging nicht hinauf. in 3 Tagen erhielt ich eine Vorladung zum Kreisleiter. vor mir stand ein großsprecheriger Tischler und sagte ich, Sie [illegible] ich ersuchte er soll mir das schriftlich geben er sagte zu was ich das brauche, ich sagte, wenn die Deutschen nach Graz kommen und ich das Schreiben vorzeige, dann werde besser behandelt als von den Deutschen.

Er sagte zu seinen Schreiber, ich sei nicht normal, sonst könne ich ihm keine solche Antwort geben.

Ich kann dir nur sagen wenn Alle solche Gegner gewesen wären wie wir, wäre es auch mit Österreich nicht so weit gekommen.

Der Kreisleiter sagte auch er lasse mich an die Mauer stellen, ich sagte ihm, das kann er schon aber sonst nichts

Liebe Burgi. lebt dein Mutter noch, mein Frau ist

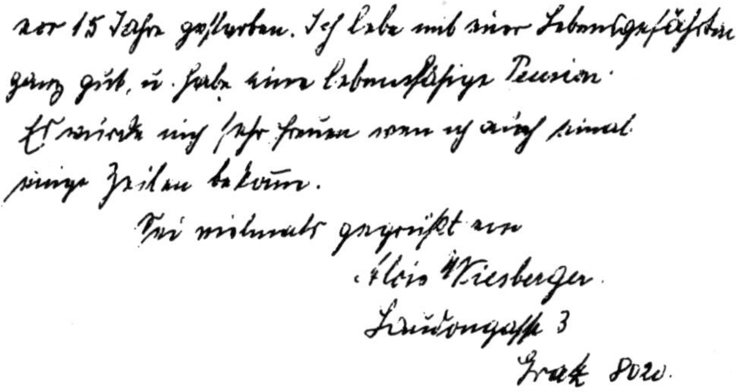

vor 15 Jahr gestorben. Ich lebe mit einer Lebensgefährtin
ganz gut, u. habe eine lebensfähige Pension.
Es würde mich sehr freuen wenn ich auch einmal
einige Zeilen bekomme.
Sei vielmals gegrüßt von
Alois Wiesberger.
Laudongasse 3
Graz 8020.

Wiesberger's Letter

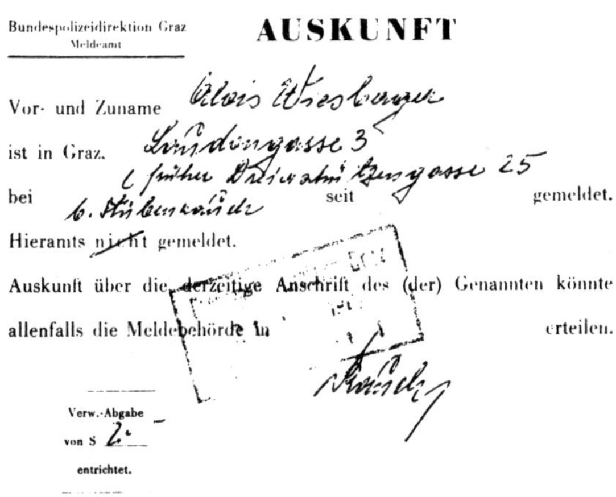

Bundespolizeidirektion Graz
Meldeamt

AUSKUNFT

Vor- und Zuname Alois Wiesberger

ist in Graz, Laudongasse 3 (früher [illegible]gasse 25)

bei 6. [illegible] seit gemeldet.

Hieramts ~~nicht~~ gemeldet.

Auskunft über die ~~derzeitige~~ Anschrift des (der) Genannten könnte allenfalls die Meldebehörde in erteilen.

Verw.-Abgabe
von S 2.–
entrichtet.

Police Identification

EPILOGUE

I owe my life to two kinds of men – the Patriots and the Villains. Most of them are dead, but there are survivors like myself who, in some cases, may wish to remain anonymous, yet I feel readers of this book have a certain right to question its authenticity.

With deep regret I state that those who died during the fight for our cause were:

Johann von Schindler, Ltn., shot by the SS in 1945, whilst escaping.

Walter Borg, Ltn., killed in Africa 1943.

Rudolf Koroschetz, executed in Jugoslavia 1943.

Werner Fink, Ltn., killed in an air crash 1944.

Sepp Schneider, SS Officer, shot himself in Poland on February 2, 1945.

Those who aided my eventful life as a Resistance-fighter and courier and who are still alive are:

Alois Wiesberger, former hotel owner.

Councillor F. Winkler, ex-shunting yard master at St. Michaels Rail Junction.

Martina Sneider, his only daughter.

Frau Lucy Koerting. Now a well known TV star.

Frau M. Oberhauser.

Dr A. Torggler.

Professor Benno Bolzano. Head of College for Commerce, Graz - Austria.
They all reside in Austria and I saw them last in 1970.

The two men directly responsible for murder and attempted murder in 1939-40 and the one who betrayed me to the Gestapo, leading to my arrest in August 1944, reside in Austria. The Graz police and Ing. Wiesenthal, the well-known "Witch-hunter" of Nazi crimes, furnished me with evidence that Herr Fritz is still living in Graz and at the same house where he murdered the old Jewish widow, but escaped punishment by an amnesty. Franz Schlager is holding a high position with the Austrian Gendarmerie, and both my husband and I met him accidently at a Graz Restaurant in 1961.

In a final assessment of my fight against the Nazis, I state, without regret, that I fought them every inch, throughout their seven year reign in Austria, using the strongest weapon at my disposal – that of a Woman. The men I have bamboozled are scattered all over Europe. They will not care to remember me nor will they concede that, judging by the outcome of the war, I served some purpose, even though my behaviour may shock many people. Those whose hearts were filled with murder, hatred and inhumanity against their fellow citizens and have not learnt from the past, need reminding of their crimes and ignorance. Unwittingly they championed my cause by their relentless pursuit of sex.

My one-woman vendetta against the most diabolical system in history was successful. The Nazi regime horrified the world with its cruelty – it cannot be forgotten – but we must never let it happen again.